PRAISE FOR JEROME CHARYN

"One of the most important writers in American literature." —**Michael Chabon**

"One of our finest writers. . . . Whatever milieu [Charyn] chooses to inhabit, . . . his sentences are pure vernacular music, his voice unmistakable."
—**Jonathan Lethem**

"Charyn, like Nabokov, is that most fiendish sort of writer—so seductive as to beg imitation, so singular as to make imitation impossible." —**Tom Bissell**

"Among Charyn's writerly gifts is a dazzling energy. . . . [He is] an exuberant chronicler of the mythos of American life."
—**Joyce Carol Oates,** *New York Review of Books*

"A fearless writer. . . . Brave and brazen." —**Andrew Delbanco,** *New York Review of Books*

"Charyn skillfully breathes life into historical icons." —*New Yorker*

"Both a serious writer and an immensely approachable one, always witty and readable and . . . interesting." —*Washington Post*

"Absolutely unique among American writers." —*Los Angeles Times*

"A contemporary American Balzac." —*Newsday*

PRAISE FOR *The Secret Life (*

"Daring." —*New York Times Book Revi*

"Audacious. . . . Seductive. . . . Charyn has ....ly. . . . A poignant, delicately rendered vision." —............... ... *of Books*

"Through a perceptive reading of Dickinson's verse and correspondence, [Charyn's] re-created her wild mind in all its erudition, playfulness and nervous energy." —*Washington Post*

"Compellingly drawn. . . . I admire Charyn's achievement in lifting the veil of a heretofore mysterious figure." —*Los Angeles Times*

"In this brilliant and hilarious jailbreak of a novel, Charyn channels the genius poet and her great leaps of the imagination." —*Booklist* **(starred review)**

"In his breathtaking high-wire act of ventriloquism, Jerome Charyn pulls off the nearly impossible: in *The Secret Life of Emily Dickinson* he imagines an Emily Dickinson of mischievousness, brilliance, desire, and wit (all which she possessed) and then boldly sets her amidst a throng of historical, fictional, and surprising characters just as hard to forget as she is. This is a bold book, but we'd expect no less of this amazing novelist." —**Brenda Wineapple**, author of *White Heat: The Friendship of Emily Dickinson and Thomas Wentworth Higginson*

The poet (left) and one of her possible muses, circa 1859
Used by kind permission of a private collector

A LOADED GUN

Emily Dickinson for the 21st Century

Jerome Charyn

Bellevue Literary Press
NEW YORK

First published in the United States in 2016 by
Bellevue Literary Press, New York

For information, contact:
Bellevue Literary Press
NYU School of Medicine
550 First Avenue
OBV A612
New York, NY 10016

© 2016 by Jerome Charyn

Library of Congress Cataloging-in-Publication Data
is available from the publisher upon request

Cover images courtesy of The Emily Dickinson Collection,
Amherst College Archives & Special Collections

Bellevue Literary Press would like to thank all its generous
donors—individuals and foundations—for their support.

 The New York State Council on the Arts with
the support of Governor Andrew Cuomo and
NYSCA the New York State Legislature

 National Endowment for the Arts arts.gov This project is supported in part
by an award from the National
Endowment for the Arts.
ART WORKS.

Book design and composition by Mulberry Tree Press, Inc.

Manufactured in the United States of America.
First Edition

1 3 5 7 9 8 6 4 2

paperback ISBN: 978-1-934137-98-7

ebook ISBN: 978-1-934137-99-4

Contents

Author's Note

I couldn't let go. I'd spent two years writing a novel about her, vampirizing her letters and poems, sucking the blood out of her bones, like some hunter of lost souls. I'd rifled through every book about her I could find—biographies, psychoanalytic studies of her crippled, wounded self, tales of her martyrdom in the nineteenth century, studies of her iconic white dress, accounts of her agoraphobia, etc. I shut my eyes, blinked, and wrote *The Secret Life of Emily Dickinson* (2010), like a boy galloping on a blind horse. I never believed much in her spinsterhood and shriveled sexuality. Yet she was a spinster in a way, a spinner of words. Spiders were also known as spinsters, and like a spider, she spun her meticulous webs, trapping words until she gathered them in a Lexicon that had no equal.

She falls in love with a handyman at Mount Holyoke in my novel. Perhaps she dreams him up in the snow outside her window, a blond creature with a tattoo on his arm of a red heart pierced with a blue arrow—that tattoo is every bit as extravagant and outrageous as her poems. Tom the Handyman could be a phantom and a whisper of her own art. He's also a burglar and a thief, an appropriate accomplice for a woman who burgled the English language; he will rescue her in Cambridge, Massachusetts, when she roams around half-blind, and she will discover him again hiding in a circus near the end of her life—Dickinson loved the circus, with its rash of red.

The poet was also in love with Susan Gilbert, as her own letters reveal. And Sue remains the most enigmatic character in the novel—volatile, brooding, dark. "She was our Vesuvius, who rained hot lava down upon our heads," as Dickinson says in my *Secret Life*. There are rides to eternity throughout Dickinson's poems, and I wrote about her own last ride as a voyage to her dead father's barn, wearing a bridal gown, all done up in tulle, but she never gets there—discontinuity has always been her habit.

And thus I travel in my Dimity and tulle, but that barn could be in Peru. I seem nearer and nearer, but never near enough. My bridal gown could be in tatters before I arrive.

As Dickinson teaches us, endings have no end. She was a master of quantum mechanics long before that science was ever born. "People like us, who believe in physics, know the distinction between past, present, and future is only a stubbornly persistent illusion," Einstein once said, and he could have been talking about Emily Dickinson. She was always at the ragged edge of time.

And there wasn't a bit of closure, even after I finished my novel. I knew less and less the more I learned about her. There was no way to shove her aside. Her poems never heal the essential wound of reading her. Even the tales of her life were tantalizing, since they reveal so little. She was an agoraphobic who could dance anywhere on her toes, a reclusive nun who wrote the sexiest love letters, a mermaid who swam in her own interior sea, a shy mouse who could pillage and plunder in her poems. All her life she was a Loaded Gun.

And while writing a novel about Lincoln, in Lincoln's voice, dealing with his staccato courtship of Mary Todd—another nineteenth-century belle who was much too complicated and whimsical for her era—and with all the brutal turns of the Civil War, I dreamt of Dickinson, who wrote some of her finest poems during the years this "still Man" inhabited the White House like a gaunt ghost. And I had to write about Dickinson again, to capture her voice—not as a novelist, but as a hunter in her own field of words.

———◦◦◦———

We all owe a debt of gratitude to Martha Nell Smith for establishing the Dickinson Electronic Archives and for her own careful scrutiny of Dickinson's texts. I would like to thank Margaret Dakin, archivist of the Emily Dickinson Collection at Amherst College, for allowing me to sift through Emily's secrets, those wondrous fragments in which she herself smashed the illusion of time and left little eternities for us all to share; I couldn't have written this book without these late fragments and letter-poems.

I would like to thank Jane Wald, executive director of the Emily Dickinson Museum, who helped me roam through Edward Dickinson's "head-quarters" at the Homestead and to wander into that "Pearl Jail" where his daughter once slept and wrote and hoarded that Lexicon of hers. I would also like to thank Dickinson scholars Polly Longsworth, Christopher Benfey, and Marta Werner, who, with poet Susan Howe, were my partners in crime, helping me unsnarl some of the *ravelments* of Dickinson's mind. And I'd like to thank poet and public health physician Norbert Hirschhorn, poet Susan Snively, graphologist Susanne Shapiro, and daguerreotype collector Sam Carlo for their own perceptions about Emily Dickinson. Most of all, I'd like to thank prima ballerina Allegra Kent, who shared her reminiscences of Joseph Cornell with me while I watched her dance toward her own "Blue Peninsula."

Symbols Used in the Text

A   Amherst College Archives and Special Collections

Fr   R. W. Franklin, editor, *The Poems of Emily Dickinson, Variorum Edition*, 1998

HCL   Harvard College Library

J   Thomas H. Johnson, editor, *The Poems of Emily Dickinson*, 1958

PF   Prose fragments from *The Letters of Emily Dickinson*, 1958, 1986

A LOADED GUN

Emily Dickinson for the 21st Century

Young Emily, circa 1847
Courtesy of Amherst College Archives and Special Collections

ONE

—∞∞∞—

Zero at the Bone

I

WHEN JULIE HARRIS DIED at eighty-seven of congestive heart failure on August 24, 2013, she was remembered most of all as an "unprepossessing anti-diva," who had a waiflike, invisible presence outside the roles she played, according to her obituary in *The New York Times*. Though she would inhabit Mary Lincoln, Joan of Arc, and Sally Bowles on Broadway, she continued to haunt the nation as "shy Miss Emily" for almost forty years. In his obit, Bruce Weber marveled at her portrait of Dickinson as a "fiercely observed, proudly literary and deeply self-conscious near-agoraphobe." Harris had played her to the hilt.

Dressed in white, like a nurse or a nun, the anti-diva appeared at the Longacre Theatre in 1976, as the Belle of Amherst, in William Luce's play. She won her fifth Tony Award and would repeat her performance in a public television special that seemed to enchant most spectators. She went on tour year after year, until Julie Harris *became* Emily Dickinson.

Such was Harris' mimetic power and the ferocity of her talent. She was like a hologram of the poet visiting us from the past. *The Belle of Amherst* presents the poet with a persona that is often funny and capricious as quicksilver. Harris was gnomic and red-haired, like Dickinson herself, and one could feel the patter of the poet's footsteps while Julie

Harris was onstage. "I first fell in love with Emily Dickinson when I read her letters," the anti-diva once wrote. "It's like listening to her heart."

Luce has her sit on a low chest, "excited. Her mind is running on one track only—publication." She's lured one of the most eminent essayists and literary critics of her time, Thomas Wentworth Higginson, into the house. But she's no Scheherazade.

"I've been waiting to hear from your own lips what you're planning for my poems. I have them right here."

She's ready to show him her entire stash, poems not even her sister knew about. And it's a pity that Higginson can't sing his own lines, else we might have had a bit of fireworks, or a wonderful comic moment. But Luce doesn't give us a single *hair* of Higginson's actual visit to her father's house, the Homestead, in 1870. Dickinson descended the stairs with two day lilies in her hand. In a letter to his wife, written that very night of his visit to Amherst, Higginson offers us one of the few genuine glimpses of Dickinson we have, without the least bit of embellishment.

> *A step like a pattering child's in entry & in glided a little plain woman with two smooth bands of reddish hair & a face . . . with no good feature—in a very plain & exquisitely clean white pique & a blue net worsted shawl. She came to me with two day lilies which she put in a sort of childlike way into my hand & said "These are my introduction" in a soft frightened breathless childlike voice—& added under her breath Forgive me if I am frightened; I never see strangers & hardly know what to say—but she talked soon & thenceforward continuously—& deferentially—sometimes stopping to ask me to talk instead of her—but readily recommencing.*   [Letter 342a]

It was the most critical encounter of her life—or at least that portion of her life we can glean from letters that still survive. She'd been waiting to meet Colonel Higginson for eight years. She had first written to him in 1862, pretending she was a neophyte—an *unborn* poet—while her letters and poems had a bewildering mastery. Yet she pretended to be his pupil, seeking his advice, sending him four of her poems like soft, seductive bombs. "Mr. Higginson, /Are you too deeply occupied to say if my Verse is alive?" [Letter 260] She didn't even sign her poems, but hid her name inside a little card. The colonel was bewitched. He wrote her right away. Dickinson replied, "I made no verse—but one or two—until this winter—Sir—" Meanwhile she'd been assembling her poems into little packets, stitched together by her own hand—close to five hundred poems, if not more. He called her poetry "spasmodic," but she hadn't really come to him for advice. She needed his intelligence, having had so few correspondents with his stature and scope. She was vampirizing the colonel, sucking at the blood inside his head.

Luce's Emily dreams on her feet about all the future editions of her poems. "And I would prefer morocco-bound." Higginson speaks, but we don't hear his voice, of course, in this "One-Woman Play." What he says unsettles her. "But my meter is new, experimental," she tells him with a decidedly twentieth-century tick. She recites to the audience:

A great Hope fell
You heard no noise
The Ruin was within . . .   [J1123]

And she vanishes into her bedroom, the heart ripped right out of her. She keeps sending him poems. "But always, from his polite replies, I get the uneasy feeling that they end up in some dusty drawer in his office."

And we're back to Emily Dickinson, the baker of black cake and victim of unrequited love. "But I'll have you know, plain or not, I had more than one suitor. And they were all married. And older than I. But there was really only one." She's been pining half her life for a particular "Christ-like man," the Reverend Charles Wadsworth, whom she'd heard preach in Philadelphia when she was twenty-four.

"His voice haunted me. I couldn't break off the enchantment, even after I returned to Amherst." She only met the preacher twice, but he became her mysterious "Master," to whom she addressed three funny, sad, heartbreaking letters that may never have been sent. All we have are the rough drafts.

> *Master.*
>
> *If you saw a bullet hit a Bird—and he told you he was'nt shot—you might weep at his courtesy, but you would certainly doubt his word.*   [Letter 233]
>
> *I've got a cough as big as a thimble—but I don't care for that—I've got a Tomahawk in my side but that don't hurt me much.* [If you] *Her master stabs her more.*   [Letter 248]

Critics have been puzzling over these letters ever since they were first discovered. For Luce, Wadsworth has become the *lesion* around which she wrote her poems, the source of her sadness and ecstasy. She also admits that one man, Judge Otis P. Lord did propose to her, and glosses right over this proposal. But Judge Lord was much more material in Emily's life than any Christ-like man. And few readers in 1976 realized that Emily Dickinson had a fling with one of her father's old friends—or even knew that he existed. Lord was considered a lion in Massachusetts, a judge of the superior court. His blue eyes blazed like bullets, and no one could return his stare. But the judge was in her thrall. She wrapped herself around him like a sexual snake. How many spectators in the audience—male or female—could have tolerated the image of Julie Harris pretending to glide over Judge Lord's erection with the blade of her hand?

> *. . . to lie so near your longing—to touch it as I passed, for I am but a restive sleeper and often should journey from your Arms through the happy night . . .*   [Letter 562, about 1878]

Instead we have a very different *erection*—the subterranean kind—as Luce's Emily recites to us her encounter with a garter snake with its "spotted shaft" that's like "a Whip lash/Unbraiding in the Sun."

> *But never met this Fellow*
> *Attended, or alone*
> *Without a tighter breathing*
> *And Zero at the Bone—*   [J986]

And that very last line defeats the whole panorama and spectacle of a play about a harmless maiden aunt who happened to write poetry. Neither the poems that weave through the monologue without much of a "Whip lash," nor the monologue itself, provide a key to Emily Dickinson's art. We don't see her demonic side. She flirts with the audience, but Luce's Dickinson is never "Zero at the Bone"—she has too much of the *reasonableness* that Luce has pumped into the play. We'd never learn from Luce that her favorite creature was the spider, or that she loved to spin her webs with the silver thread of her Lexicon, and capture her prey—words or young widows and married men.

But it isn't Luce's fault. The Dickinson he offers us had been around for eighty-six years, ever since she was first published in 1890, half the deviltry of her language and punctuation rubbed out, some of it by Higginson himself, who thought he was doing Dickinson a favor by presenting her as a lovelorn recluse and village savant. She was half-forgotten by the turn of the century, a poet whose ragged lines had the registers of a spinster who pined away. But a war developed among Dickinson's heirs. Her brother's mistress, Mabel Loomis Todd, had a cache of letters and poems (she'd been Higginson's co-editor and was the first to transcribe Dickinson's manuscripts). Emily's sister-in-law, Susan Dickinson, had another cache. And their daughters, Martha Dickinson Bianchi and Millicent Todd Bingham, would become involved in the battle—whole new gatherings of poems suddenly appeared like "a Bomb, abroad." [Fr360] But the myth of the recluse remained, the half-cracked poetess who had to renounce her love. Few of us had read her letters. We knew her by a little "menagerie" of poems, memorized in high school. We'd never heard of Judge Lord, and we wouldn't have believed the tale of *our* Emily romping around on the family sofa with a man her father's age. We could only imagine the Queen Recluse in a virginal white dress.

And this was the creature Julie Harris inhabited in 1976—with her freckles and black cake—until that *other* Emily, seductive, spiteful, cruel, with the reckless anger and eruptions of a volcano, was swept under the carpet.

2

STILL, SOMETHING HAPPENED around the time *The Belle of Amherst* was first produced. Adrienne Rich, who had won the National Book Award for her poetry in 1974, was utterly obsessed with Dickinson. "For months, for years, for most of my life, I have been hovering like an insect against the screens of an existence which inhabited Amherst, Massachusetts, between 1830 and 1886." But Dickinson was hard to capture. "Narrowed-down by her early editors and anthologists, reduced to quaintness or spinsterish oddity by many of her commentators, sentimentalized, fallen-in-love with like some gnomic Garbo, still unread in the breadth and depth of her full range of work, she was, and is, a wonder to me when I try to imagine myself into that mind." Rich didn't see any quaintness at all. This gnomic Garbo had to find the means to survive. There was nothing pathological about her life as a hermit in her father's house: her self-styled isolation was her survival kit as a poet. She was, as Rich says, a most practical woman, who understood her gifts. "I have come to imagine her as somehow too strong for her environment, a figure of powerful will, not at all frail and breathless, someone whose personal dimensions would be felt in a household."

As much as she was frightened of her father, he must have been a little wary of her smoking intelligence and wit. And in 1975, a year before Julie Harris broke through as *The Belle of Amherst*, mesmerizing audiences in her white dress, Rich published "Vesuvius at Home: The Power of Emily Dickinson," an essay that dynamited many of the shibboleths about the Belle of Amherst. The gnomic Garbo was suddenly gone, and in her place was a woman who had to exercise a good deal of cunning in a society where most men, including her father, often considered females little more than voluptuous, intelligent, child-bearing creatures with their own mysterious charm; Emily might go to school, but she had to remain outside history. She could not even carry her father's name into marriage— daughters were swallowed up by husbands, fathers, brothers. Is it any wonder Dickinson never married? Her elder brother, Austin, was Edward Dickinson's favorite. Father and son fought all the time, but Edward missed him the moment he was out of sight. He cherished his son's school compositions, called them better than Shakespeare, and wanted to have them published in a morocco-bound book, while his daughter's poems would always be invisible to him. And when Austin considered moving to Chicago with his bride (Susan Dickinson was Emily's dearest friend and perhaps her greatest love), Edward bribed him to remain in Amherst by building a house for him and Susan—the Evergreens—next door to the Homestead.

Those were the confines of Emily's world; she baked her father's bread, she gardened, and was able to wheedle the best room in the Homestead from him, in the southwest corner, where she could look at the Dickinson meadow from her writing desk. Adrienne Rich made a pilgrimage to that room. "Here I became, again, an insect, vibrating at the frame of the windows, clinging to panes of glass, trying to connect. The scent here is very powerful. Here in this white-curtained, high-ceilinged room, a red-haired woman with hazel eyes and a contralto voice wrote about volcanoes, deserts, eternity, suicide, physical passion, wild beasts, rape, power, madness, separation, the daemon, the grave. Here, with a darning needle, she bound these poems—heavily emended and often in various versions—into booklets, secured with darning thread, to be found and read after her death." And somehow she thrived. She might call Higginson her Preceptor, but she had none. She was utterly self-taught, self-schooled. She had her Bible and her Lexicon, but she couldn't have learned much about the "Whip lash" of words from her favorite authors—Elizabeth Barrett Browning, the Brontë sisters, Dickens, Emerson, George Eliot, George Sand, Keats. (Perhaps Shakespeare was her Master—her only one). Her poems were like hymnals, but they didn't come from any church. That strange polyphony was born inside her head. But she lived with all the constraints—"the corseting of women's bodies, choices, and sexuality [that] could spell insanity to a woman genius." She could out-Puritan the Puritans in her poems. She was fierce—and cruel—like some rebel preacher in their midst. God was terrifying and aloof, but he was also impotent and maimed.

Those—dying then,
Knew where they went—
They went to God's Right Hand—
That Hand is amputated now
And God cannot be found—   [Fr1581]

But from that amputation grew her own power, her power to summon her energies and to subvert. "It is always what is under pressure in us, especially under pressure of concealment—that explodes in poetry," wrote Adrienne Rich. It was the poetry of a renegade, who could *unsex* herself if she had to, masquerade as a man, or shift from sex to sex, like Virginia Woolf in *Orlando*. She could be male or female, according to her desire. She was drawn to women and men with powerful minds and a particular beauty. Her letters read like a catalogue of seductions, and her poems are often fired up with pain, in the coded language of a failed love affair, real or imagined. She was in love with Susan Gilbert, however we may define that love.

Sue wasn't a patrician like Dickinson herself, who could practice her craft like a spider with "a Silver Ball," in her father's house. [Fr513] Sue had run away to Baltimore and tried to support herself as a schoolteacher—the experiment failed. She had to find a suitor. She was dark, strong-willed, with an almost masculine beauty. She chose Emily's brother, who was considered a catch. Austin was handsome and haughty, the son of the most powerful man in Amherst. And she was fond of his father. Both of them had become Christians on the same day in 1850, joined the First Church of Amherst as members of the "elect." She had a nervous fit after her engagement to Austin. Her hair fell out. She stayed in bed a month. She had to have a nurse. Finally, she did marry Austin, though she remained dubious about male affection.

Her favorite sister had died shortly after giving birth, and Sue was suspicious of "a man's requirements." Still, she would have three children of her own, and soon had the finest salon in Amherst—Bret Harte and Ralph Waldo Emerson stayed at the Evergreens. And for a while, Emily visited with her dog, Carlo. She may have been in love with one of Sue's guests, editor Samuel Bowles, with his "Arabian presence." She would write to Bowles—a married man who enjoyed having a "menagerie" of women around him—with her own kind of cryptic passion. Scheherazade living under a *vail* of words. She had a weakness for married men who could test her own intelligence; with them she would weave her Silver Ball.

I suspect that Colonel Higginson was another one of her "suitors"; like Bowles, he had a sickly wife. And she revealed herself to him—and the foibles of her family—as she did with no other man. Ten days after her very first letter to Higginson, she writes, "I have a Brother and Sister—My Mother does not care for thought—and Father, too busy with his Briefs—to notice what we do—He buys me many books—but begs me not to read them—because he fears they joggle the Mind. They are religious—except me—and address an Eclipse, every morning—whom they call their 'Father.' But I fear my story fatigues you—I would like to learn—Could you tell me how to grow—or is it unconveyed—like Melody—or Witchcraft?" [Letter 261, April 25, 1862]

And Adrienne Rich resurrects a poem that baffled most critics in 1975 and was seldom discussed—a poem about Dickinson's creative demon that was central to her "addiction" to male Preceptors, like Higginson and Bowles. "I think it is a poem about possession by the daemon, about the dangers and risks of such a possession if you are a woman, about the knowledge that power in a woman can seem destructive, and that you cannot live without the daemon once it has possessed you. The archetype of the daemon as masculine is beginning to change, but it has been real for women up until now. But this woman poet [in "My life had stood a loaded gun"] also perceives herself as a lethal weapon," a weapon that guards her Master's life. [Fr764]

> *To foe of His—I'm deadly foe—*
> *None stir the second time—*
> *On whom I lay a Yellow Eye—*
> *Or an emphatic Thumb—*

The narrator of the poem—woman as Loaded Gun—has become a kind of Annie Oakley in her Master's house, the "blonde Assassin" [Fr1668] with a murderous Yellow Eye. The poem whips between surrender and rage, as if Dickinson herself were caught in a sadomasochistic dream about her own identity. She is both the hunter and the hunted, has become her very own prey.

> *And now We roam in Sovreign Woods—*
> *And now We hunt the Doe—*

The gun, Rich tell us, *speaks* for her Master. "If there is a female consciousness in this poem it is buried deeper than the images: it exists in the ambivalence toward power, which is extreme. Active willing and creation in women are forms of aggression, and aggression is both 'the power to kill' and punishable by death."

Rich realizes that she cannot unravel the poem, crack all its essential codes. The speaking gun is too perverse, as if the very act of creation for a woman in the nineteenth century was impossible to bear and would have broken any other poet with a lesser will. Dickinson could not have survived without her own "Yellow Eye." It was, for Dickinson, "an extremely painful and dangerous way to live—split between a publicly acceptable persona, and a part of yourself that you perceive as the essential, the creative and powerful self, yet also as possibly unacceptable, perhaps even monstrous."

And that was Dickinson's dilemma. The poet on the second floor was like a monster in her lair. And it shouldn't startle us that there was a strange flutter about her—she was carrying bombs in her bosom, under the white dress that has tagged her as a harmless old maid for at least a hundred years, the very recluse we meet in Luce's play, who spills all her secrets to an audience of strangers, when she was a woman with volcanic powers—whose lightning rhythms and ragged rhymes seem to mirror our postapocalyptic age, and whose lyrics grow more and more modern. We can barely keep up with her leaps of language.

> *Title divine—is mine!*
> *The Wife—without the Sign!*
> *Acute Degree—conferred on me—*
> *Empress of Calvary! . . .*
> *Born—Bridalled—Shrouded—*
> *In a Day—* [Fr194]

It's as if she were sending us telegrams or tickets from the moon. Her finest poems often have the brutal starts and stops of a telegraphic "tongue" that's difficult to decipher. Her dashes, which can curl up or descend like a cliff, seem to suggest some sort of violent rupture; her mind itself could be ripping as she moves from image to image. Her language is seldom stable, like the contours of our own world; shapes shift. And we're hunters in the dark, looking for traces of Emily Dickinson, while she's a target who never sits still.

3

COMMENTARIES ON HER POEMS began 125 years ago, when Colonel Higginson's little article, "An Open Portfolio," appeared in *The Christian Union* on September 25, 1890, two months before Dickinson's first batch of poems was published by Roberts Brothers of Boston. It was meant to give readers a pre-taste of the poems. Perhaps Higginson was a nervous impresario and worried that his name was attached to a book that might be mocked, and that he himself might be ridiculed as the presenter of Emily Dickinson.

Emerson, he said, had once talked about "The Poetry of the Portfolio," the work of poets who never sought public acclaim, but "wrote for the relief of their own minds." Higginson damned and blessed such primitive scratchings—"there will be wonderful strokes and felicities, and yet an incomplete and unsatisfactory whole." And thus he presented his own "pupil," whom he had reluctantly rescued from oblivion. "Such a sheaf of unpublished verses lies before me, the life-work of a woman so secluded that she lived literally indoors by choice for many years, and within the limits of her father's estate for many more—who shrank from the tranquil society of a New England College town." And yet he was startled by what she was able to dredge up from "this secluded inland life." And he presented a few of his pupil's poems, *regularizing* them as much as he could. The ellipsis was gone; so was every single dash.

Yet he was also a shrewd observer. "Her verses are in most cases like poetry plucked up by the roots; we have them with earth, stones, and dew adhering, and must accept them as they are. Wayward and unconventional in the last degree; defiant of form, measure, rhyme, and even grammar; she yet had an exacting standard of her own, and would wait many days for a word that satisfied." He saw her wildness, and didn't really know how to deal with it.

He must have assumed that these "wayward" poems would be buried overnight. But "An Open Portfolio" had helped create the legend of the recluse in her inland village who could weave her verses "out of the heart's own atoms." Higginson's article succeeded in ways he couldn't have imagined—the book went through printing after printing and sold eleven thousand copies. The village poet had come right out of the cupboard.

In October 1891, in the thick of all this flurry of sales, Higginson received a letter from a wealthy banker-writer, Samuel G. Ward, who *revealed* this wild poet to her coeditor.

MY DEAR MR. HIGGINSON,

> *I am, with all the world, intensely interested in Emily Dickinson. No wonder six editions have been sold, every copy I should think to a New Englander. She may become world famous, or she may never get out of New England. She is the quintessence of that element we all have who are of Puritan descent* pur sang. *We came to this country to think our own thoughts with nobody to hinder. . . . We conversed with our own souls till we lost the art of communicating with other people. The typical family grew up strangers to each other, as in this case. It was* awfully *high, but awfully lonesome. Such prodigies of shyness do not exist elsewhere.*

Ward goes on to describe Dickinson's poetry in perfect pitch. "She was the articulate inarticulate," that lone voice out of the Puritan wilderness. And we haven't gotten much closer to Dickinson's puzzling rhymes, even after more than a century of criticism. We've put back into order the little bound booklets—fascicles—that Mabel Loomis Todd ripped apart. We've studied the shifts in her handwriting. We have her secret stash of poems and whatever letters we could find— Jay Leyda, a man almost as cryptic as Dickinson herself, believed that we may have uncovered only a minuscule portion of her letters—as little as one tenth. And her letters are every bit as bewildering as the poems, perhaps even more so, because they *pretend* to give us a clearer picture of the poet. We soon come to realize that's she's wearing an assortment of masks—sometimes she's Cleopatra *and* an insignificant mouse in the same letter.

It wasn't always like that; in her earliest letters, she's chatty and reliable; the voice is never disembodied, never drifts. She's like a female Mark Twain, a teller of tall tales. Here's Emily at eleven and a half, writing to Austin:

> —*the other day Francis brought your Rooster home and the other 2*
> *went to fighting him while I was gone to School—mother happened*
> *to look out of the window and she saw him laying on the ground—he*
> *was most dead—but she and Aunt Elizabeth went right out and took*
> *him up and put him in a Coop and he is nearly well now—while he*
> *is shut up the other Roosters—will come around and insult him in*
> *Every possible way by Crowing right in his Ears—and then they will*
> *jump up on the Coop and Crow there as if they—wanted to show*
> *that he was Completely in their power and they could treat him as*
> *they chose—Aunt Elizabeth said she wished their throats would split*
> *and then they could insult him no longer—*   [Letter 2, May 1, 1842]

With a bit more vernacular, Huck Finn could be talking here. And at fourteen, she writes to her friend Abiah Root: "I am growing handsome very fast indeed! I expect I shall be the belle of Amherst when I reach my 17th year." [Letter 6, May 7, 1845]

But something happens to that chatty exuberance by the time she's in her twenties. The letters grow shorter and shorter, have much more violent shifts. And when she first writes Higginson in 1862, seducing him with her poems, compelling him with her leaps, she's like a huntress with poison arrows.

"I had a terror—since September—I could tell to none—and so I sing, as the Boy does by the Burying Ground—" [Letter 261, April 25, 1862]

Higginson didn't have a chance. And neither do we. But it's hard to grasp how and where that sudden mastery arose. It had to come from more than craft. It's as if she had a storm inside her head, an illumination, like a wizard or a mathematical genius. Dickinson was reinventing the language of poetry, not by examining poets of the past, but by *cannibalizing* the words in her Lexicon. Jay Leyda was the only one who understood this. In his introduction to *The Years and Hours of Emily Dickinson* (1960), he talked about the "omitted center" in her letters and poems—all the tiny ribs of language that were left out. But Leyda was much more optimistic than I am about where those ribs came from. She told riddles: "the deliberate skirting of the obvious— this was the means she used to increase the privacy of her communication; it has also increased our problems in piercing that privacy." Leyda assumes she always had a reader in mind, that all the missing keys depended upon a specific audience, and that Sue or Austin would know what that "omitted center" was about. Hence he gives us the minutia surrounding Dickinson's life. And *The Years and Hours of Emily Dickinson* is a monumental book that reads like a musical composition or collage, filled with every sort of scrap. That sentimental legend of a lovelorn Emily "*isolates* her—and thus much of her poetry—from the real world. It shows her unaware of community and nation, never seeing anyone, never wearing any color but white, never doing any housework beyond baking batches of cookies for secret delivery to favorite children, and meditating majestically among her flowers."

Leyda was already anticipating *The Belle of Amherst,* years before it was produced. But he believed that Dickinson was no more isolated from the world than most other artists, that "she wrote more *in time,* that she was much more involved in the conflicts and tensions of her nation and community, than we have thought." Yet she remained a riddler, like Leyda himself. Perhaps that's why he was able to penetrate her personality—crawl right under her skin—before any other critic. It's difficult to uncover where Leyda was born, or who raised him. Leyda's "omitted center" is as elusive as Dickinson's. He still believed that hers was *recoverable.*

I'm not so sure. Leyda understood the limits of his "rag-picking method . . . most of our biggest questions about her must remain unanswered." But he still persisted, like some magnificent collagist, still hoped to find the missing keys.

Suppose the keys weren't missing at all, but were part of some private, internal structure. And suppose her definition of poetry was different from ours, and she was a very different kind of poet, more like an explorer and discoverer, who meant to subjugate her Lexicon, rather than juggle words. She would share some of her discoveries in her letter-poems, sing a verse or two to a favorite cousin, but she shared her hand-sewn fascicles with no one; these were very private catalogues, complete in themselves, meant for her own consumption; and the variants to a particular word that she wrote in the margins were like magical flowers, not meant to cancel one another, but to create a cluster, or bouquet. That "omitted center" was less a mask than the sign of her modernity. For those critics who swear she was *feminizing* a male-dominated culture of language constructions, I would say that there's something strange about the femininity of her attack. Camille Paglia best describes the force and "riddling ellipsis" of Dickinson's style. "Protestant hymn-measure is warped and deformed by a stupefying energy. Words are rammed into lines with such force that syntax shatters and collapses into itself." It's that same Yellow Eye of the blonde Assassin. "The brutality of this belle of Amherst would stop a truck."

But more than a century after Higginson first introduced Emily Dickinson to her public, we're still having a hard time unraveling most of her riddles. We've examined her in every sort of context, have peered into her culture and seen how women behaved with other women, and how nineteenth-century courtship rites distanced them from the language of their male suitors. We've seen Dickinson's own sexual ambiguity. Sam Bowles seemed to have a crush on Sue's former schoolmate Kate Scott, but so did Emily Dickinson, who knit a pair of garters for the ravishing young widow, and had the garters sent over to the Evergreens (while Kate was in residence), with the following lines:

> *When Katie walks, this simple pair accompany her side*
> *When Katie runs unwearied they travel on the road,*
> *When Katie kneels, their loving hands still clasp her pious knee—*
> *Ah! Katie! Smile at Fortune, with* two *so* knit *to thee!*

It's hard to imagine that Dickinson was unconscious of how erotic these lines were—it's almost as if she were caressing Kate with her own "loving hands," but whether she was conscious or not, the garters still leap out at us like a pair of seductive spiders.

Yet all her puzzles didn't have such keys, no matter what Leyda said. We may have Kate's reminiscence (in 1917) of Emily at the Evergreens in 1859, "with her dog, & Lantern! often at the piano playing weird & wonderful melodies, all from her own inspiration, oh! She was a choice spirit!" These "weird and wonderful" riffs do mirror the music of her poems, and we can see how Dickinson loved to improvise, but she remains a moving target, hard to find. "Biography first convinces us of the fleeing of the Biographied—" she wrote to Higginson in 1885. [Letter 972]

I believe she suffered horrendously as a woman; dream brides drift in and out of her poems like a continual nightmare—yet she did not want to be "Bridalled." Sometimes she was married to God, with her "Title divine," sometimes to the Devil. Like Sue herself, she had a genuine fear of male sexuality, that infernal "man of noon," who scorches and scalds every little virgin flower—"they know that the man of noon, is *mightier* than the morning and their life is henceforth to him. Oh, Susie, it is dangerous, and it is all too dear, these simple trusting spirits, and the spirits mightier, which we cannot resist! It does rend me, Susie, the thought of it when it comes, that I tremble lest at sometime I, too, am yielded up." [Letter 93, 1852]

She had a plan for Sue and herself, a lifetime of love and devotion to the one craft that was open to women—"we are the only poets, and everyone else is *prose*." [Letter 56, October 9, 1851] Together they might defeat or outfox "the man of noon." But Sue was an orphan in search of a home. She couldn't practice her craft in the poorhouse. And so she yielded herself up to Austin, this willful girl who seemed to have such a sway over Emily all her life. So many of Dickinson's poems and letters are like dream songs, where she had to borrow from Shakespeare to change her sex, morph into some Marc Antony trying to conquer that Cleopatra who lived next door. . . .

I believe that her rebellion against the culture of nineteenth-century Amherst was of another kind. She was promiscuous in her own fashion, deceiving everyone around her with the sly masks she wore. She was faithful to no one but her dog. Her white dress was one more bit of camouflage, to safeguard the witchery of her craft. It may have been an act of impersonation, as Sandra M. Gilbert and Susan Gubar suggest in *The Madwoman in the Attic*, but I don't agree that Dickinson, decked in white, became "a helpless agoraphobic, trapped in her room in her father's house." There's a different tale to tell.

She played the role of little girl that nineteenth-century women were meant to play. But she was far from a little girl, even if she told Higginson, "I have a little shape—it would not crowd your Desk—nor make much Racket as the Mouse, that dents your Galleries—" [Letter 265] It was one more act of seduction. She must have sensed her own monstrous powers—this Vesuvius at Home. The Brain, she would write, is wider than the Sky.

> *The Brain is just the weight of God—*
> *For—Heft them—Pound for Pound—*
> *And they will differ—if they do—*
> *As Syllable from Sound—*   [Fr598]

She may have sent her letter-poems to favorite friends like little bombs of love, but I don't believe she ever meant to share her own "experiments" with anyone else. Higginson was reluctant to unclasp her Portfolio—poems plucked up from the roots of her mind. But she wasn't boasting when she said—twice—that he had saved her life, not because he had much to say about her poems. He didn't. But he cared for his half-cracked poetess, must have sniffed her greatness and her suffering. He wasn't a fool. He just couldn't read the future very well, couldn't have seen that the twentieth century would soon explode into slant rhymes that would render him obsolete. Yet Dickinson desperately needed him. He was her lifeline—not to the literary culture of Boston; she wasn't much interested in that. But she could *practice* her own intelligence—and her craft—on him. And so much of what we will ever know about her comes from her letters to Higginson; with him, she could wear the mask of a poet.

If I read a book [and] *it makes my whole body so cold no fire ever can warm me I know* that *is poetry. If I feel physically as if the top of my head were taken off, I know* that *is poetry. These are the only way I know it. Is there any other way.* [Letter 342a, Higginson to his wife]

Not as far as Dickinson's poetry is concerned. And that's why we pay homage to this outlaw. She wasn't one more madwoman in the attic. She was the mistress of her own interior time and space, where she delivered "Dirks of Melody" that could delight and stun. She was the blonde Assassin who could dance with "the man of noon" and walk away at will—in her poetry.

"I cannot dance upon my Toes—/No Man instructed me—" she declared in one of her most striking poems. But she needed no instruction. Dickinson was dancing all the time. Few people in Amherst ever caught that dance, not even Sue. She danced right past her father's eyes, made herself invisible in her white dress. And Allen Tate, one of a handful of poets and critics who rediscovered Emily Dickinson in the twentieth century, paid her the highest sort of compliment when he said: "Cotton Mather would have burned her for a witch."

4

I WANTED TO FOLLOW THE WITCH'S WAKE, so I went on a pilgrimage to Mount Holyoke College, in western Massachusetts, to breathe in some of the atmosphere the poet had breathed for two semesters, in 1847 and 1848, and to interview Dickinson scholar Christopher Benfey, who teaches a course on Emily Dickinson's time at Mount Holyoke Female Seminary, as the college was then called. But it was like trafficking in ghosts, since the seminary's main building, with its elaborate portico and line of chimneys, no longer exists. And from the window of Benfey's office near the main gate, I looked out upon the little serene pockets and hills of the college lawn. "We did an archaeological dig," he said, "so where you see that oak tree"—in a lacuna on the lawn—"is perhaps the footprint of the building. . . . And the road you came in on is the same road. So Dickinson was right here. Dickinson stood right here where you're sitting—lived right here."

Most scholars, including Alfred Habegger, dismiss the importance of Dickinson's stay at Mount Holyoke. "We know of no new friends she kept up with after leaving. In later years she hardly mentioned the place." Yet I'm convinced that her *grounding* as a poet started here, in South Hadley. It was Dickinson's first extended leave from Amherst as an adolescent—it troubled her, made her feel horribly homesick, but she found a kind of solace in words; there's a sudden *thrill* in language itself as she writes letter after letter to Austin, and we can sense her plumage gather, like some songbird startled by the sound and texture of its own song.

A Menagerie performs outside her window, with its pet monkeys and bears. "The whole company stopped in front of the Seminary & played for about a quarter of an hour, for the purpose of getting custom in the afternoon I opine. Almost all the girls went & I enjoyed the solitude finely." [Letter 16, South Hadley, October 21, 1847]

She needed that solitude—and the distance from her family, so that she could lick her own feathers. As Benfey says about Dickinson, "We put that little mountain range between ourselves and our mother and our father and our sister and our brother, and we think, I'm separate from them. I'm alone with language in a new way. I'm writing letters with a new intensity. For the first time, we have that sense of Dickinson writing these letters that go across mountains and across rivers. And for the first time, she has the sense that words travel, that they have wings," like the hummingbird and its "Route of Evanescence" that Dickinson loved to write about.

> *And every Blossom on the Bush*
> *Adjusts its tumbled Head—*
> *The Mail from Tunis— probably—*
> *And easy Morning's ride—*   [Fr1489A]

But it wasn't simply her solitude that sharpened her. She met her first real antagonist, Mary Lyon, within the school's walls. Lyon was a formidable foe. The founder and headmistress of Mount Holyoke Female Seminary, Lyon came from a much humbler background than the poet and believed in educating rich and poor alike as female soldiers in Christ. But no matter how wily she was, the headmistress in the severe white bonnet couldn't get Dickinson to profess her faith, couldn't rescue her soul. Emily Dickinson was one of the few "unsaved" seminarians. The battle was less about God and the Devil than about two women with strong wills, one of them a sixteen-year-old girl whose father was almost as tyrannical as Mary Lyon. None of Lyon's little Christian soldiers could *persuade* the poet. She learned whatever she wanted to learn, and discarded all the rest.

Benfey was still bemused by Dickinson as a young scholar. "I like to joke that she spent a year here and still thought *i-t-apostrophe-s* was the possessive of *it*, a word that she would write in a particular way." But that allowed her to give *any* word "a color, a taste, a feel, a texture, an intensity" that no other poet could duplicate.

Yet Benfey still broods over the year Dickinson spent at Mount Holyoke. He's surrounded by the college's earliest catalogues on his shelves, but insists, "We don't really know what Mount Holyoke was like. I'm sitting in this office with a direct connection to Mary Lyon and Emily Dickinson. I think I know as much about that period as anyone alive and I know nothing. . . . I know more about the questions. I know that Mary Lyon is as mysterious a figure as Emily Dickinson, that if we could begin to understand who Mary Lyon was, we might begin to understand how complex that relationship was.

"I speak as a biographer here, a self-torturing biographer. But every account of Dickinson feels wrong. I can't pretend that I can say, *'And then Dickinson entered Mount Holyoke, a really important transitional milestone'*—it feels false from the first letter put down on the page."

And this is the dilemma we all have, that impossible plunder of capturing whoever she was. We fling out words like a chorus of arrows to find some mark, to *brand* Emily Dickinson, mythologize her in some way, and she hints at all the dangers, gives us a wicked slap in the face.

Finding is the first Act
The second, loss,
Third, Expedition for the "Golden Fleece"

Fourth, no Discovery—
Fifth, no Crew—
Finally, no Golden Fleece—
Jason, sham, too— [Fr910]

5

BENFEY AGREES WITH W. H. AUDEN "that language finds certain people and lives through them, almost the way a virus lives by finding a host, I think language lives by finding hosts. . . . It found a way to live in Shakespeare. Infested him. Got all it could out of Shakespeare and then moved on."

"It didn't disappear," I say. "It went into the ground—"

"For a long time, and found Emily Dickinson."

And then the virus moved on. "You listen to those early songs of Bob Dylan, and you think, Whoa, how could he have written them? But he doesn't know. Just as Dickinson wouldn't have been able to say, *'Well, I first thought of the loaded gun image when I was sitting in my father's room and there was a gun in the corner and I thought, I'm like that gun.'* We have no idea."

And the letters she wrote were as puzzling as that loaded gun.

"We still don't know how to read them," Benfey says. "We assume the difficulty of the poems. And we assume the availability and relative intelligibility of the letters. It's gotta be the opposite, because with the poems, we have some idea what rhyme and meter are. But with the letters, we have no fucking clue what the rules for reading and writing letters are. The 'Master Letters' have gotten a ton of attention, but it's the other letters . . ."

We talk about the cunning and the craft of her letters to Higginson. "She doesn't need him as a mentor," I say, and Benfey agrees.

"That's where we get the sense of her as a performance artist. She walks downstairs to see Higginson, carrying the two day lilies, and says, 'These are my introduction' in a breathy voice, and it was the most amazing sort of ballet imaginable. You know. The white dress . . ."

Higginson served as "a mirror, a conduit, a messenger—a publicist. Somehow she identifies both [her] publicists, Higginson and Mabel Loomis Todd. And damned if they don't pair up and sell her to the world.

"She performs for both of them. She gives them just the amount they need; she withholds access in just the right way." She tantalizes Mabel, never reveals herself. "'You may see me when I'm in my ultimate box, in my coffin. That's when you'll see me for the first time, in my box.'"

She "micromanaged" her own funeral, like another ballet, "with the Irish Catholic men carrying her out through the open barn—and put her in another box, the tomb, another box on top of it. The whole thing was orchestrated beyond belief."

Yet I'm not convinced that her final performance was to have a pair of messengers, Mabel and Higginson, *entomb* her poems in yet another box and publish them. The "phosphorescence" of her poems was from a very private glow. She spelled the way she wanted to spell, constructed her poems like hieroglyphics with all the weird minuscules and majuscules of her own hand, until you could no longer tell the difference between them; it was the deepest sort of play.

> *My Basket holds—just—Firmaments—*
> *Those—dangle easy—on my arm,*
> *But smaller bundles—Cram.*   [Fr358]

She had no time for those "smaller bundles" of recognition and career. It's not that she disregarded her own worth as a poet, but she saw that worth in a messianic way.

> *The Poets light but Lamps—*
> *Themselves—go out—*
> *The Wicks they stimulate*
> *If vital Light*
>
> *Inhere as do the Suns—*
> *Each Age a Lens*
> *Disseminating their*
> *Circumference—*   [Fr930]

And she was out "opon Circumference," where she wasn't hindered by custodians of culture, and could explore as she pleased. *"Finite— to fail, but infinite—to Venture—"* [Fr952] She tore language from its roots, created an internal Teletype that is still difficult for us to comprehend. *None* of us knows her motives. We have to pry, like clumsy surgeons. We attach ourselves to whatever clues we can. And we try to listen, crawl into that hole in time where her creativity began.

The Clock strikes One
That just struck Two—   [Fr1598D]

TWO

———∞∞———

The Two Emilys—and the Earl

I
—

IN 1956, R. P. BLACKMUR, who was as much of an autodidact and outsider as Emily Dickinson, and grew up less than fifty miles from where she was born, wrote about her in *The Kenyon Review*: "One exaggerates, but it sometimes seems as if in her work a cat came at us speaking English." This is what Colonel Higginson must have intuited, without ever being able to articulate it—this strange woman, who had "the playful ambiguity of a kitten being a tiger," according to Blackmur. She must have scratched Higginson many a time with her "claws," while she called herself his Scholar and his Gnome; she crawled right under his skin. She bombarded him with letters and poems, even while he was away at war. He returned from battle like a wounded ghost, settled in Newport, had to take care of his sick wife. He tried three times to lure Emily out of her *carapace* and have her come to Boston, where she could listen to him lecture, converse with other poets, and attend meetings with other women at the aristocratic and exclusive Women's Club. And Dickinson refused him three times. ". . . I do not cross my Father's ground to any House or town," she wrote to the colonel in 1869. It's Dickinson's credo of defiance and probably her most famous line. [Letter 330, June 1869]

Dickinson scholars love to toss this credo back at us as hard evidence of her growing agoraphobia. But it's evidence of nothing more than her swagger, her delight in shocking the colonel. Meanwhile, she plotted in her own way, kept inviting Higginson to Amherst. Finally, after corresponding with her for eight years, he did go to see his half-cracked poetess, in August 1870. The death of an older brother, who had lived nearby, gave him the excuse to visit. It was one of the great encounters in American literature. A gentle soul who swore he loved danger walked right into Emily Dickinson's lair and met the Satanic, catlike sibyl whom R. P. Blackmur would write about almost a century later. She glided down the stairs of her father's house and said, "Forgive me if I am frightened; I never see strangers & hardly know what I say—" [Letter 342a, Higginson to his wife] and talked continuously for an hour, sucking all the energy out of the colonel.

And when Higginson finally got a word in and asked the reclusive sibyl "if she never felt want of employment, never going off the place & never seeing any visitor," the sibyl said, "'I never thought of conceiving that I could ever have the slightest approach to such a want in all future time' (& added) 'I feel that I have not expressed myself strongly enough.'" [Letter 342a]

That sounds more like a poet plucking her feathers and pruning her resources than an agoraphobic who was careening out of control.

And then she uttered something that was even odd for a sibyl. She asked Higginson if he could tell her what "home" is. "I never had a mother," she said. "I suppose a mother is one who to whom you hurry when you are troubled." [Letter 342b] She was thirty-nine years old. And in not one of her previous letters—to Higginson or any other correspondent—had she ever spoken of herself as a motherless child. Nor had she said *anything* unkind about her mother, Emily Norcross Dickinson—Emily Sr., as some scholars call Mrs. Dickinson to distinguish her from her poet daughter. She appears in one of Dickinson's very first letters, where she helps save Austin's sick rooster from oblivion. She's a whirlwind of activity—cooking, sewing, gardening, and going off to "ramble" with her neighbors, bringing them crullers or another delight, and "she really was so hurried she hardly knew what to do." [Letter 52, September 23, 1851] Sometimes she suffers from neuralgia, where one side of her face freezes up. And in 1855, after Edward Dickinson moved his family back to the Homestead, *his* father's former house, she fell into a funk that lasted four years. But her daughter was just as uneasy about the move. ". . . I am out with lanterns, looking for myself." [Letter 182, about January 20, 1856]

Both mother and daughter had frequent bouts of melancholy. Both took part in Amherst's most publicized event, the annual Cattle Show, where they baked pies and bread and served on committees. And even after her sibyl-like remark to Higginson, she still recognized the presence of her mother, as she wrote to her cousins Louise and Frances Norcross: ". . . Mother drives with Tim [the stableman] to carry pears to settlers. Sugar pears, with hips like hams, and the flesh of bonbons." [Letter 343]

Then, in 1874, she wrote to Higginson:

> *I always ran Home to Awe when a child, if anything befell me.*
> *He was an awful Mother, but I liked him better than none.*
> [Letter 405]

Here she was doubly unkind. Not only didn't she have an anthropomorphic mother, but the mother she did have—*Awe*—had a male identity. She was now forty-three, long past her most productive period, as most Dickinson scholars believe. And why did she suddenly parade in front of Higginson with one of her letter bombs and *annihilate* her own mother? But it wasn't only Mrs. Dickinson who was in her line of fire. In 1873, while both her parents were still alive, she wrote to Mrs. J. G. Holland, one of her most trusted friends:

> *I was thinking of thanking you for the kindness to Vinnie.*
> *She has no Father and Mother but me and I have no Parents but*
> *her.* [Letter 391]

It had to have been more than some momentary crisis. She adored her father—and feared him. He was constantly present in her mental and material life. She'd become a creator in her father's house, in that corner room, with her Lexicon, her lamp, and her minuscule writing desk.

Sweet hours have perished here,
This is a timid [mighty] *room—* [Fr1785A]

But the two biting remarks to Higginson about her mother would have a scattergun effect. In 1971, psychoanalyst and Dickinson scholar John Cody published *After Great Pain: The Inner Life of Emily Dickinson*, a five-hundred-page study that presents Dickinson as a mental case whose only manner of survival was writing her cryptic and very private poems. Cody argues that Dickinson could never have become a poet without her *delinquent* mother—she was indeed a motherless child, emotionally abandoned by a woman who was "shallow, self-centered, ineffectual, conventional, timid, submissive, and not very bright." Mrs. Dickinson was utterly responsible for her daughter's "*infantile* dependence . . . and compulsive self-entombment." And, says Cody, "one is led to conclude that all her life there smoldered in Emily Dickinson's soul the muffled but voracious clamoring of the abandoned child."

Cody isn't the only culprit. For many critics, Dickinson has remained the madwoman entombed in her own little attic. Even Alfred Habegger, one of her most subtle biographers, believes that Dickinson's "great genius is not to be distinguished from her madness." And for Sandra M. Gilbert and Susan Gubar, Emily Dickinson may have posed as a madwoman to insulate herself, but became "truly a madwoman (a helpless agoraphobic, trapped in a room in her father's house)." Whatever theories we may hold about madness and art, or about some great psychic wound Dickinson suffered—a relentless blow that Dickinson herself described—

A Death blow— is a Life blow— to Some
Who, till they died,
Did not alive—become—   [Fr966A]

her letters and poems are not the work of a madwoman, or someone
trying to cover up her own debilitating tremors and attacks. In a letter to Colonel Higginson, Sue wrote that Emily "hated her peculiarities, and shrank from any notice of them as a nerve from the knife."
Why don't I believe her? Dickinson's entire life was a singularity; she
could have been one of Melville's "isolatoes," living in the interior
continent of her own mind. How else could she have thrived? But
Sue had a terrifying need to normalize her sister-in-law, turn her into
one more village poet, scribbling about unrequited love. She couldn't
bear to look at Emily's deep rage and urge to destroy. Dickinson never
shrank from any knife—she loved knives. It was her task at Mount
Holyoke to clean the knives and collect them, like some kind of knife
thrower in the making. She could wound us all with "Dirks of Melody." [Fr1450] Mutilation had become a central motif in her letters
and poems. "Here is Festival," she wrote to Sue in 1864, exiled in
Cambridge for nearly eight months while a Boston ophthalmologist
dealt with her irritated eyes. "Where my Hands are cut, Her fingers
will be found inside—" [Letter 288]

It's one of Dickinson's most disturbing images, as if Sue and Emily
were sisters bound together by mutilation, but where had this mutilation come from? Had Emily cut herself, or had Sue crept inside her like
some ghoul, with a dirk of her own? There's a lot of bile and savagery
in that image. And perhaps it might help us understand her own sudden, brutal remarks to Higginson about her mother, like Blackmur's
cat breaking into English. Dickinson wasn't a madwoman, but she was
maddened with rage—against a culture that had no place for a woman
with her own fiercely independent mind and will. Yet that annihilation
of Emily Sr. was also about something else. Dickinson had to reinvent
herself, or be stifled and destroyed by all the rituals around her—she

was the daughter of the town patriarch. Cody believes that Dickinson was doomed to become a spinster because she was "too uncertain of her attractiveness and too fearful of heterosexuality to consider marriage." That hardly stopped most other women of her class, and it wouldn't have stopped the Belle of Amherst. I suspect that what disturbed her more than giving in to the "man of noon" was the notion of having to give up the Dickinson name. She could only become "The Wife—without the Sign!" [Fr194A] Her brother was the adored one, the pampered one—he would perpetuate the Dickinson line. Emily and her sister were household pets. Edward would school the girls, send them both to a female seminary, but he never mapped much of a future for them. Born into a genteel caste, the two sisters "suffered the tormenting paralysis of women deadlocked by a culture that treated them as both servant and superior," according to Susan Howe in *My Emily Dickinson*, a kind of love song from one poet to her nineteenth-century sister. And so we have the picture of Emily Dickinson as the perpetual child, a pose she often adopted with Higginson and others as one of her many masks. But that childish whisper of Emily's wasn't her natural voice—her own hoarse contralto wasn't a whisper at all. She was, as Howe insists, a woman "with Promethean ambition." She would remain a Dickinson, but parent herself, become a creature of both sexes, defiantly original and androgynous.

> *A loss of something ever felt I—*
> *The first that I could recollect*
> *Bereft I was—of what I knew not*
> *Too young that any should suspect*
>
> *A Mourner walked among the children*
> *I notwithstanding went about*
> *As one bemoaning a Dominion*
> *Itself the only Prince cast out—*   [Fr1072]

And it was as "the only Prince cast out" that she lived her life, searching for the "Delinquent Palaces" of her childhood—and her art. We can feel that streak of rebellion when she unconsciously sympathizes with a maverick student at Mount Holyoke. She had only been there a little longer than a month and was still homesick when she wrote to Austin:

> *A young lady by the name of Beach, left here for home this morning. She could not get through her examinations & was very wild beside.* [Letter 17, November 2, 1847]

It was this wildness that frightened and attracted Emily, a wildness that would haunt the dreamscape of her poems. We never learn what happened to Miss Beach, whether she settled down with some "man of noon" or remained a maverick—another "Prince cast out." But Dickinson had to rebel in a much more secret and convoluted way, as the village Prometheus, who stole whatever she could from her Lexicon and the local gods of Amherst, and manufactured her very own fire.

Self-born, self-tutored, she had to tear apart all ties to her mother, the one creature who had done the most to shape her sensibility. Emily Dickinson's own elliptical songs are like a hymn to her mother's repeated silences and melancholy. But who was Emily Norcross Dickinson and why do we know so little about her?

2

P ART OF IT IS EMILY SR.'S OWN FAULT. She suffered all her life from logophobia, a fear—and distrust—of the written word. Vinnie, the daughter who was closest to her, who could knit and sew and clean the house like a dervish, suffered from a bit of the same fear.

> *. . . though I've always had a great aversion to writing, I hope, by constant practice, the dislike will wear away, in a degree, at least.*

But Vinnie wasn't shy, the way her mother was. Vinnie loved to flirt. She was also a mime and a reader of books. And she overcame her word blindness enough to write seventeen poems that still survive.

The fire-flies hold their lanterns high
    To guide the falling star,
But, if by chance the wicks grow short
    The stars might lose their way.

Vinnie has almost a kind of fictional glow; we can imagine her fat little fingers, her brown hair and brown eyes, her plump arms, her growing army of cats, her waspish tongue—she assumes mythical proportions and powers in the eyes of her poet sister. Vinnie could be "full of Wrath, and vicious as Saul—" [Letter 520, September 1877]

And during the presidential campaign of 1880, Emily wrote to Mrs. Holland:

Vinnie is far more hurried than Presidential Candidates—I trust
in more distinguished ways, for they have only the care of the Union,
but Vinnie the Universe—   [Letter 667, 1880]

Emily hurls a lot of her own Promethean fire on Edward, Vinnie, Austin, and Sue. We can recall her father stepping like Cromwell, or wandering in his slippers after a storm, to feed the hungry birds; and Dickinson scholars have examined and reexamined Austin, who would become a sad clown in purple pantaloons and coppery green wig; Sue remains the Dark Lady of Dickinson scholarship—volatile, complex, and ultimately unfathomable; we follow her tracks and can only find more and more mysterious lines. It's hard to determine what she really thought about *anything*. She excites us, as she excited Emily. We can imagine her dark, smoldering face, masculine and feminine at the same time. But we cannot imagine the least wisp of Emily Norcross Dickinson. We have her daguerreotype and a silhouette of her, but she still remains invisible, as if her steps can never be traced.

This was true of most women in the nineteenth century, privileged or not. But in 1975, Carroll Smith-Rosenberg published a controversial essay, "The Female World of Love and Ritual: Relations between Women in Nineteenth-Century America," which revealed that women had their own remarkable and secret history. Smith-Rosenberg believes they "did not form an isolated and oppressed sub-category in male society. Their letters and diaries indicate that women's sphere had an essential integrity that grew out of women's shared experiences and mutual affection. . . . Continuity, not discontinuity, characterized this female world."

Women had their own signs and symbols, their own love codes. "Girls routinely slept together, kissed and hugged each other," and they continued to kiss and hug even after they were married. Men made "but a shadowy appearance" in this landscape of women, if they ever appeared at all. But Smith-Rosenberg seems to oversimplify the almost mystical power that women shared among themselves. Men intruded everywhere, before and after marriage. "Women of Dickinson's class and century existed in a legal and financial state of dependence on their fathers, brothers, or husbands, that psychologically mutilated them," according to Susan Howe. After their father died, Emily and her sister went around like paupers and could hardly make a purchase without Austin's approval. They were wards of a male world.

But there's another distortion in Smith-Rosenberg's study of female friendship and ritual. She writes about women who were highly literate and could articulate their wishes and their woes, thus giving them a power and a perspective that many men and women did not have. There must have been a far greater unwritten record—of women who never mastered the art of writing. They might have been part of the same society that Smith-Rosenberg writes about, kissing, exchanging secrets, and trooping from home to home in an endless social knot as they presided over births and deaths. But they cannot share their pain, their joy, and their melancholy with us. They are the invisible ones, and Emily Norcross is among them.

She was born on July 3, 1804, in Monson, a rural community twenty miles south of Amherst. Her father, Joel Norcross, was a rich farmer who helped found Monson Academy, a school that admitted females as well as males. Joel believed in the education of his daughters—he had three of them and six sons, several wiped out by consumption, a disease that plagued the family. His wife, Betsy Fay, would die of it at fifty-one. Emily was the eldest daughter. She was attached to her one surviving sister, Lavinia, born in 1812, a feisty girl who loved to scribble letters and poems.

Rich as her father was, Emily Norcross didn't have an easy time at home. Joel had only one servant to care for an enormous barn-like house that had once been a tavern. Most of the chores fell on Emily. Joel took in boarders, and Emily also had to care for them. Her mother couldn't do very much; she was sick a good part of the time. And we can imagine how erratic Emily's schooling must have been. She still managed to attend a fancy girls' boarding school in New Haven for several months when she was nineteen. There's no record of her having met Edward Dickinson, who was also in New Haven at the time, about to graduate from Yale.

Emily returned to Monson, her education over. She would meet Edward three years later at a "Chemical" lecture on January 1, 1828—it happened to be his birthday. Edward had just turned twenty-five; she was twenty-three, practically an old maid in Monson. Edward was a law student who had to struggle, since his father couldn't seem to juggle his own accounts. Samuel Fowler Dickinson was still one of the most prominent men in Amherst. Cofounder of Amherst College, he had run—unsuccessfully—for Congress. He wanted to bring a law school to Amherst. He would claim that Edward had been the valedictorian of his class at Yale. It was a bald lie. Samuel had to yank his boy more than once from New Haven, and Edward barely had enough time and money to graduate. The "Squire," as Samuel was called, continued to remain involved with Amherst College, and he sank whatever small fortune he had into paying the school's bills. He lived on loan after loan, until there was little left to borrow.

Meanwhile, Edward was now a major in the Massachusetts militia And he hadn't come to Monson to study chemistry, but to preside over a military court. He had to pass judgment over a reckless lieutenant colonel who had vanished from camp. And we have to wonder if Edward was wearing his uniform, with it ceremonial sword and sash, at the lecture. Is that what caught Emily's eye? And what did Edward see in this silent girl? He must have been bewitched by her. He wrote his first letter to her on February 8 and never stopped writing. But he realized soon enough that Emily Norcross wasn't much of a correspondent. She didn't answer him until March. He had made her aware that he was looking for a bride. He proposed marriage on June 4—marriage by mail. He received no reply. He wrote to her father, who was just as silent. Joel Norcross wasn't that eager to relinquish a daughter who had become the workhorse of his family. This accumulation of silences couldn't discourage Edward, who continued to press his case, like a lawyer and militiaman. But Emily wasn't unmoved. She must have been fond of her suitor's red hair and barrage of long letters. Finally, at the end of October, she agreed to marry him, more or less.

That's when the torture began. He couldn't get much of a commitment out of Emily. He visited Monson, but she wouldn't introduce him to any of her friends, as if his marriage plans were secret to everyone, including herself. Edward complained:

> . . . *for, I think, if you intend to be seen with me at all, you can not have much delicacy in accompanying me to a neighbor's house, after I have shewn myself* publicly *to the good people of Monson . . . with no particular* business *to make my visits so frequent, except what I have transacted with you. I begin to be plain, you see. Don't you think it is time?—*

Often he rages like King Lear to prove his constancy and devotion, but it is a Lear made of tin, alas.

> *I cannot tell when I shall visit you again—I will let your people know in season to prepare for* a storm—*Let the winds howl—let the storms beat—let my horses die!—let my sleighs break—let all the elements conspire against me. I can not, so long as my person is safe—I shall not be discouraged . . . Let us continue virtuous & we shall be happy.*

He sounds like a very odd suitor, his letters stuffed with bewildering banalities. "I know not what is in store for us—We may be happy—We may be the reverse—We may be fortunate. We may be unfortunate," he writes to her on September 24, 1827. There isn't much blood or fire in Edward's remarks. He could be ordering a *perfect* bride out of a catalogue. He promises to be "the lawful promoter" of her "lasting enjoyment." His letters grow longer and longer, while he also promises "not to send another of such an unmerciful prolixity." But he cannot keep his promise. He wants to control her every move. He's like an intelligence officer spying on his future wife.

It gets him nowhere. Emily isn't unkind. "Pleasant dreams to you dear Edward," she writes in September of 1827, after a lapse of six weeks. She has her own wayward sense of grammar and punctuation. Her spelling is perverse, as her poet daughter's would be. Her handwriting is beautiful and precise, almost sculpted; not a single line wavers. We can imagine the care that must have gone into every word. Vivian Pollak, who edited *A Poet's Parents: The Courtship Letters of Emily Norcross and Edward Dickinson*, believes that Emily had the upper hand in this battle of words between Edward and his reluctant bride-to-be. She used silence as a strategy, as her armor against Edward's maneuvers and warlike advances.

I'm not so sure. I suspect her silences masked a kind of shame. She would be marrying a lawyer. "My education is my inheritance," he wrote her at the beginning of their romance. He'd gone to Yale, and she was a farmer's daughter who had mastered the art of penmanship, but that itself was a ruse; all the curlicues covered up a genuine hysteria about the deeper twists of language. Yet we're always touched by what she writes, while Edward's sentences have their own hard shellac. He just won't understand that she may love him and still be afraid of marriage. "I have many friends call upon me as they say to make their farewell visit. How do you suppose this sounds in my ear But my dear it is to go and live with you."

She kept delaying the wedding date, wouldn't even visit him in Amherst. "Have I not reason to fear that you will think it best to remain at Monson after we are married?" he writes. She still refused to visit him, and sent Lavinia as her surrogate. And poor Lavinia, now fifteen, was lonely from the instant she arrived in Amherst.

Emily was determined about one thing: She wanted a wedding "with as little noise as possible." There would be no bridesmaid or bridesman. They were married in Monson on May 6, 1828, in her father's house, while her mother was mortally ill.

Edward had established himself as a lawyer in Amherst; and he moved his bride into *half* the widow Jemima Montague's house, near his office. We know almost nothing about the widow Montague or her house. All we know is that she wouldn't provide Edward with any milk, and he had to keep a cow. Emily didn't have a single male or female friend—Amherst might as well have been Antarctica. She had to take in student boarders, or they could never have afforded to live in Jemima Montague's house. Edward's parents and siblings were very little solace. His mother, Lucretia Gunn Dickinson, was a cold, bitter woman with a sharp tongue. His father was sinking into bankruptcy. Emily was all alone. Edward couldn't even take her to Monson to see her mother—he was much too busy with his career.

No one but Lavinia understood her pain, her loneliness, and grief. A few years later, she would write:

Sister! Why that burning tear
Stealing slowly down thy cheek
To my friendly listening ear
All thy little sorrows speak.

Meanwhile, Austin Dickinson, named after one of her dead brothers, was born on April 16, 1829. Emily hadn't seen her mother once. And she wouldn't visit Monson until a few days before Betsy Fay Norcross died that September. She had to grieve alone. She didn't even have the security of her new home. A year after Austin's birth, Edward moved out of the widow Montague's and into his father's house, the Homestead; built by Samuel Fowler Dickinson in 1813, it was the first brick mansion in Amherst. But the Squire was swimming in mortgages and had to sell the Homestead to one of his cousins; he remained in the eastern half as a tenant, while Edward purchased the western half of the house.

Emily had almost nothing to do with Edward's siblings, and she was like a sibling herself. She didn't get along with Lucretia Gunn Dickinson; no one did. And on December 10, 1830, Emily Elizabeth Dickinson was born in Squire Dickinson's former house, presumably at five o'clock in the morning. Whatever gifts she had or developed with such tenacity didn't come from that stilted language revealed in her father's courtship letters. She inherited his red hair, not his writing voice.

"Language is first made in the mother's body," writes Aífe Murray in *Maid as Muse*. For Emily Dickinson, it may have been a very sad song. Her mother was plaintive most of her life. And, says Murray, "No language acquisition will ever be so sensate as the learning of our mother tongue." But that mother tongue was shaped by the sounds and movements of a young wife in a house that must have sometimes felt like half a prison—and a morgue. Her melancholy didn't come out of nowhere. Less than a month after she gave birth to Emily Elizabeth, her father, Joel Norcross, married again, to Sarah Vaill, a much younger woman. Lavinia was perturbed by her father's decision to remarry so soon after her mother's death. She would write to her sister on December 6, 1830:

> *I know of no one that I should prefer to her* [Sarah Vaill] *from what I have heard of her character & I hope it will be for Father's happiness & the happiness of his family—but we can not tell—what shall I call her? Can I say Mother.*

We have no written record or reaction of how Emily Sr. felt. But she must have continued to grieve for her mother, and locked that grief inside herself. That hardly means she abandoned Austin and little Emily. Yet Dickinson's psychoanalytic biographer, John Cody, makes this wildly reductive remark. "A warmer relationship with her mother would probably have made her a housewife," as if Cody had found the dynamics of Dickinson's art. But I suspect another dynamic was at play here, that Dickinson absorbed her mother's pain, and was her own little mourner—that mourner would become Vesuvius at Home, a poet filled with a crackling rage.

> *The soul has moments of escape—*
> *When bursting all the doors—*
> *She dances like a Bomb, abroad . . .*   [Fr360]

3

EMILY Sr. SUFFERED THE WAY most other women suffered in nineteenth-century New England, however rich or poor. If she wanted to marry, she had to leave her parents' home like a vagabond in a bridal gown, shelve herself inside her husband's surname, learn to live with this man who was little more than a stranger, no matter what courtship rites were followed, and become subservient to this stranger's kin and to all his sexual needs and desires. Women were trained by their mothers and older sisters to give in to "a man's requirements" and "the low practices" of sexual intercourse. They were told to lie still and to seek no pleasure for themselves. There was no pleasure to be had in this kind of ritualized rape. They were harlots if they ever moved or groaned with delight. There were, of course, exceptions to this rule—women who were a bit more adventurous, and husbands who were gentler and more *feminized*. Women and men were both trapped within the same Calvinist culture, and were often victims of an identical patriarchy. If they didn't profess their faith, they would rot in hell—husbands might be separated forever from their wives and children. And so there were constant religious revivals, mass professions of faith. But there were no female pastors. Men ruled the church, just as they ruled the banks and the law courts, and ruled Amherst College. Mount Holyoke Female Seminary wasn't founded until 1837; even if Emily Norcross had been a better student, she would have had nowhere else to go after she returned from her boarding school in New Haven. And Susan's daughter, Martha Dickinson Bianchi, who was an unreliable narrator in anything to do with her aunt, still understood the merciless repertoire of every single Amherst belle: "between the abrupt ending of school routine and the fatal hour of marriage there was for every girl a chasm to be filled in."

Emily Norcross was a farm girl, not the daughter of an Amherst squire; she must have cleaned and scrubbed from the age of ten. And she had to grow up with all the fears and mystery that surrounded childbirth; so few children survived that they often weren't given a proper name until they reached the age of one. Austin and Susan's firstborn wasn't given a name at birth; soon he was called "Jacky," until he survived six months and now had an official name, Edward, or Ned.

There was no anesthetic; childbirth was not only dangerous, it was also filled with shame; a male doctor, rather than a midwife, poked around in your waters. He delivered your child with medieval instruments and his own bloody hands. Women often went from pregnancy to pregnancy, with little time to recover; but being pregnant didn't *deliver* them from their chores. We have to imagine Emily Sr. in her isolation at the widow Montague's, or at the mansion on Main

Street, with Lucretia Gunn Dickinson as the real mistress of the house. Edward was seldom there; he was part of the fire brigade and would soon be running for public office. Little Emily must have *felt* her mother's loneliness; she was like a primitive Geiger counter, "a Goblin with a Guage" [Fr425]; that was her particular genius. Soon she had a little sister; Vinnie, named after her own aunt Lavinia, was born on February 28, 1833, at nine o'clock in the morning. But Mrs. Dickinson couldn't seem quite to recover, and she would never have another child. Vinnie herself was ill for a while. Perhaps it's why Mrs. Dickinson seemed to favor her.

When Emily was two and a half, she was sent to stay in Monson with her aunt Lavinia while her own mother and little sister continued to convalesce. We have a remarkable record of the trip in Jay Leyda's *The Years and Hours of Emily Dickinson*, as Lavinia wrote her sister about the various stages of this voyage to Monson. Scholars have picked Lavinia's letters apart to look for signs of Mrs. Dickinson's abandonment of her little daughter. But the letters are poignant and funny, and offer our first glimpse of "Elizabeth," as Aunt Lavinia called Emily Dickinson. She and her little niece left Amherst sometime in the spring of 1833 and found themselves in the middle of a thunderstorm.

> *Just after we passed Mr Clapps—it thundered more & the thunder and lightning increased—Elizabeth called it* the *fire—the time the rain wind and darkness came we were along in those pine woods—the thunder echoed—I will confess that I felt rather bad. . . . We tho't if we stopped we should not get home* [to Monson] *that night—Elizabeth felt inclined to be frightened some—she said "Do take me to my mother" But I covered her face all under my cloack to protect her & took care that she did not get wet much . . .*

On May 9, she wrote to Edward, her brother-in-law, that little Elizabeth had learned to play the piano—"she calls it the *moosic.*" Later that month, she wrote that Elizabeth was now a perfect little member of the family. Joel Norcross was "much amused" by the little girl. And Lavinia now played the perfect aunt. She groomed the little girl, got her "a little gingham apron [and] some new *hose.*"

> *She speaks of her father & mother occasionally & little Austin*
> *but does not express a wish to see you—Hope this wont make you*
> *feel bad—She is very affectionate & we all love her very much—*
> *She don't appear at all as she does at home & she does not make*
> *but very little trouble—When I wish you come for her I will let*
> *you know . . .*

John Cody and other Dickinson sleuths read this as a clear sign of the little girl's deprivation and distance from her mother. But Aunt Lavinia's remarks reveal more about herself than about the two Emilys. She had a new stepmother and was never comfortable around her. She was in love with her own first cousin, Loring Norcross, and would marry him the following year, but alliances between first cousins were practically forbidden, and her own alliance was frowned upon by all her relatives in Monson. She wrote to her sister about Loring:

> *Emily—no wonder you are astonished to hear—of the attach-*
> *ment between cousin Loring & myself—You expressed your surprise*
> *when I was at A[mherst] you recollect—One year ago I thought of*
> *no such thing but I know that now my heart is devoted to him. . . .*
> *I have had many sorrowful hours—for we are connected & we have*
> *been brought up together . . . If I love him, It is sufficient—& I*
> *have banished those doubts & fears—Whether it be right for cous-*
> *ins to marry or no—*

And so it was important for Lavinia to have Elizabeth around; the little girl distracted her from her dilemma over Loring, and allowed her to become a kind of mother, or at least a motherly aunt. And she writes on June 11, just after *her* Elizabeth had been returned to the Homestead.

> *I cant tell you how lonely I was—it seemed so different & I wanted*
> *to weep all the time—the next Morning after Emily was gone I saw a*
> *little apron that she left & you cant think how I felt . . .*

Aunt Lavinia was the deprived one, who suffered the loss of not having Elizabeth —note how she calls her Emily again once the little girl is gone. Emily Dickinson was much too young to understand Lavinia's predicament and stubborn will. She would love Aunt Lavinia all her life, and love Lavinia and Loring's children, Frances and Louisa— Fanny and Loo—and would board with them in Cambridge when her eyes bothered her. She wrote some of her warmest letters to Fanny and Loo, called them her "little brothers," and no matter how landlocked she was in her "Pearl Jail" at the Homestead, she never denied them anything on their visits to Amherst.

But Aunt Lavinia also provided a kind of symbolic key for the future poet. By marrying her first cousin, Lavinia would guard her maiden name—she remained a Norcross. It must have been a magical quotient for Emily Dickinson. Of course, she never found a first cousin of her own. And there wasn't one to marry. But it had to give her some delight.

When Aunt Lavinia died of the Norcross disease—consumption— in 1860, Emily wrote the following to Loo:

> *"Mama" never forgets her birds—*
> *Though in another tree.*
> *She looks down just as often*
> *And just as tenderly,*
> *As when her little mortal nest*
> *With cunning care she wove—*
> *If either of her "sparrows fall",*
> *She "notices" above.*   [Fr130]

Dickinson could just as well have been writing about her own mother—I'm sure the two sisters were "entangled" in her mind. And we have to rid ourselves of the negative notions that have fallen upon Emily Sr. and threaten to wipe out whatever little traces we have of her, as if the poet's father had such significance in her life and Emily Sr. had none. Habegger calls her a woman with a "relatively inelastic spirit." Sewall speaks of "this fluttery, timid woman." Lyndall Gordon, in *Lives Like Loaded Guns*, pretends she didn't exist at all: "the mother, the usual provider of emotional nourishment, is strangely absent."

Sewall himself relented a bit in a letter to Jay Leyda:

> *Even Mrs. Dickinson's distaste for writing letters is blown up to account (in part) for Emily Dickinson's scorn of her mother, her taking over the mother's role with Austin and writing the letters for her, etc. Whereas she seems to me to be much like many people I know (including my wife) who express themselves in non-literary ways. They hate to write letters (Til would rather be hanged by the thumbs). Mrs. Dickinson sent flowers & fruit & food to her friends and made pies for her family.*

But she was a little more fiery and independent than that. There's an apocryphal tale about Emily Sr., who, having hired a paperhanger, Lafayette Stebbins, against her husband's wishes, "went secretly to the paper hanger and asked him to come and paper her bedroom. This he did, while Emily was being born."

Of course it never happened, at least not in that way. But it's fun to imagine Emily Dickinson, who at times liked to think of herself as a mermaid, coming out of her mother's waters while Lafayette Stebbins was papering the walls. And it does reveal a stubborn streak in Mrs. Dickinson, who found her own way to defy Edward before and after their marriage. He was the invisible bridegroom at his own wedding, because the bride was so ambivalent about abandoning her family. And if she didn't have the intellectual curiosity of the rest of the Dickinson clan—even Vinnie was a religious reader of *The Atlantic Monthly*—it's partly because Edward managed to stifle whatever native rebellion she might have had. He couldn't control her while she was still in Monson, though he tried to smother her in a constant barrage of instructions, telling her how she ought to behave and whom she ought to see. Once she was married and the mother of three small children, she had very little maneuverability. He stifled her and his children, insisting that they avoid the cold weather and dark streets of Amherst while he was away—and it seems he was away a good part of the time, either as a member of the legislature or on some urgent errand. And his wife did rebel, a little. "I attended church all day yesterday," she wrote on March 13, 1838. "I felt quite like a widow."

Little Emily Elizabeth also rebelled. In that same year, while Edward was politicking somewhere on Beacon Hill, his wife wrote:

> *And I do indeed truly rejoice that the time is so near at hand when I hope to embrace my husband. . . . [Emily] sais she is tired of living without a father . . .*

Mrs. Dickinson may have suffered from bouts of melancholy, like her poet daughter, but we trivialize her and distort her life if we consider her a chronic invalid, or someone who spent half her days dusting the stairs. She was probably up and about by 4:00 A.M., as Aífe Murray suggests, dealing with stove ash, and firing up a stove that had come with her all the way from Monson; attending that stove was "primitive, complex, and continuous." Murray also suggests that the kitchen was the most creative room in the house; it was her mother who taught the poet various household witcheries—baking, gardening, and sewing would become "key silent texts, a place for words to pour into and disappear from," just as "needlework, brooms, and spider webs" would appear and reappear like witchcraft in Dickinson's poems.

Dickinson was a redhead, and she didn't have her mother's gray eyes. But she might not have become a poet without her mother's magical stove; she baked words with the same intensity that she baked her father's bread.

In 1864, two years after she lured Higginson into her spiderweb with that first letter of hers— *"Are you too deeply occupied to say if my Verse is alive?"*—she wrote a poem that could have been the autobiography of her mother:

She rose to His Requirement—dropt
The Playthings of Her Life
To take the honorable Work
Of Woman, and of Wife—

If ought She missed in Her new Day,
Of Amplitude, or Awe—
Or first Prospective—or the Gold
In using, wear away,

It lay unmentioned—as the Sea
Develope Pearl, and Weed,
But only to Himself—be known
The Fathoms they abide—   [Fr857]

Of course it's hazardous to interpret the poem in relation to a particular person, even her mother, but I still believe that her mother's shadow is in every line. She wrote it between 1861 and 1865, when poems must have come to her with the speed of a comet or a fireball. It was during the Civil War. And critics have their own little wars over what all that butchery meant to her. She would write her Norcross cousins that "Sorrow seems more general . . . since the war began," and that she herself "sang off charnel steps." [Letter 298, 1864?] Such sorrow seeped into her poetry in some mysterious manner. "The subterranean stays—" she would write to Higginson in 1879. [Letter 593]

And "She rose to his requirement—dropt" is filled with a kind of subterranean remorse. The poet might have imagined herself *wearing* her mother's clothes, giving up her "Playthings" for the honorable "Work" of wife. But the word *honorable* seems ominous here, as if it prefigures some cruel act of castration. "She rose to His Requirement" suggests both punishment and sexual play. The poet distances herself, speaks to us in the third person, as a dream wife watching her own dream—of diminishment. The wife has to survive without "Amplitude" and without "Awe," has to live utterly in the mundane. Even the "Gold" of her wedding ring—her status as wife—will "wear away," as Helen Vendler suggests.

But now the poet intercedes for her mother-wife. Lying "unmentioned" and alone, that pale, bitten "Gold" might "Develope Pearl" in the immense water of her own mind. "Pearl"—like "Snow" or "Diadem" or "Possibility"—is a trigger word, the secret signature of her craft. And here we have a curious conflation. As a dream wife, married to her own father, she cannot *rise* to "His Requirement," can only protect herself with "Pearl."

The poem suggests a sympathy for her mother that she seldom allowed herself to reveal—she was her father's, the best little girl in town. But in an undated prose fragment she summons up her own past, a past in which her father doesn't appear:

> *Two things I have lost with Childhood—the rapture of losing my shoe in the Mud and going Home barefoot, wading for Cardinal flowers and the mothers reproof which was* [for] *more for my sake than her weary own for she frowned with a smile . . .* [PF 117]

This frowning with a smile would haunt Emily Dickinson and become her Haunted House. It also suggests another way of reading her poetry. We have to get rid of the idea of an Emily Dickinson "canon," obliging her poems to move like an elongated ladder in some direction that coheres and has a logic all its own. We'll never tame the cat that leapt at us speaking English; nor will we ever cure it. All we can do is listen harder to the cat's *moosic*.

As noted earlier, Emily talked in her second letter to Higginson of a certain terror that came "since September," when she sang like a boy in a boneyard, because she was afraid.

Afraid of what? Was it the terror of love? A romance that had ripped her apart? Was it about that unknown Master who had inspired those three lyrical, half-crazy, and suicidal letter-poems? We'll never uncover who her Master was, or if he ever existed at all. But I think that terror had to do with something else. Was she performing for Higginson? Yes—and no. I suspect she was frightened of the Vesuvius inside her, the energy that took hold of her entire being, like some monster she craved and couldn't get rid of.

It wasn't about her "Scarlet prison" upstairs, or the booklets she was sewing together in her sanctuary. It was the sheer creative drive; she was writing one—two—poems a day. She'd moved with her family out of the mansion on Main Street when she was ten, had lived in a house on North Pleasant Street, a house whose rear windows bordered upon Amherst's cemetery; Mrs. Dickinson had been much happier here, without the ghost of her mother-in-law, Lucretia Gunn. Austin had built a wall of pine trees—evergreens. Vinnie had fallen in love with Joseph Lyman, one of her brother's former classmates, now at Yale. Emily had a "coven" of girlfriends, loved all her teachers, became her mother's scribe, incorporating bits and scraps of her voice into letters to Austin.

And then, in 1855, Edward bought back his father's house, the Homestead, had it refurbished, added a conservatory, so that Emily could have her own winter garden and winter flowers; and that November, the Dickinsons moved a quarter of a mile—to Main Street. Edward's poet daughter felt like some pioneer coming from Kansas. Her father had bribed her a little, with that winter garden, and he gave her the best room in the mansion, on the southwest corner of the second floor. But Mrs. Dickinson was completely shattered by the move; the Homestead had been a haunted house for her, where she had to cope with a mother-in-law who made her feel like an intruder while her own children were very small; even after Samuel Fowler Dickinson moved to Ohio in 1836, and his own family followed him there, Mrs. Dickinson was still uncomfortable; there were too many recollections of a divided family and a divided house. Samuel Fowler Dickinson died on April 22, 1838, in total disgrace—he'd bungled the account books at a college near Cleveland. Lucretia Gunn Dickinson wanted to move back in with Edward at the Homestead, but Edward wouldn't have her. She "complained about boils, dizziness, and the ingratitude of children."

Edward was now the new Squire of Amherst; he had a terrible temper, kept beating his horse. Townsmen would walk to the other side of the street whenever the Squire loped along. Elected to Congress in 1852 as a Whig, he was the town's most famous citizen, and one of its wealthiest. But when the Dickinsons returned to Main Street, Emily Sr. sank into a deep melancholia that would last four years. Her poet daughter was one of the first to notice this decline.

> *They say that "home is where the heart is." I think it is where the house is, and the adjacent buildings. . . .*
>
> *Mother has been an invalid since we came* home, *and Vinnie and I "regulated," and Vinnie and I "got settled," and still we keep our father's house, and mother lies upon the lounge, or sits in her easy chair. I don't know what her sickness is, for I am but a simple child, and frightened at myself.* [Letter 182, about January 20, 1856]

Emily was more than a bit disingenuous in this letter-poem to Mrs. Holland about the consequences of the move. She was putting on her feathers again, playing the innocent child. But there was a good deal of anger underlying the chatty, quicksilver narrative. She knew what her mother's sickness was all about—her inability to rebel, to express her own rage against her husband about the return to this homeless home. There were too many phantoms, even with a new cupola. But she sat in her own silent rage. Emily wasn't her father's only daughter—and here

Mrs. Dickinson might be considered just another "simple child," who couldn't openly rebel against her husband-father.

In an 1852 letter to Austin, Vinnie described one of Edward's whippings:

> *Oh! Dear! Father is killing the horse . . . whipping him because he didn't look quite* 'umble' *enough . . . Emilie is screaming to the top of her voice. She's so vexed about it.*

And once, after visiting Sue and another friend, Emily returned at 9:00 P.M. and "found Father is great agitation at my protracted stay—and mother and Vinnie in tears, for fear that he would kill me." [Letter 42, to Austin, June 8, 1851]

Edward had barely changed since his courtship ritual—he couldn't control Emily Norcross while she was still in Monson, but he could smother her once she arrived in Amherst with her magical stove. And he would smother his children in much the same way, watchful of their every move.

"I do not go out at all, lest father will come and miss me," Emily wrote in the midst of her mother's crisis, "or miss some little act, which I might forget, should I run away—Mother is much as usual. I know not what to hope of her." [Letter 191, to Mrs. Joseph Haven, early summer, 1858]

One might imagine the turmoil she was in—an invalid mother and tyrannical father whom she also loved. She must have had a deep sympathy for her mother—we can sense this in a dream she had right after she arrived at Mount Holyoke; it was her first extended period away from "head-quarters," as Austin liked to call their father's house.

> *Well, I dreamed a dream & Lo!!! Father had failed & mother said "our rye field which she & I planted, was mortgaged to Seth Nims." I hope it is not true but do write soon & tell me for you know "I should expire with mortification" to have our rye field mortgaged . . .* [Letter 16, to Austin, October 21, 1847]

Father may be commander in chief, but Emily and her mother planted the rye field and are in danger of losing it. And for once, Emily Dickinson decided to become her own commander in chief in that Pearl Jail her father had assigned to her at "headquarters." She couldn't leave her father's house, or rise to any man's "Requirements" and take on another name. She would write her poems as a Dickinson, poems lashed with anger and pain. She was far from a model prisoner in her Pearl Jail—she assumed the sounds of her mother's sadness as she rebelled against her father in the best way she could. She pitied him, and loved him, and feared him, but she was her mother's child in her letters and poems. Her conservatory, her bedroom, the pantry, and her mother's kitchen became "boundaries within boundaries," where she could *dance* with a kind of invisible precision in her father's house, but removed from his gaze—and his control.

In her very best writing, "she explored the implications of breaking the law just short of breaking off communication with a reader," Susan Howe reminds us. And the law she broke was the patriarchal rules of punctuation and grammar, the very language passed down from her beloved Lexicon. Dickinson's private Lexicon grew out of her mother's tangled, chaotic grammar. One can read her very act of writing as a willful war with her father—Edward Dickinson was both God and the Devil, both her enemy and ideal reader, who never even read her poems. "We don't *have* many jokes tho' *now*, it is pretty much all sobriety," she wrote to Austin in 1851, "and we do not have much poetry, father having made up his mind that its pretty much all *real life*." [Letter 65]

Her *real* life was inside that Pearl Jail, where her secret songs remained locked in a drawer. She could have recited her poems at some women's club, charmed Sam Bowles, met Ralph Waldo Emerson in Sue's parlor, or performed the "surgery" that Higginson requested, if she wanted to publish her poems. And the one certain letter we have of hers to her father is a letter never sent! It appears in pencil, on a piece of stationery, and on the back of a poem:

Knock with tremor—
These are Caesars—
Should they be at Home
Flee as if you trod unthinking
On the Foot of Doom . . .   [Fr1333]

And what did Dickinson's undelivered letter say?

Dear Father—

[blank space]

   Emily—   [A 265]

Edward often appeared in Emily's poems as the unnamed "Earl." She would dream of him every night after he died and couldn't walk past his room without feeling his ghostly presence. Perhaps she wasn't even aware of her anger against him, or what fueled her poems. Dickinson saw her father in the grandest terms, as a giant who could terrorize an entire town, as he terrorized his horse. But Higginson recalls a very different man. "I saw Mr. Dickinson this morning a little—thin dry & speechless. I saw what her life has been." [Letter 342b, August 1870]

Edward wasn't much of a squire—or an earl. He was a backwoods politician who couldn't hold on to his seat in Congress and never really understood the rumblings that led to the Civil War. He didn't have a clue of what his poet daughter's life was like, might never even have wandered into her Pearl Jail, nor did he have a pinch of poetry in his own life; he was a stern, humorless man who read the Bible every morning to his children and his wife. Emily was able to catch at least a glimpse of his hollow, frozen core. In a letter to Joseph Lyman, sometime during the 1860s, she writes:

Father says in fugitive moments when he forgets the barrister &
lapses into the man, says that his life has been passed in a wilderness
or on an island—of late he says on an island.

But Father's island wasn't her "Blue Peninsula," where one could "perish—of Delight." [Fr535] It was much starker and mundane. She never judged that Earl. And we have to be cautious when we judge Emily Dickinson, much more cautious than R. P. Blackmur, who wrote with blind bravura in 1956: "We cannot say of this woman in white that she ever mastered life." She was born and died a Dickinson, and the white wrappers she began to wear were the costume of a gardener, a baker, and a poet who had little time for corsets and fanciful clothes. She was always the mistress of her own life, and the agoraphobia we prescribe to her is our own facile way to deal with the mystery of creation. She was the "blonde Assassin" who turned her mother's silent pain into her own "noiseless noise" [Letter 271], a language that stuns and mutilates, even while it soothes. There's nothing else remotely like it. Dickinson sings to us from another time, yet her Yellow Eye seems much more modern than our own baffling and bewildered image in the mirror—we are its steady target.

THREE

Daemon Dog

1

NONE OF US CAN REALLY SAY how reclusive Dickinson was, but one thing is certain: She had a companion for sixteen years—a big, slobbering brown dog named Carlo, a Newfoundland as tall as she was, Dickinson loved to boast, and who must have weighed a 150 pounds. Soon after her poems were published and Higginson deified her as the virgin recluse, a note appeared in the *Commercial Advertiser*, dated August 23, 1893. Dickinson had acquired her own sudden fame, like a thunderclap across New England, and a certain Grace Smith, now Mrs. Luther W. Bodman of Chicago, summoned up the walks she once took with the poet when she was a little girl, while Dickinson's "huge dog stalked solemnly beside them. 'Gracie,' said Miss Dickinson, 'do you know that I believe that the first to come and greet me when I go to heaven will be this dear, faithful old friend Carlo?'"

This was one of the first bits of apocrypha about the poet, half her fire already swallowed up by Mabel Todd, who was deeply bothered by Dickinson's "carelessness of form. . . . I admired her strange words and ways of using them, but the simplest laws of verse-making were ignored, and what she called rhymes grated on me."

It would take more than half a century to undo the damage Mabel had done; and in all this time, Dickinson remained the virgin recluse, who talked about eternity to little girls while she "bribed" them with baskets of gingerbread hanging down from her window. But her letters reveal another picture of the poet. She was never fond of yapping about eternity. As she told Higginson on June 9, 1866:

> *You mention Immortality.*
> *That is the Flood subject. I was told that the Bank was the safest place for a Finless Mind.*   [Letter 319]

Grace Smith might have accompanied Carlo and his mistress across Amherst more than once, but I suspect she told readers of the *Commercial Advertiser* what they wanted to hear about a woman who took a carriage ride to eternity in one of her poems. I doubt Dickinson would ever have talked about the "Flood subject," even to a little girl.

Yet it was Jay Leyda who unearthed this bit of apocrypha, and other tales about Emily Dickinson and her prodigious dog—by recapturing Dickinson's days and hours, he was quick to understand the dog's worth. It seems she was mesmerized by Maj. E. B. Hunt, a Civil War hero and husband of Helen Fiske Hunt, who had first met Dickinson when both were schoolchildren and would become a celebrated poet and novelist after Major Hunt was killed in an accident at the Brooklyn Navy Yard. Dickinson was reintroduced to Helen Hunt and the major at one of her father's receptions for Amherst College, sometime in the 1860s.

> *Major Hunt interested her more than any man she ever saw. She remembered two things he said—that her great dog "understood gravitation" & when he said he should come again "in a year. If I say a shorter time it will be longer."*

Most Dickinson scholars have paid scant attention to Carlo, even though that big brown dog haunts her letters and her poems. Carlo isn't even listed in the index of Cynthia Griffin Wolff's six-hundred-page biography. And John Cody, who spends page after page analyzing Dickinson's psychic dilemma as a love-starved woman and poet, mentions him only once. "Carlo seems to have accompanied Emily on all her rambles, and it is clear that she became fond of him." But he finds no connection at all between Carlo and the poet's "inner life."

I suspect that Carlo occupied more psychic and physical space than any other creature; she couldn't have thrived without him. With all her aristocratic mien, she was little more than an expensive chattel who couldn't even buy her own writing paper and pens without her father's funds. She and Vinnie were kept on an invisible leash and were the real pets of the family, not Carlo. That brown dog was Dickinson's one and only possession . . . if we're willing to admit that anyone can ever "own" a dog. Not according to Adam Gopnik, who got a caramel-colored Havanese named Butterscotch for his daughter and wrote about this experience in *The New Yorker:* "Dog Story: How Did the Dog Become Our Master?"

Gopnik ventures back into ancient history. "Dogs began as allies, not pets, and friends, not dependents." Prehistoric man didn't steal cubs from wolf packs and tame them—wolves will always return to the wild. But certain breeds of wolves began to collect around human garbage dumps, and these "tamer, man-friendly wolves produced more cubs than their wilder, man-hating cousins." Such "willing wolves" morphed into dogs who became our hunting companions and the playmates of our children. For Gopnik, dogs chose us and chose to become dogs. He deconstructs the whole man-dog relationship. The best of dogs are neither kind nor heroic. "The dog will bark at a burglar; but the dog will also bark at a shirt."

I wonder if Gopnik's Ur-dog really describes Carlo. He doesn't believe in dogs of mythic proportion. But it's hard to imagine Carlo in any other way. Perhaps it's because of Carlo's prodigious size, and the fact that the Newfoundland was the archetypical dog of the nineteenth century, great swimmers who were known to rescue men from the sea with a wide flick of their webbed paws. Lord Byron had a Newfoundland called Boatswain. The most notorious poet of his time, he swam the Hellespont despite his "clubfoot," had love affairs with married women, Greek boys, and his own half sister, Augusta Leigh, and was adored and reviled by the men and women of New England—there had never been a New Englander remotely like him. Byron's dog died of rabies in 1808, and Byron wanted to be buried in the same tomb with Boatswain; the dog was five years old. Boatswain's anniversary is still celebrated more than two hundred years after his death.

There was also a Newfoundland in Charlotte Brontë's *Jane Eyre*, a novel Dickinson adored. "A lion-like creature with long hair and a huge head . . . with strange pretercanine eyes," the dog, whose name is Pilot, belongs to Jane's own moody master, Edward Rochester. She's a governess at Rochester's mansion on the Yorkshire moors, while Rochester's mad wife lives in the attic—Jane has come to a haunted house. Still, Pilot remains loyal to Rochester and loyal to her. Yet Dickinson named her own Newfoundland after *another* dog in the novel—old Carlo, a pointer who belongs to St. John Rivers, a stern, unsmiling missionary—"cold as an iceberg"—who doesn't love Jane but wants to marry her and make her his missionary wife.

Dickinson read the novel in 1849, and her dog must have arrived in the late autumn or early winter of that year. Vinnie was away at school in Ipswich, Austin attended Amherst College and caroused with his friends and classmates, and Emily felt abandoned. "I am very puny alone," she confessed to a friend. [Letter 32, early 1850?] And her father gave her the dog to console her and watch after her while he was away. The first mention of Carlo was in a mock Valentine sent to George Gould, one of Austin's classmates; there is some speculation that Gould was in love with Emily but was rejected by her father as a possible suitor.

> *Sir, I desire an interview; meet me at sunrise, or sunset, or the new moon—the place is immaterial. . . . Don't be afraid of it, sir, it won't bite. If it was my* Carlo *now! The Dog is the noblest work of Art, sir.*

I may say the noblest—his mistress's rights he doth defend—although it bring him to his end . . . [Letter 34, February 1850]

Carlo must have been more than a puppy by this time, though an enormous puppy could have defended Dickinson's "rights." But it's still puzzling why she named her dog after St. John River's pointer rather than Rochester's noble Newfoundland. Perhaps Rivers reminded Dickinson of her father in his cold, relentless manner. She was the consummate puzzle master, as Jay Leyda reminds us. And a loveless missionary and his pointer might have appealed to her in some perverse way.

What we do know is that the tiny, freckled woman and her big brown dog soon became a fixture in Amherst. She would be out exploring with her lantern and Carlo. Her schooling was over. She'd become close to Sue. Her father, Sue, and Vinnie would profess their faith and join the First Church that same year—1850. Her mother had professed her faith nineteen years earlier, in 1831, when Emily was six months old. And much of her sadness had come from the fear that she would not meet her own family in heaven. Austin would also join the Church, but Emily was the one who remained adamant all her life. She would keep her own Sabbath within her mind, locking the doors of her "election," as she hovered somewhere between God and the Devil. She herself was a fallen angel. But she had few antecedents as a writer, almost none. And it's not clear when she turned from being the village rhymester without a real vocation—like a hundred other poets in a hundred other villages—and grew into that aberration we know as Emily Dickinson. It never should have happened. Every idiot has her lexicon, her own book of words. Dickinson's experiences weren't richer or any more vital than those of other aristocratic New England daughters.

And it was almost impossible for a woman to declare herself, secretly or not, as a writer. As Susan Sontag reminds us almost a century and a half after Dickinson's own struggles, silence had become the female writer's bitter reward. "Silent not merely for want of encouragement. Silent because of the way that women are defined and therefore, commonly, define themselves. For the obligation to be physically attractive and patient and nurturing and docile and sensitive and deferential to fathers (to brothers, to husbands) contradicts and *must* collide with the egocentricity and aggressiveness and the indifference to self that a large creative gift requires in order to flourish."

Sontag offers up the example of Alice James, the brilliant sister of Henry and William, who fell into a deep depression at nineteen, dreamt of suicide, traveled abroad, and lived most of her life in bed, suffering from the "all too common reality of a woman who does not know what to do with her genius, her originality, her aggressiveness, and therefore becomes a career invalid." Cody sees Dickinson as much the same "career invalid," who could have occupied Alice James' bed, and who turned her own bedroom into a hermitage—and a mausoleum. And a host of other scholars agree with him. Sewall himself says that her unwillingness to leave her father's house can be regarded "as an unfortunate eccentricity or as a symptom of profound psychic fear." But suppose it was neither of the above. What choice did she really have? She was a birdlike woman with red hair who had to summon up her own powers. Critics talk of her breakdowns but can never point to a single one.

Brenda Wineapple, in *White Heat*, her narrative about the complicated and curious ballet between Higginson and his half-cracked poetess, seems to understand that most of Dickinson's tentative dance steps were strategies of survival and maneuvers of a woman at war—"her backbone made of steel, she pretended fragility." Dickinson, Wineapple says, "seems to exist outside of time, untouched by it. And that's unnerving. No wonder we make up stories about her: about her lovers, if any, or why she turned her back on ordinary life . . ."

Where else did Dickinson have to go? She didn't have a novelist and a philosopher in her family, the way Alice James did. Her own father, brother, and sister were quite ordinary and wouldn't be remembered for five minutes if they hadn't been related to the Belle of

Amherst—whatever fame they have comes from her twists and turns. Sue might have had *some* of Emily's intellect, but she would grow much more conventional after her marriage. She would have buried Dickinson's poems in a communal grave if she'd had her wish. She didn't want to see them published. She'd rather have printed them privately. As she wrote to Higginson on December 23, 1890:

> *I sometimes shudder when I think of the world reading her thoughts minted in heartbroken convictions. In her own words (after all the intoxicating fascination of creation) she as deeply realized that for her, as for all of us women not fame but "Love and home and certainty are best." I find myself always saying "poor Emily."*

Poor Emily indeed.

We don't have a whole lot of clues about where her brilliance came from. She may have been writing poems since she was fourteen, but the earliest ones don't reveal very much. It's only in her love letters to Sue that we feel a kind of genius; there's a sudden thrust in her language, an urgency that's shaped and defined—and filled with a kind of sexual somnambulism as Dickinson sees herself and Sue being yielded up to some *union* with a man.

> *. . . how it will take* us *one day, and make us all it's own, and we shall not run away from it, but lie still and be happy!* [Letter 93, early June 1852]

Dickinson can bear it as long as Sue is also sacrificed to the man of noon and "scorched" by him. But she cannot bear it when Sue is out of reach—"your absence insanes me so—" [Letter 107, March 12, 1853] And when she discovers that Sue is really out of reach, she loses all control—walks the streets alone at night—as her language gathers more and more control, and she will now "appear like an embarrassed Peacock, quite unused to its plumes." [Letter 177, late January 1855]

But 1855 will be a fateful year. She has to leave her haven over the cemetery—on North Pleasant Street—and move back to her father's house with all the other Dickinsons, while Edward has a ducal manor— the Evergreens—built for Austin and Sue, so he can bind them to him with an invisible cord. None of the Dickinsons will ever leave him now, not his *useless* daughters, nor his son, whom he has made a partner in his law firm.

We have fewer letters from Emily in 1856—only five or six—and none at all in 1857. Some scholars, including Cody, see this as evidence of a breakdown—a kind of psychic paralysis over Sue's marriage to Austin and final abandonment of her. But I don't see this at all. Sue has become one more Phantom in her box of Phantoms, no matter how often Emily visits the Evergreens with her lantern and her dog.

Something else happened in 1857. Emily was different—she knew that, had a much quicker wit than the men and women around her, and a rage she couldn't reveal. She was a Gnome with red hair who wanted to be Bearded, like a man. Why should she become another man's cow, and carry his children? She wanted to father her own prog- eny—and she did. And it was her mountain of a dog who gave her a bit of courage. Dogs, as Adam Gopnik tells us, "are the only creatures that have learned to gaze directly at people as people gaze at one another, and their connection with us is an essential and enduring one."

She must have gazed into Carlo's eyes and seen a mirror of her own wants—Carlo was her one ally, clever and dumb at the same time. He didn't have strings of language in his skull, but he had something bet- ter: He could listen to her recite. Aífe Murray believes that from the moment Carlo appeared in her life, she was much more creative, and that "tramping abroad with her dog might have shown this aspiring writer how walking can loosen the subconscious and become a way to compose."

Language must have come to her in its own enigmatic flash, or we couldn't have that "Whip lash" of images. She speaks of her creativity, I think, and how it controls her, when she writes:

I felt a Cleaving in my Mind—
As if my Brain had split—
I tried to match it—Seam by Seam—
But could not make them fit—

The thought behind, I strove to join
Unto the thought before—
But Sequence ravelled out of Sound—
Like Balls—opon a Floor—　[Fr867B]

Her genius had little to do with logic and order, but with Sequence—
the cohesion and coherence of a poem—*ravelling* out of Sound, twist-
ing and tearing asunder, beyond the reach of Sound, she says, "Like
Balls—opon a Floor." But are these balls of yarn that unwind and ravel
out into silence? I'm not convinced of that. *Ravel* is too strong a word;
it feels like a scratch, a rip that we can taste and hear. And those could
also be billiard balls that echo without end, as if a poem could ricochet
into eternity, *Beyond the Dip of Bell—* [Fr633]

She doesn't give us much room for resolution. Dickinson never
did. And that deep silence of 1857 was like going into a dark well.
Her genius might always have been there, perhaps even from the first
words she spoke, with her Aunt Lavinia, when she was riveted to the
thunder and lightning on her voyage to Monson and called it "the
fire." But did she have that aggression Sontag talks about, that *violence*
to nurse her own creative gifts, the ability to declare herself as a poet?
The simplest act of aggression in women was frowned upon, and so
she masked herself as the woman-child, whispered like a child, ran
from the door when a stranger knocked. But it was part fear, part performance. As she would declare to her cousin Loo: "Odd, that I, who
run from so many, cannot brook that one turn from me." [Letter 245,
December 31, 1861]

She had what she needed: a room of her own, a writing desk, a
conservatory for her winter plants and perennials, and a big brown

dog. She was akin to the village clown, the eccentric daughter of Squire Dickinson. She confided in no one but Carlo, and Carlo nuzzled her and never talked back.

2

Y ET CARLO REMAINED MOSTLY INVISIBLE in her correspondence— until 1858, when he appears all of a sudden in a letter to Sue, appears in a comic, almost pathetic way.

> *Vinnie and I are pretty well. Carlo—comfortable—terrifying man and beast, with renewed activity—is cuffed some—hurled from piazza frequently, when Miss Lavinia's "flies" need her action else-where.*   [Letter 194, September 26, 1858]

It's hard to imagine anyone cuffing Carlo and hurling him off the Dickinson porch, except in some mock fashion, as if Emily's New-foundland had become a captive clown, like the poet herself. And now Carlo will appear in other letters, as Emily's sidekick and alter ego, her voiceless voice, and one of her many masks. On December 10, 1859, she writes to Mrs. Sam Bowles:

> *I cannot walk to the distant friends on nights piercing as these, so I put both hands on the window-pane, and try to think how birds fly, and imitate, and fail. . . . I talk of all these things with Carlo, and his eyes grow meaning, and his shaggy feet keep a slower pace.* [Letter 212]

But the tenor shifts in 1862, once she starts her correspondence with Colonel Higginson—these letters are part of her poet's blood, no mat-ter how she masks herself, and how many plumes she wears. She will send him her poems, play the amateur, the village crank, but what she really wants to talk about is her craft, that subterranean life of hers—and Carlo is part of that life.

You ask of my Companions. Hills—Sir—and the Sundown—and
a Dog—large as myself, that my Father bought me—They are better
than Beings—because they know—but do not tell [her secrets]—
and the noise in the Pool, at Noon—excels my Piano.   [Letter 261,
April 25, 1862]

She tells Higginson an outright lie that August, says she had no
"Monarch" in her life, when her father ruled her and all the Dickinsons
from the day she was born, kept his wife and Vinnie as aging, grown-
up children, and harmed Austin—tethered him—by holding him as
an exalted prisoner next door. Austin never crept out from under his
father's shadow, even after his father's death. And his poet sister's only
escape was to crawl inside her own head and crumble half of Squire
Dickinson's world in her poems, attack God and the Devil, and twist
the entire universe into her own "prophetic vision of intergalactic nothingness." Language itself was a kind of Ice Age for Dickinson, utterly
autistic—soundless sounds.

The colonel asks her why she shuns "Men and Women," and she
answers—"they talk of Hallowed things, aloud—and embarrass my
Dog—He and I don't object to them, if they'll exist their side. I think
Carl[o] would please you—He is dumb, and brave—" [Letter 271,
August 1862] Carlo has become a mirror of her wants, a silent *medal-*
lion. She mentions her dog in almost every letter to Higginson, is eager
to have him know how essential Carlo is to her.

One of her next letters to the colonel is critical—he's gone off to war
without even telling her, and she barks at him—like her "Shaggy Ally,"
as she now calls Carlo.

I should have liked to see you, before you became improbable. . . .
I found you were gone, by accident, as I find Systems are, or Sea-
sons of the year, and obtain no cause—but suppose it a treason of
Progress—that dissolves as it goes. Carlo—still remained . . .

She continues to bark and bite—lets him know that Carlo is loyal to her, even if he is not. But she relents a bit and calls herself his Gnome. [Letter 280, February 1863]

She writes to him from Cambridge in early June of 1864; she's staying with her Norcross cousins while having her eyes looked at by a noted Boston ophthalmologist, Dr. Henry Willard Williams—"The Physician has taken away my Pen." Fanny and Loo read Shakespeare to her while she writes in secret with her pencil. Higginson had received a mysterious wound in July 1863 and had to leave his regiment.

> *Are you in danger—*
> *I did not know that you were hurt . . .*
> *I was ill since September, and since April, in Boston, for a Physician's care—He does not let me go, yet I work in my Prison, and make Guests [poems] for myself—*
> *Carlo did not come, because that he would die, in Jail . . .*
> [Letter 290]

Her next letter to the colonel isn't until late January 1866—it's one line long, with a salutation and a postscript.

> *To T. W. Higginson*
> *Carlo died—*
> *E. Dickinson*
> *Would you instruct me now?* [Letter 314]

She never really recovered from Carlo's death. "I wish for Carlo," she would write to Higginson later that year. [Letter 319, June 9, 1866] "I explore but little since my mute Confederate [died]."

We know that her long explosion of creativity continued in 1865, when she worked on 229 poems, even while she was stranded in Cambridge for seven months, exiled from her home and her dog, and half-blind. But the explosion *seemed* to end in 1866, when her output plummeted to ten new poems. Some scholars believe that Dickinson's creativity collided with the Civil War, that some inner drama was worked out in the war's own drama and butchery, that she responded to the slaughter with a woman's *deeper* emotions. But I'm not convinced. She was always ambivalent about the war.

> *I shall have no winter this year—on account of the soldiers—Since*
> *I cannot weave Blankets, or Boots—I thought it best to omit the season*
> . . . [Letter 235, to Mrs. Sam Bowles, about August 1861]

She could cry over the "slaughter" of Lt. Frazer Stearns—"His big heart shot away by a 'minie ball'" [Letter 255, late March 1862], but Frazer had been her brother's friend, was the son of Amherst College's president, and was part of her social class. Dickinson was hardly a democratic goddess; she'd always been an aristocrat and a snob. She didn't cry much for any common soldiers. "A Soldier called—a Morning ago, and asked for a Nosegay, to take to Battle. I suppose he thought we kept an Aquarium," she wrote to Sam Bowles. [Letter 272, about August 1862] She was putting on her feathers, trying to shock Bowles a bit. But cruelty was one of her measuring sticks and part of her mental apparatus. It's not that she couldn't write about the war, and sing off charnel steps about "Battle's—horrid Bowl."

> *It feels a shame to be Alive—*
> *When Men so brave—are dead—*
> *One envies the Distinguished Dust . . .* [Fr524]

Or when she writes to Higginson: "I can't *stop* to strut, in a world where bells toll." [Letter 269, summer 1862?] Yet it's hard to decipher where her sympathies lay. Her father was an old-fashioned Whig, who couldn't have borne "Black Republicans," those who wanted to end slavery at any cost. Her cousin Perez Dickinson Cowan was an Amherst College student from Tennessee. And Joseph Lyman, Vinnie's "lost" suitor, would spend the war fighting on the Southern side.

She didn't end her habit of stitching her poems into booklets on account of the Civil War; it was rather because of rheumatic iritis—her irritated eyes didn't allow her to sew. And for her, the war ends in a kind of comedy—with the capture of Jefferson Davis, disguised as a woman, in "Skirt and Spurs" [Letter 308].

To the author of "My life had stood a loaded gun," killing was a natural habitat. She was the "blonde Assassin," after all. The universe had become an "abattoir," according to Camille Paglia. War was her own special landscape—she was also in rebellion, like the South, with Carlo as her "mute Confederate." She'd been writing poems with a brutal intensity, the White Heat of "unanointed Blaze" [Fr401]. And suddenly some of that heat was gone.

"Magic, as it electrifies, also makes decrepit—" she would write to Higginson in 1879. [Letter 622] "A Spell cannot be tattered, and mended like a Coat—" [Letter 663, to Sue, about 1880] And she could not mend her own powers. She was in her mid-thirties the year Carlo died. And if we consider her language—her Witchcraft—as a kind of lyrical mathematics, then it shouldn't startle us. A lot of mathematicians have lost their own siren's call by the time they're thirty-five. Dickinson had stopped dancing "like a Bomb, abroad" [Fr360], or perhaps she was dancing in a different way, and all the carnage had used her up. Carlo's death had jolted her, and she would mourn him for the rest of her life. He was very old for a Newfoundland when he died—almost seventeen. Most Newfoundlands don't live beyond the age of ten; they're often born with defective heart valves; and so Dickinson had her big brown dog for a very long time.

She no longer wandered through the village and the countryside, without her Newfoundland. It would have been treasonous to have another dog—Carlo couldn't be replaced. He'd been part of her thoughts and desires, had mirrored her own reticence, her shyness. Deprived of that walking mountain, she would turn inward, seldom leave her father's house.

3

"HALF THE PLEASURE OF HAVING A DOG," writes Adam Gopnik, "was storytelling *about* the dog: she was a screen on which we could project a private preoccupation." In addition to a real dog, Gopnik "had a pretend version, a daemon dog," who lived inside the real one. His own fictive dog was a companion who liked long walks and "listening to extended stretches of tentatively composed prose." And Carlo was also a daemon dog, real and fictive at the same time. We can imagine Dickinson reciting the melody of her lines to Carlo on *their* long walks. And that daemon dog appears in one of her most disturbing poems, written long before Carlo died, a poem that summons up a strange, miraculous adventure in the middle of a walk.

I started Early—Took my Dog—
And visited the Sea—
The Mermaids in the Basement
Came out to look at me—

And Frigates—in the Upper Floor
Extended Hempen Hands—
Presuming Me to be a Mouse—
Aground—opon the Sands—

But no Man moved Me—till the Tide
Went past my simple Shoe—
And past my Apron—and my Belt
And past my Bodice—too—

And made as He would eat me up—
As wholly as a Dew
Opon a Dandelion's Sleeve—
And then—I started—too—

And He—He followed—close behind—
I felt His Silver Heel
Opon my Ancle—Then My Shoes
Would overflow with Pearl—

Until we met the Solid Town—
No One He seemed to know—
And bowing—with a Mighty look—
At me—The Sea withdrew—   [Fr656]

How can we enter this journey, through which porthole or door? The poem is as difficult and daunting as "My life had stood a loaded gun." The first two lines don't indicate the peril of the poem, the fear of being swallowed up and ravished by some imagined male sea. Suddenly there are "Mermaids in the Basement," as if the speaker had tumbled upon that perverse porthole of her own mind. But these mermaids aren't threatening. They won't seduce or bite. They're curious about the poet, want to have a look. Mermaids are a crucial piece of property in Dickinson's Lexicon. She herself is a mermaid astray on dry land. And the mermaids in the poem are like a welcoming mirror.

She would reveal the nature of her poetics to Higginson in her fourth letter to him: "When I state myself, as the Representative of the Verse—it does not mean—me—but a supposed person." [Letter 268, July 1862] Perhaps she wasn't even conscious of her own lie. This "supposed person" is one more bit of camouflage. The speaker is always Emily Dickinson, the poet-wanderer, whether she appears as male or female, child, hummingbird or bee, or a ghost talking to us from the other side of the grave. It doesn't really matter what persona she inhabits—it's a reckless version of herself. But she can afford to be reckless in this poem—she has her dog.

The speaker here could be Little Alice, going through the looking glass, or down a rabbit hole—the poem has the same enchantment and menace as Alice in Wonderland, and the same sexual perversity.

She can shrink or grow enormous, as Alice does, become both power-ful and puny.

The Frigates on the Upper Floor of her mind presume her to be a Mouse adrift upon the Sands. But they don't crush the poet. They extend Hempen Hands. She's not as meek as they imagine. "But no Man moved Me"—until the Tide appears and almost submerges her in its own will. It rides past her "simple Shoe," past her Apron, and her Belt, past her Bodice, too, with its own menacing and hypnotic caress. But she resists this tide—the male sea—and she emphasizes his male-ness twice. "And He—He followed—close behind," with his "Silver Heel" of seduction until her *simple* shoes "overflow with Pearl"—per-haps the secret tides of her own creation—and she manages to escape the sea, with the dog as her silent witness, and arrives at the "Solid Town," the safer and more conscious perimeters of her mind, where the sea isn't known and has little sway—and bowing to Dickinson, the sea departs, with a "Mighty look" at the poet.

Nothing is really stable in the poem—"nature is so sudden she makes us all antique," Dickinson once jotted down in a fragment that may have been sent to Judge Lord. [PF 82] Perhaps the poem is about the entan-glement and confusion of her sexual and creative force. "All power," writes Susan Howe, "including the power of Love [and the power to cre-ate], all nature, including the nature of Time, is utterly unstable." There are no truths to discover, "only mystery beyond mystery."

She was frightened of her own powers, and her daemon dog must have soothed her a bit. She could saunter in and out of some treacher-ous dream with Carlo and still stay alive. Carlo was her mute Confeder-ate—she and her dog were both rebels, who would weave bandages or blankets for no one. She wasn't blind to the battle reports. And she was as warlike as the generals in both camps. Her most revealing glimpse of the carnage was written long after she had lost her mute Confederate.

'Tis Seasons since the Dimpled War
In which we each were Conqueror

And each of us were slain
And Centuries 'twill be and more
Another Massacre before
So modest and so vain—
Without a Formula we fought
Each was to each the Pink Redoubt—
[Fr1551, about 1881, in pencil, on a scrap of paper]

And there was no room for Emily or her daemon dog on that Pink Redoubt, where *decoration* dwelled—like some murderous jewel—rather than the rectitude of war.

NOTE: Rebecca Patterson, who was the first to describe Dickinson's love for Kate Scott, believed that this poem charts the lost romance of two women—Dickinson and Kate—and their Pink Redoubt; Patterson could be right, but like most of Dickinson's poems, meaning upon meaning abounds.

FOUR

~~~~~~~~~

Judith Shakespeare and Margaret Maher

1

IN 1929, VIRGINIA WOOLF PUBLISHED a short book, *A Room of One's Own*, that would become a war cry for all women writers. *A Room of One's Own* rumbles on for forty pages, until Woolf decides "to draw the curtains" and describe how women lived in Elizabethan England. "For it is a perennial puzzle why no woman wrote a word of that extraordinary literature when every other man, it seemed, was capable of song and sonnet."

And Woolf comes to a rather somber conclusion about Elizabethan women. "Imaginatively she is of the highest importance: practically she is completely insignificant. She pervades poetry from cover to cover; she is all but absent from history. She dominates the lives of kings and conquerors in fiction; in fact she was the slave of any boy whose parents forced a ring upon her finger. Some of the most inspired words, some of the most profound thoughts in literature fall from her lips; in real life she could hardly read, could scarcely spell, and was the property of her husband."

She was, in Woolf's own words, "a worm winged like an eagle." She had no private income and a room of her own, the two essential ingredients for a female writer. She could only strut and prance about in some male poet's mind. And to support her case, Woolf imagines that Shakespeare had a sister—Judith—with his extraordinary gifts.

How could she have possibly thrived? Judith might have been "as agog to see the world" as Will. Her father wouldn't have sent her to school—there were no schools for girls. She might have picked up one of her brother's books, taught herself to read, considering she had some of his genius. If she were lucky, she could have written a page or two in her father's apple loft, and that would have been the end of her career as a scribbler.

She still had her own secret ambition and wasn't going to tie herself for life to some bony, half-witted boy. So she breaks her father's heart, prepares a tiny bundle of her belongings, climbs down a rope from her window, and runs off to London—not yet seventeen, but with "a gift like her brother's for the tune of words."

She arrives at the stage door with that bundle on her back. She wants to act, she says. The stage manager and all his cronies laugh in her face. There are no females on the London stage; boys have all the women's parts. And what is Judith Shakespeare to do? She can't learn her craft, can't even have dinner at the local tavern—she would be considered a slut. Yet she has Will's gray eyes and beautiful brows. But the manager, Nick Greene, pities her in his own way, knocks her up, and with all "the heat and violence of the poet's heart when tangled in a woman's body," she kills herself one winter's night, and now her bones lie buried beneath some London crossroad. And, says Virginia Woolf, any woman born with Judith Shakespeare's gifts in the sixteenth century "would certainly have gone crazed, shot herself, or ended her days in some lonely cottage outside the village, half witch, half wizard, feared and mocked at." And she would not only have been harmed by the people around her but would have been ripped to pieces by her own contrary instincts.

Suppose by some miracle Judith Shakespeare had survived, had written plays, like her brother; she could never have signed them. "That refuge she would have sought certainly. It was the relic of the sense of chastity that dictated anonymity to women even so late as the nineteenth century." And so we have George Eliot, George Sand, and Currer Bell, aka Charlotte Brontë, all beloved by Emily Dickinson. George Eliot's picture hung on her bedroom wall, together with Elizabeth Barrett Browning, whom she loved and admired all her life. When Sam Bowles visited Europe in 1862, Dickinson wrote:

> *Should anybody where you go, talk of Mrs. Browning, you must hear for us—and if you touch her Grave* [in Venice], *put one hand on the Head, for me—her unmentioned Mourner—*   [Letter 266, early summer 1862]

Elizabeth Barrett was born in 1806, near a tiny village in northeast England, and grew up at Hope End, an enormous estate of woodlands near Wales that would become her own Deserted Garden. She couldn't go to boarding school, unlike her brothers, but read *Paradise Lost* before she was ten, studied Latin and Greek on her own, translated Aeschylus, began to publish her poems, without ever signing her name—proper young ladies didn't become poets. But she wasn't Judith Shakespeare, forlorn and alone in London. She managed to educate herself. She'd had a troubled adolescence, with terrible backaches, and would soon become an invalid. She may have suffered from scoliosis, an abnormal curvature of the spine, though doctors couldn't really diagnose her condition. For months she had to lie still in a "spine crib," a hammock that seemed to float in the air four feet above the ground. But that didn't prevent her from writing. Pampered by her father, who was strict with his other children but proud of his "Poet Laureate," she was soon encouraged to publish under her own name. He wasn't quite as sanguine when she eloped with Robert Browning; he'd forbidden his favorite daughter—and all his other children—to marry.

It isn't hard to imagine what hold that secret marriage must have had on Emily Dickinson, who was fifteen at the time. She was mesmerized by "that Foreign Lady" with her long eyelashes and long dark curls, while she, the Belle of Amherst, with her freckles and weak chin, morphed into "the only Kangaroo among the Beauty." [Letter 268, to Higginson, July 1862]

> *I think I was enchanted*
> *When first a sombre Girl—*
> *I read that Foreign Lady—*
> *The Dark—felt beautiful—*   [Fr627]

And Dickinson crept into that magic spot—"noon at night"— where creativity began. Barrett Browning never betrayed her. At her first meeting with Higginson, nine years after Mrs. Browning's death, she wouldn't let him leave without one of her prize possessions, a photo of the Foreign Lady's tomb.

She modeled herself on Mrs. Browning, not in her poetry—that electric leap from line to line is all her own—but in the way she lived. The Foreign Lady hid herself, ran from strangers, and saw only a few friends. This would become Dickinson's own *style* and battle plan as a poet. Someone who was truly agoraphobic couldn't have warded off Professor Joseph Chickering the way she did—with such humor and élan. Chickering was a graduate of Amherst College and taught English there for thirteen years. He was also Dickinson's neighbor and had befriended her and Vinnie several times. He knew about her poetry, and when he wanted to visit, she wrote:

> *I had hoped to see you, but have no grace to talk, and my own*
> *Words so chill and burn me, that the temperature of other Minds is*
> *too new an Awe—*   [Letter 798, early 1883]

There's a bit too much art in her *agoraphobia*, and a touch of malice. She could sing nonstop to Higginson, suck the blood out of his bones, until he was worn down, and had to retreat with his little memento of the Foreign Lady, but she didn't want to talk about her poems to a college professor.

She'd rather read and reread *Aurora Leigh,* Barrett Browning's epic portrait of the artist as a young woman, first published in 1856, around the time that Dickinson was flirting with her own powers as a poet— and daring to write in her Pearl Jail. *Aurora Leigh* would serve as a road map and rallying cry for Dickinson's own struggles as a poet. It's a great big clunky book that enthralled a whole generation of readers, male and female. Sam Bowles adored every line and could recite entire sections by heart. Virginia Woolf captured all its contradictions, more than half a century later:

> *Stimulating and boring, ungainly and eloquent, monstrous and exquisite, all by turns, it overwhelms and bewilders. . . . We laugh, we protest, and complain—it is absurd, it is impossible, we cannot tolerate this exaggeration a moment longer—but, nevertheless, we read to the end enthralled.*

But it was far from monstrous for Emily Dickinson. She would mark up the copies she had, and Jay Leyda uncovered several of these markings. Aurora's aunt had lived "a cage-bird life," leaping mindlessly from perch to perch, and loving every leap.

That was not the life for Emily, or Aurora Leigh.

> *The works of women are symbolical.*
> *We sew, sew, prick our fingers, dull our sight,*
> *Producing what? A pair of slippers, sir . . ."*

And to her cousin Romney, who wants to marry her and bridle her will to create, Aurora answers:

> *. . . I may love my art.*
> *You'll grant that even a woman may love art,*
> *Seeing that to waste true love on any thing*
> *Is womanly, past question.*

Leyda believed that one or two of these markings may have been a secret dialogue with Dickinson's own father. She couldn't have known anything about Shakespeare's imaginary sister, of course. But she would have understood Judith Shakespeare's suffering and suicide. "I knew a Bird that would sing as firm in the centre of Dissolution, as in it's Father's nest—" Dickinson wrote in 1881. [Letter 685]

She was that bird, and she was still in her father's nest. She had a room of her own, like Virginia Woolf, and even if she didn't have a private income, her father paid for all her wants. She also had "a cage-bird life," but she didn't leap mindlessly; she leapt into song. And Judith Shakespeare must have lived inside her blood, unbeknownst to her, with all the other phantoms of lost female genius. And this is the rage that flew out of her, "a sumptuous Destitution—/Without a Name—" [Fr1404]. And if we want to celebrate her as a Civil War poet, talking about the bloodbath "In Yonder Maryland—" [Fr518A], we had better look twice—she was a poet of apocalypse. We cannot shackle her to one side or another—her compass didn't read North and South. The poet dreams of the dead rather than the living. When a townswoman—Mrs. Adams—loses her *second* boy during the first year of fighting, Dickinson writes to one of her Norcross cousins about ghost riders: "Poor little widow's boy, riding to-night in the mad wind, back to the village burying-ground where he never dreamed of sleeping!" [Letter 245, December 31, 1861]

She was also a ghost rider in her father's house, flitting around in her white dress, without anywhere else to go. She could "touch" the universe with her mind, and all alone—

A speck opon a Ball—
Went out opon Circumference—
Beyond the Dip of Bell—   [Fr633]

And that's where she lived most of the time, after Carlo died; not with her sister-in-law, a hedge away, though she sent 252 poems, often like love missiles, across the lawn, according to R. W. Franklin's count; not with Austin, who had distanced himself from her world of poetry and allowed Edward to entomb him in the Evergreens; not with her mother, who had become more and more morose once she moved back to the Homestead and would suffer a stroke in 1875; not with Vinnie, who was a stranded mermaid, like her sister, but had come up from a different well. Her argument was with her father, dead or alive. The martial spirit in her poems, her warlike rumbles, her constant riddling, was a dialogue with Edward Dickinson, in slant rhyme. "Out opon Circumference," she was his secret son. In the poet's psyche, Judith Shakespeare had suddenly turned into Will. She was Edward's heir apparent.

> *Amputate my freckled Bosom!*
> *Make me bearded like a man!* [Fr267]

It's not that she wanted to do away with her brother—she adored him. But she couldn't attend Amherst College, or become a lawyer, so she became a lawyer in her poems—her lines swell with legal terms. Here she writes a legal brief *against* a spider, who has occupied her place in the privy.

> *Alone and in a Circumstance*
> *Reluctant to be told*
> *A spider on my reticence*
> *Assiduously crawled*
>
> *And so much more at Home than I*
> *Immediately grew*
> *I felt myself a visitor*
> *And hurriedly withdrew—*
>
> *Revisiting my late abode*
> *with articles of claim*
> *I found it quietly assumed*
> *as a Gymnasium*
> *Where Tax asleep and Title off*

The inmates of the Air
Perpetual presumption took
As each were spectral Heir—
If any strike me on the street
I can return the Blow—
If any take my property
According to the Law
The Statute is my Learned friend
But what redress can be
For an offense nor here nor there
So not in Equity—
That Larceny of time and mind
The marrow of the Day
By spider, or forbid it Lord
That I should specify—   [Fr1174]

The poem rumbles out in all directions. Dickinson often sees herself as the spider-artist, spinning meticulous webs of Pearl. And here the spider has usurped her place in the privy. So she's become the plaintiff against herself. Still, she argues her case. We should also remember that Austin seldom appeared in court. He was never his father's "bulldog," never a trial lawyer. But the poem itself has a special Circumstance; it also happens to be a piece of constructivist art, "and is one of the oddest in all of Dickinson's writings," as Christopher Benfey acutely observes in *A Summer of Hummingbirds*.

Right in the middle of the poem is a collage, with Dickinson's own spiderlike handwriting swirling around the central image. [A 129] Dickinson has pasted a three-cent stamp "sideways," with a pair of tiny cutouts from the May 1870 edition of *Harper's Monthly Magazine*. One of the cutouts reads "GEORGE SAND," the other is simply the name of Sand's novel "Mauprat," and they *fly* out of the two left corners of the stamp, like "a bird with wings outstretched."

Sand, of course, was one of Dickinson's heroines, who wrote about the "White Heat" of her love affairs; she also flaunted her independence by dressing as a man. But the stamp itself is part of the extravaganza; it depicts a locomotive with smoke "streaming from its pyramidal smoke-stack," while the train, as placed "is traveling upward like a rocket, the smoke cascading down," almost into the language of the poem.

It was Edward who first brought the railroad to Amherst. Emily would write about it in one of her most celebrated poems, "I like to see it lap the miles" [Fr383], where the locomotive, with its pyramid of smoke, ends up "docile and omnipotent/At its own stable door," just like the carriage horses her father loved to drive. He's the phantom conductor of the train, as well as her secret interlocutor in the earlier poem—Edward's trace is everywhere.

Is it any wonder that she was so reluctant to "print," to see her lines—and her name—in some public auction of the soul? And yet she seemed to mimic the art of publication, as if she were preparing a secret oeuvre; but how could anyone ever have published a poem with a locomotive in the middle? Still, there was "divine Sense" to what she was doing—she survived with the lightning inside her head. And after Carlo died, she would find another ally: Margaret Maher.

2

J AY LEYDA WAS THERE FIRST, AS HE OFTEN IS. Long before scholars ever considered the importance of servants at the Homestead and the Evergreens, Leyda wrote about Margaret Maher, the Dickinsons' Irish maid, in his essay "Miss Emily's Maggie." Leyda wasn't inter-ested in the usual smoke screens; he wanted to dig under the false legends and reports that surrounded the poet. Minutiae, he believed, might unlock some of the secrets that surrounded Dickinson's "sur-prising poems and equally surprising life." Minutiae would help reveal "warm and wild and mighty" Maggie, as the poet came to call her. [Letter 907, early August 1884]

But it hadn't always been that way. Dickinson never lost her patrician manner, and was on guard against the Irish, who worked on her father's railroad and lived near the railroad tracks. As Leyda tells us: "Every fence was employed to isolate the Irishman from the community," his Catholicism "an excellent barrier to the tightly buttoned Congregationalist villages of western Massachusetts." There was no place for an Irishman among gentrified Whigs like her father; the wild Irish had to join the Democratic Party if they wanted any political clout. *Scribner's* and the *Springfield Republican* constantly made fun of the Irish. And for the poet herself, they were barely human, blushing as easily as some savage child from the railroad tracks.

Several months after Margaret arrived at the Homestead, in 1869, Dickinson wrote to Loo about her father's Irish handyman and his expertise with horses:

> . . . *Tim is washing Dick's feet, and talking to him now and then in an intimate way. Poor fellow, how he warmed when I gave him your message!* [Tim must have been kind to Loo on her last visit]. *The red reached clear to his beard, he was so gratified; and Maggie stood as still for hers as a puss for patting. The hearts of these poor people lie so unconcealed you bare them with a smile.* [Letter 337, late 1869]

Yet she would learn to trust Margaret, to depend on her, as she trusted no one else. Margaret might deliver a message to the poet's sister-in-law, keep strangers out of her hair, protect her from every prying eye. They formed a powerful unit—mistress and maid. Dickinson stored her stash of poems with Margaret; all her fascicles lay at the bottom of Margaret's trunk, in that tiny room above the kitchen where Margaret slept. Emily was still the same patrician, but by 1881 she would write to her Norcross cousins:

> *Maggie's brother is killed in the mines, and Maggie wants to die, but Death goes far around to those that want to see him. If the little cousins would give her a note—she does not know I ask it—I*

think it would help her begin, that bleeding beginning that every
mourner knows.

Before she came to the Homestead, Margaret worked for the Boltwoods, who were every bit as prominent in Amherst as the Dickinsons.
She had moved to Hartford with Clarinda Boltwood and her husband,
but after her brother-in-law, Tom Kelley, lost his arm in an accident—
he fell off a building and tumbled thirty feet—Margaret returned to
Amherst to be with the rest of her family. The Boltwoods still wanted
to keep her; Margaret was quite attached to Clarinda, and wrote as
often as she could.

. . . I don't know whether it is day or night since I left hartford . . .
the dath of dear father lies in a cloud *of sadness on me and I can't*
get over it he died in my armes . . . how nice it would be to have all
friends lay down and die so that we would not have to suffer the loss
of those that gone . . .

Edward had had a difficult time finding and keeping servants. As
one former seamstress said, "The Dickinsons didn't like strangers . . .
Outsiders weren't welcome there." Particularly if they were Irish.

Margaret was well into her twenties when she came to work for
Edward Dickinson; she had no real desire to stay in his service. Born
in Tipperary in 1841, she had come to America with bits and pieces of
her family, and wanted to join her brother in the Far West—or move
back to Hartford to be with the Boltwoods—but couldn't seem to get
out from under Edward's grip.

. . . Mr. Dicksom said he would Pay me as much more wages
soner then let me go so that I have decided to stay for the Preasant . . .

The "Preasant" soon became thirty years; she would outlive all the
Dickinsons who had ever employed her—father, mother, Emily, Austin, Vinnie—but five years after the poet's death, she still signed her
letters "Miss Emily's and Vinnia's Maggie."

Yet even as Leyda hunts down Margaret and uncovers as much minutiae as he can, he still can't tell us much about Margaret's relationship to her mistress's poetry. Neither can Richard Sewall and the poet's other biographers; she's not even mentioned in John Cody's psychoanalytical study, though Dickinson spent more time with Margaret, "the North Wind of the Family," than she ever did with Sue. It's only in the twenty-first century, when most class distinctions have long disintegrated, and we've had more than a hundred years of mining the poet's art and life, that we can find a much more subtle and *searing* portrait of Edward's "Irish girl."

As Aífe Murray writes in *Maid as Muse*, "There was an invisible story within an invisible story," about Irish, Native American, and black gardeners and maids who worked for genteel families like the Dickinsons but remained unrecorded ghosts, outside time and history. Margaret would also have remained a ghost if her mistress hadn't become *our* Emily Dickinson. But Aífe Murray is the only one who has grasped that Margaret helped shape the poet's interior landscape. Her maid would keep alive a counternarrative of "a cacophonous tumbling kitchen 'world.'" If, as Murray suggests, the parlor was the stern, almost morbid, fixture of Puritan Amherst, the kitchen was "the most creative room in the house[,] dominated by a mix of voices and purposes." But it was also beyond the pale of Puritan culture.

The kitchen, pantry, and back rooms belonged to the "architecture of the unseen," where servants could disappear from view and never be noticed. The poet learned to intrude upon this hidden architecture. She often scribbled bits of poems in the pantry and worked with Maggie in the kitchen, particularly after her mother had a stroke. And Murray doesn't see the poet's mythic white dress as a mark of seclusion. It had a much more practical bent. The white wrapper allowed her to move unimpeded from her garden to the kitchen, and to her writing desk upstairs. It also brought her much closer to Margaret's world. Murray senses a "seamlessness between the motions of maid and mistress . . . as one mixed and the other measured, as quick remark of one was met by quick remark of the other."

How much of Margaret's cadences broke into Emily's *moosic* is difficult to surmise. Murray can feel Margaret's presence in every single one of the poet's celebrated dashes, which "provide a halting, almost rollicking gait," like Margaret's own. But I find Dickinson's dashes much more violent, and not part of any particular "chant." Her dashes decapitate lines and words, until syntax shatters and we're left with sharp little strings of language, like lonely, isolated islands.

Yet Margaret still managed to influence Dickinson's fate. She would become the poet's accomplice, a female master sergeant. Margaret was the guardian of her mistress's "Snow," the stitched and unstitched booklets, and isolated scraps written on recipes and chocolate wrappers. Dickinson had ordered Margaret to burn the entire stash upon her death. But Margaret removed the poems from her trunk and put them back in her mistress's bureau, where Vinnie discovered them. Murray believes the poet knew all along that Margaret would never destroy her "Snow" and was counting on her maid's loyalty and shrewd judgment.

I'm not so sure. Dickinson was very careful and precise about other matters. She had Judge Lord prepare her will—Margaret was one of her witnesses. She orchestrated her own funeral, asked for a simple white coffin, and wanted six of the family compound's Irish laborers to carry her out the back of the house, through the barn, and across the fields to the burial ground—one of these six men was Margaret's brother-in-law, Tom. Yet she was so reckless and nonchalant about the fate of her poems, that spider's material she had accumulated for almost thirty years. Perhaps she wasn't reckless at all, and really preferred that the poems be destroyed. It was a form of "suicide"—she didn't want to leave a trace of herself.

She could rant to Higginson about the unbearable burden of publication:

> *If fame belonged to me, I could not escape her—if she did not,*
> *the longest day would pass me on the chase—and the approbation of*
> *my Dog, would forsake me—then—My Barefoot-Rank is better—*
> [Letter 265, June 7, 1865]

But she wasn't Barefoot in the swirl of her mind. She had an audience to play against in her letters; she could dance on invisible toes, pirouette for some imperfect Other, except perhaps in her "Master Letters," where the Other may never be defined, or could have been her own invented male self. The poems were often *secretions* within the letters themselves, like the markings of a snail, and she might shift a word or a line to suit a particular correspondent, like some poet-tailor. But all her lines, altered or not, still had their own very private life. She may have worn as many masks as she could in her letters, but here she was pirouetting for herself. And though it's dangerous to intuit her intentions about her poetry from a particular poem, we might find a couple of clues:

> *I would not paint—a picture—*
> *I'd rather be the One*
> *It's bright impossibility*
> *To dwell—delicious—on—*
> *And wonder how the fingers feel*
> *Whose rare—celestial—stir—*
> *Evokes so sweet a torment*
> *Such sumptuous—Despair—*
>
> *I would not talk, like Cornets—*
> *I'd rather be the One*
> *Raised softly to the Ceilings—*
> *And out, and easy on—*
> *Through Villages of Ether—*
> *Myself endued Balloon*

By but a lip of Metal—
The pier to my Pontoon—

Nor would I be a Poet—
It's finer—Own the Ear—
Enamored—impotent—content—
The License to revere,
A privilege so awful
What would the Dower be,
Had I the Art to stun myself
With Bolts—of Melody!   [Fr348]

This is Dickinson's portrait of the artist—in the midst of a disappearing act. I don't believe the poem is about painters, musicians, and poets, but concerns itself with the primacy—or "celestial—stir"—of image and sound. The speaker-poet does wonder how her fingers might feel had she that "bright impossibility" to paint a picture, and it evokes a "sumptuous—Despair."

And she doesn't want to be a Cornet, but would rather ride softly to the Ceilings with the sound, into "Villages of Ether," while *clothed* as a Balloon, moored by some phantom metal string.

In the third stanza, Dickinson denies her own identity. She'd rather not be a Poet, but the poet's *instrument*—her Ear—with all its contradictions and sweet torment: "impotent," because the Ear cannot create, but has "the License to revere"; and the speaker wonders what her "Dower"—or divine reward would be:

Had I the Art to stun myself
With Bolts—of Melody!

Dickinson is teasing herself, of course, wearing yet another mask. She understood her own genius and the "sumptuous—Despair" of song.

"I would not paint a picture" is still a puzzle within a puzzle. A lot more than whimsy is at stake. If, as I believe, she was her own essential audience, then that Balloon in the Ether is more than a fanciful ride—balloons mattered to Emily Dickinson, as poet Susan Snively suggests: "balloons embody her imagination's pilgrimages of discovery"—her means of travel. "Vehicles of beauty and danger—like poetry itself . . . balloons involve the dynamic pull of opposites: hope and disgrace, life and death, exultation and despair, renewal and destruction," and the very breath of language, its rise and fall.

The poem itself is a long balloon ride through the Ether of her own intellect; she'd rather sail on the balloon of language, pelted by the brain's own black mud and wind, and be the *instrument* of song, with a Metal lip, than be mangled and swallowed up in the persona of a poet.

3

THAT LEAVES MARGARET MAHER. And we shouldn't take her for granted. "Surely," says Aífe Murray, "Emily intuited that her maid would resist the order to burn her poems." I'm not convinced. Lavinia burnt all the letters, as she had been told by her sister. But Margaret wasn't a Dickinson. She was a maid, without a single right. This is quite apparent in the poet's letter to her Norcross cousins in 1873:

> *Austin went this morning, after a happy egg and toast provided by Maggie, whom he promised to leave his sole heir.* [Letter 394, September 1873]

Austin could promise Margaret half the world, and wind and rain, as any master might amuse himself with a servant—he left her nothing at all. The poet left her nothing, though she had little to leave, and Vinnie also left her nothing. Maids were always visibly invisible, no matter how valuable they were. She might have been the poet's "muse, lookout, and beckoner," as Murray insists, but we still aren't sure how her last name was pronounced. It couldn't have mattered much to the Dickinsons, since she was their Maggie.

And if she did salvage the poems, rescue them from oblivion, it might not have been as a favor to her dead mistress. She wasn't tinkering with history. She returned the poems to her mistress's drawer, and let her other mistress decide—"Miss Vinnia." She also saved the daguerreotype we have of the poet—taken at sixteen—that no one in the family ever liked, not even the poet herself, who would deny to Higginson that she had ever had her portrait taken. Father, she said, "has Molds of all the rest—but has no Mold of me" [Letter 268, July 1862], and then proceeded to paint her own portrait, declaring that she was small, "like the Wren," and had eyes "like the Sherry in the Glass, that the Guest leaves—Would this do just as well?" It was perhaps her most artful bit of seduction.

The daguerreotype should have disappeared. But Margaret had a fondness for the picture, and wanted a memento of her mistress. It became known as "Maggie's daguerreotype." And once the poet was res-urrected, brought back from the dead, her publishers, Roberts Broth-ers, craved a portrait of their rising star. Vinnie and Austin objected to the daguerreotype, considered it too solemn. Vinnie told Roberts Brothers that the daguerreotype did not represent her sister's "most interesting & most startling face." She had a Boston miniaturist create a "bowdlerized" version of the daguerreotype—the poet suddenly had curls and a high, ruffled collar; her image was altered again and again after Vinnie's death, the curls washed with color, until Emily Dickin-son looked like a cross-eyed Scarlett O'Hara. The original daguerreo-type was found again in 1945, as if it had risen right out of Vinnie's grave; the poet's sister, it seems, had swiped the silvered copper plate back from Margaret Maher, then palmed it off on a distant cousin, who had kept it "in storage" for over fifty years and turned it over to Mabel Todd's daughter, Millicent.

But behind this whole farrago stands Margaret Maher, without whom we'd never have had the poems or the silvered plate. While she was with the Dickinsons, she liked to sign her letters "your unworth but true Maggie Maher." As Aífe Murray tells us, "unworth" was just a mask of meekness that servants often had to wear—a pretense for their masters.

Margaret wasn't meek at all. But she had to pick her way "with aplomb" over her mistress's land mines. As Higginson realized after one hour, it was impossible to live around the poet. He had to flee Amherst as fast he could. But Margaret remained with Dickinson during the last seventeen years of her life. The poet was "making a loaf of cake with Maggie," on June 14, 1884, when she fainted for the first time—it might have been a small stroke. [Letter 907, to Fanny and Loo, early August 1884] She kept to her bed much of the time after that. "The Dyings have been too deep for me," she wrote that autumn. [Letter 939] Her mother, an invalid for years, had died in 1882. The Reverend Charles Wadsworth, whom many scholars still consider the most likely candidate for her "Master Letters," also died in 1882. Gib, her favorite nephew, fell ill with typhoid fever in the fall of 1883. He was eight years old and might have sipped some water from a "poisoned" well; accompanied by Maggie, Dickinson went across the lawn for the first time in years to visit the dying boy, but the odor of carbolic acid in the house sickened her, and she had to return to her bedroom, more feeble than ever.

A year later, Judge Lord died. We cannot choreograph their romance; we have only the drafts of certain letters that may never have been sent. But that romance was real enough to upset the judge's niece, Abby Farley, who might have lost her inheritance if Lord had ever married the poet. "Little hussy," she said years later of the poet. "She was crazy about men. Even tried to get Judge Lord. Insane too."

Abby Farley's hostile image of the poet wasn't unique. Dickinson had become "the most dangerous type of alien—a poet," according to Jay Leyda. The town thrived on any "revelation" about her—"madness was one of the gentler accusations." Hence, she and Maggie were both exiles of a sort in Amherst: the Irish maid and that eccentric spinster in white who was capable of any folly. It was Margaret who must have helped her when she was much too weak to wash, Margaret who might have sung Irish lullabies to her. We can feel the poet's affection when Maggie herself fell ill with typhoid fever in 1882, and had to "abandon" both Dickinson sisters and stay with her own sister and brother-in-law. The poet played on that abandonment in a letter to Maggie:

> *The missing Maggie is much mourned, and I am going out for "black" to the nearest store.*
> *All are very naughty, and I am naughtiest of all.*
> *The pussies dine on sherry now, and humming-bird cutlets . . .*
> *What shall I send my weary Maggie? Pillows or fresh brooks?*
>

Her grieved Mistress.
[Letter 771, October 1882]

That's the one and only letter we have from Dickinson to Margaret Maher. And we're lucky to have it. How often was Margaret ill with typhoid, and how often was she away from the house? But we have nothing in return from Margaret—not a word about her mistress. We know that she hated Vinnie's cats. When she first arrived at the Dickinson house, she wrote to her former mistress:

> *. . . one grate trouble that I have not half enough of work so that I must play with the cats to Plase Miss Vinny you know how I love cats . . .*

But what did she really think of the poet? Did they plot together to *ruin* Vinnie's empire of cats? Did they laugh in the kitchen? "To see is perhaps never quite the sorcery that it is to surmise," Dickinson wrote in 1878. [Letter 565] Yet it's hard to surmise Margaret's untold story, even after Aífe Murray describes her as the poet's muse. I can't find much of Margaret's lilt in Dickinson's *moosic*—her lightning came from another source. But Margaret must have loved that lightning in her own way, guarded it, even if she hadn't read a line. We'll never know how she grieved for her mistress. But I can still imagine her in the sunlight, accompanying the bier carried by the six Irish workmen to the grave site. ". . . Maggie is getting corpulent," Dickinson wrote to her Norcross cousins in 1881. [Letter 727] Corpulent Maggie was forty-five at the time of the funeral;

there's no record of her ever marrying or "keeping company" with a man. We know what she looked like—before she was corpulent; we have a photo of her from the early 1870s, taken with her one-armed brother-in-law and his own daughter, who also worked for the Dickinsons, and was known as "Little Maggie."

Margaret looks into the camera with her dark eyes; her smile is half a frown, as if she had a much stronger will than the photographer; she's wearing a white scarf and a silk three-piece dress; the hand she has on Tom Kelley's shoulder is small and delicate. Her chin is very strong. She's not a maid who could have been trifled with. And I wonder how she mourned her mistress. Was it with a brooding Irish eye?

We do have at least one record of their conversation. In 1880, two and a half years after Sam Bowles had died, Dickinson wrote to his son, "Samuel Bowles the younger":

> —*A servant who had been with us a long time and had often opened the door for him* [Sam Bowles], *asked me how to spell* "Genius," *yesterday—I told her and she said no more—Today, she asked me what* "Genius" *meant? I told her none had known—*
> *She said she read in a Catholic Paper that Mr. Bowles was "the Genius of Hampshire"* [Hampshire County], *and thought it might be that past Gentleman—*   [Letter 651]

There's more than a touch of snobbery as the poet trumpets Sam Bowles at Margaret's expense. She's back in the world of patricians, where her maid is left out. But we can forgive her as we understand the poignancy of Margaret's remarks. She must have known that her mistress was also a "Genius," even if she couldn't spell the word. And it made her fiercely protective and proud. I like to think she would have cherished those seventeen years, even if the poems had never been removed from her trunk and Dickinson remained one more undiscovered poet, as invisible as Margaret herself.

———◦〰◦———

FIVE

Ballerinas in a Box

1

THOSE FORMIDABLE MALE POETS and critics—Conrad Aiken, Yvor Winters, Robert Frost, R. P. Blackmur, Archibald MacLeish, and John Crowe Ransom—who rediscovered Dickinson and rescued her in the first half of the twentieth century were always a bit condescending about the nature of her art, as if she were that strange cat who'd come out of a New England closet with her slant rhymes. "Most of us," MacLeish admitted, "are half in love with this dead girl we all call by her first name." Her genius, Aiken said, was as erratic as it was brilliant, and the reader had to adjust himself to that "spinsterly angularity" of the poet. Winters felt caught within the tangle of her poems, where beautiful lines were "wasted in the desert of her crudities. . . . In this respect, she differs from Melville, whose taste was rich and cultivated."

Shrewd enough to grasp that they were in the presence of a master, they still couldn't welcome her into their private pantheon of male poets, though not a single one of them, including Robert Frost, had her demonic powers and monstrous wit, nor would they haunt our new century the way she has done. She would remain for them the village spinster and virginal poetess who suffered through an unrequited romance with some mysterious male suitor.

Only Allen Tate, who with his fellow southerner, John Crowe

Ransom, belonged to the Fugitives, a gang of agrarian poets that despised the avaricious heart of modern America, understood her worth as a poet. In a seminal essay on Dickinson that first appeared in 1932, Tate struck at the prejudice of male readers who were convinced that "no virgin can know enough to write poetry." Her powers came with a certain mystery. "We shall never learn where she got that rich quality of mind." But that didn't seem to bother Allen Tate. Dickinson, "a dominating spinster whose very sweetness must have been formidable," didn't have to travel much farther than her upstairs room at the Homestead. "Her life was one of the richest and deepest ever lived on this continent."

Still, most critics were completely unprepared when Rebecca Patterson, an obscure college instructor at the University of North Carolina, published *The Riddle of Emily Dickinson* (1951), a book that redefined this same village spinster as a sexual outlaw who had a romance with another woman, Kate Scott. Patterson was convinced that without Katie, Dickinson might never have become a poet. The book was mocked and reviled by most male critics. George Whicher, the preeminent Dickinson scholar of his time, called it "probably the worst book on Emily Dickinson yet written, and that is saying a good deal."

Kate Scott Turner Anthon—she was widowed twice—was born on March 12, 1831, in Cooperstown, New York, the lair of novelist James Fenimore Cooper, whose father had founded the tiny village in 1786 on one of his own enormous tracts of land. Three months younger than Susan Gilbert and Emily, Kate was sent to Utica Female Academy when she was seventeen—a tall, voluptuous beauty with dark hair and dark eyes. It was hard for men and women to resist "Condor Kate," as Emily would discover ten years later. But her history with Kate really began at this female academy, where Susan Gilbert had also been sent and was the first to feel Kate's seductive twitch. Assigned as a new monitor at the academy, Sue stopped at Kate's door as part of her duties, and without warning, Kate leapt out and kissed her on the cheek. Kate never recovered from that kiss:

> *Dear, dear Sue, I have loved you always, since the first night you were "monitoress." And I hardly knew you, but kissed your dear face simply because I could not help it! Your sweet eyes looked into mine, and I could never forget them!*

The two young women remained friends, but Sue was a bit of a rag doll, and she couldn't reconnect with Kate on her own terms until after she married Austin and became mistress of the Evergreens. In 1855, Kate had married Campbell Turner of Cooperstown, a young medical doctor, sick with consumption, who died in 1857—Kate had been more nurse to him than wife, and after Campbell's death, she began calling herself Kate Scott again.

This is how Patterson describes Kate's first visit to the Evergreens:

> *On a day of early March, 1859, a tall young woman, swathed in long furs, her dark hair crowned by a fashionable black hat, her dark eyes brilliant behind a widow's black veil, stepped down from Austin's sleigh to the snowy driveway of the Austin Dickinson house.*

She would stun both households, the Homestead and the Evergreens, and there's little doubt that Sam Bowles, who was visiting Austin and Sue at the time, fell in love with "Mrs. Kate." He kept asking about the tall goddess dressed in black who descended upon this puritanical town like some nineteenth-century femme fatale. But Kate wasn't really interested in Mr. Sam. A certain freckle-faced poet appealed to her much more in Patterson's novelistic rendering of Emily Dickinson. "Upon the dead, and somewhat desolate, calm of Emily's twenty-ninth year, this lonely, emotional young widow broke with the destructiveness and terrible beauty of a spring storm. For years afterwards Emily Dickinson was occupied in gathering up the wreckage of her life."

And Patterson maps the progress of their romance. They met in March (actually, it was a couple of months before that), were immediately drawn to each other, and the young widow would return to Amherst at least four times in the next two years and bewitch the poet's mind and imagination. Dickinson's own letters reveal this intoxication. In a letter to Kate near the end of 1859, she writes:

Katie—

Last year at this time [before she met Kate at the Evergreens] *I did not miss you, but positions shifted, until I hold your black in strong hallowed remembrance. . . . I am pleasantly located in the deep sea, but love will row you out if her hands are strong, and don't wait till I land, for I'm going ashore on the other side—* [Letter 209]

And in 1860, suffering through a spell without Kate, she conjures up Kate's image in its own *phantom niche.* "I touch your hand—my cheek your cheek—I stroke your vanished hair, Why did you enter, sister, since you must depart? Had not its heart been torn enough but *you* must send your shred? Oh! our Condor Kate! Come from your crags again!" [Letter 222]

Cooperstown was far more sophisticated and sensual than a town of farmers, students, and hell-fire preachers, where young men and women had to dance or play cards and read novels in secret, and Katie would become the poet's first—and last—genuinely sinful pleasure, according to Rebecca Patterson. "Having spent her entire capital on one venture, and suffered bankruptcy, she dared not try again." Condor Kate flew from Emily and Amherst in 1861; she sailed off to Europe three years later, lived among the blue skies and waters of Barrett Browning's beloved Italy, and in 1866 Kate married a rich lawyer and classical scholar, John Anthon, two years younger than she herself, and moved to Manhattan, where she immediately fell out of love with the metropolis.

Meanwhile, Emily mourned Kate, shrouded herself in white, and hovered close to insanity. Kate was the hulking condorlike shadow that looms behind every poem. Hence, we have the *riddle* of Emily Dickinson, who arrived at her craft by sheer accident, and was "stirred to poetry by a chance encounter"—with Kate. During one of her visits to Amherst in 1860, Kate talked to Emily about *Aurora Leigh,* Barrett Browning, and their own escape to the blue Italian seas, where they could defy the Calvinist codes of Amherst and live like outlaws, away from New England's fierce *inquisition*. And out of this dreamlike, impossible longing for Italy grew the key poem that would unmask Dickinson's desires, after Kate had abandoned her.

> *I am not used to Hope—*
> *It might intrude opon—*
> *It's sweet parade—blaspheme the place—*
> *Ordained to Suffering—*
>
> *It might be easier*
> *To fail—with Land in Sight—*
> *Than gain—My Blue Peninsula—*
> *To perish—of Delight—*   [Fr535]

And for Patterson, this "Blue Peninsula" marked the poet's obsessive, boundless love for Kate. But after Kate's marriage to John Anthon, Emily had fewer and fewer "sweet parades," as her own interest in poetry declined, and she withdrew into the near silence of her white shroud. From this moment on, Dickinson herself becomes a wraith and virtually disappears from Patterson's book, and we follow Kate after her second husband dies and she wanders across Europe, moving from one address to another every five or six months. She takes up with a much younger woman, Florence Eliot, or "Florrie," the daughter of an Anglo-Indian widow who wasn't much older than

Kate. And they become an odd threesome, traveling together, living together, with Florrie often hopping between Kate and her mother until she leaves Kate flat and marries her own young man. Kate can barely endure this abandonment and neglect. And in some perverse high-wire act, Patterson has her morph into Emily Dickinson. "She was no happier than Emily had been on a like occasion in 1864. If she had been a poet, she could now have written the entire canon of Emily Dickinson." Condor Kate seems to have cannibalized the book, as if Patterson were telling us that Dickinson's genius had come out of some generic sense of grief, a black bottle filled with pain that could be patented for potential poets.

There has never been such a bottle, but at least one reader was intrigued by the "twinning" of Emily Dickinson and Condor Kate. Artist Joseph Cornell had heard about Dickinson in the 1920s, after reading Marsden Hartley's *Adventures in the Arts* (1921), where the poet was presented as a prankster and an imp shaping and reshaping words in her own celestial garden. That childlike quality appealed to Cornell, the maker of shadow boxes that were like intricate miniature toys entombed in glass and wood. He had found a copy of Rebecca Patterson's book at the Flushing Public Library, perhaps at the prodding of Jay Leyda, one of his mentors. And in 1953, while Leyda was working on Dickinson's manuscripts, assembling all the different scraps, he told Cornell about these mysterious fragments and constructions, such as an envelope refashioned into a house to encase one of her poems:

> *The   way*
>   *Hope   builds   his*
> *House*
> *It   is   not   with   a   sill* . . . [Fr1512; manuscript: "A 450"]

Credit: Fr1512; manuscript: "A 450," Amherst College Archives and Special Collections

The lines are split up to form their own tiny edifice, as if Dickinson were building a cathedral inside a paper tomb. Cornell understood the wicked play of her art, and in appreciation of Leyda's sharing some of these "assemblages" with him, he sent Leyda an assemblage of his own—a pencil called "Lovely," with a rush of color on its wooden tube like psychedelic waves; the pencil is encased in a piece of cardboard, like the words inside Dickinson's paper house. Cornell, a very shy man, believed that Leyda, who was "more conversant with the lines of Miss Emily," might see the connection between her controlled chaos and "this liquid swirl encoffined" in cardboard. [Letter to Jay Leyda, June 19, 1953]

But it was Emily's "Blue Peninsula" that appealed to Cornell most, her land of longing, and he must have felt like some Frankenstein monster in relation to her, Emily's malformed modern twin, who stalked Manhattan like some pitiless scavenger, looking for artifacts and clues to his own existence. Cornell needed Emily's "Blue Peninsula" as much as she ever did.

2
—

H E WAS BORN JOSEPH I. CORNELL (the sixth in a line of Cornells with the identical name), on Christmas Eve, 1903, in Nyack, a resort town on the Hudson that was crumbling into ruin, yet had once been famous for its mansions and luxurious hotels. Edward Hopper had come from the same town: Haunted, half-empty hotels, where humans in their isolation barely left a trace, would mark both their work like some terrifying motif—the void of hotel rooms would breathe its own primitive fire in Hopper's paintings and Cornell's collages and shadow boxes; in fact, Hopper's canvases were like mammoth shadow boxes, where the walls were about to collapse. And Cornell's shadow boxes always seemed to carry the crumbling debris of some lost hotel.

His father, Joseph I. Cornell the fifth, a successful textile designer, was a dapper man who dressed in Sulka shirts and took part in local theatrical productions, but didn't have his wife's aristocratic credentials. Helen Ten Broeck Storms Cornell may have lacked her husband's panache, but she could trace her Dutch ancestors back to the American Revolution—her grandfather was one of the richest men in Nyack and had an avenue named after him.

Cornell had two younger sisters, Elizabeth and Helen, and a baby brother, Robert, who was afflicted with cerebral palsy at birth and never learned to walk. A year before her marriage, Helen had studied to become a kindergarten teacher, and though she never taught, she would remain a kind of kindergarten teacher most of her life, taking care of *two* handicapped sons, Robert and Joseph, who could never seem to crawl out from under his mother's control.

He didn't have the least bit of artistic bent. "I've never called myself an artist," he would declare, long after he had become famous with his shadow boxes. "I can't draw, paint, sculpt, make lithographs." But even as a boy, he loved to collect things and to watch people, as if every gesture of theirs was a private performance for Joseph Cornell, who lived in his very own circus. His favorite *performer* was Harry Houdini, the ultimate escape artist, whom Cornell had seen several times at the Hippodrome in Manhattan. No box or shackles could hold Houdini, who practiced a brand of "white magic" that would enchant Cornell for the rest of his life. Every one of his shadow boxes was an homage to Houdini, where ballerinas or birds and birdlike poets were often escape artists, who were on the point of fleeing, or had already flown.

The boy also liked to think of his father as a magician, who would disappear on a train and suddenly reappear several days later with candy and trinkets in his coat pocket, dime-store merchandise that would become intricate parts of his son's shadow boxes—potions of "white magic." The magician grew more and more affluent, and by 1912 the family was living in an enormous house on a hill right above the Hudson. But his father developed "pernicious anemia" and died in 1917, when Cornell was thirteen. He was still able to attend Phillips Academy in Andover, Massachusetts, perhaps the most prestigious prep school in the nation—Benjamin Spock and Walker Evans were among his schoolmates. The family fell on hard times, but Cornell's tuition and expenses were paid by his father's former employer, who befriended the boy. This would be Joseph's first and last forage away from home. A mediocre student, whose one memorable effort was a term paper on Houdini, he spent three and a half years in Andover but failed to graduate because he couldn't complete requirements in history and mathematics. And while his classmates went on to college, Cornell slipped off to a modest house in Bayside, Queens, where Helen had moved with the rest of her family.

Now eighteen, Cornell went to work as a "sample boy"—a cloth and wool salesman—at a Massachusetts textile wholesaler with an office in Manhattan at 25 Madison Avenue; long and lean, he looked like a wraith with ferocious blue eyes as he carried around his enormous sample trunk

from one menswear manufacturer to the next. He felt an incredible ela-
tion on his trips from Bayside to Manhattan, on his wanderings through
the city, with or without his sample trunk, and on his lunchtime breaks
in Madison Square Park. His shadow boxes were his own miniature sample trunks, and they grew out of his constant treasure hunts for trinkets,
his "*trouvailles*," as he would later call them. He haunted penny arcades,
cafeterias, and the secondhand bookshops on Fourth Avenue. He was a
scavenger and voyeur, looking to collect a past for himself, not his own
past in Nyack, but a reconstructed past of nineteenth-century Europe.
It's not clear how much French he knew, but it was the one subject
that had excited him at Andover, and most of his favorite writers were
French—Rimbaud, Baudelaire, and particularly Gérard de Nerval, who
despised the material world and believed in his own visionary powers.
Nerval would wander the streets of Paris with his pet lobster, Thibault,
on a leash of pure blue silk; he suffered several breakdowns after the
death of actress Jenny Colon, whom he loved but who couldn't love him
back, recorded his own nightmares and hallucinations, and hanged himself from a window grate when he was forty-six.

Cornell must have imagined his own pet lobster on his wanderings through the city, and re-created a thousand Jenny Colons. The
most iconic of these women was Fanny Cerrito, a "lost" nineteenth-
century ballerina from Naples, whose image he first discovered in
a Fourth Avenue bookstall in 1940, and immediately had what he
would call an "unfoldment"—an epiphany that was akin to Nerval's
hallucinations, where several hidden truths were revealed to him in
a flash as Cerrito leapt from the stall and danced in front of his eyes.
"The figure of the young danseuse stepped forth as completely con-
temporaneous as the skyscrapers surrounding her." He would have
another "sighting" of Cerrito that same year, when he discovered her
on the roof of a Manhattan storage warehouse, in the uniform of a
male guard. This shift in persona would become a staple of Cornell's
work, where one's sexual identity was never reliable or safe.

He burrowed deep into the ballerina's life, collected whatever material he could find about her (it would eventually fill a suitcase), saw himself as her double—he, too, could flit from male to female, like Fanny Cerrito disguised as a guard in the modern city, but he was frightened (and enthralled) by the mature female form; that's why he was obsessed by *fées,* young androgynous girls he would spy on in the streets of Manhattan or Flushing, where his mother had bought a modest Dutch Colonial house in 1929, with white shingles and a blue trim. He would live there for the rest of his life, on a nondescript street in the middle of nowhere. Ballerina Allegra Kent, to whom he would devote a series of boxes, said about her own excursion into that invisible country of Queens: "His greeting was joyous and happy, although somehow visits were always hard to arrange. . . . It might have been easier to travel to Russia than to Utopia Parkway."

He set up his own workshop in the kitchen, where he would constantly tangle with his mother over the colossal mess he made; even after he moved his workshop to the cellar, these battle royals would go on and on; he stored his shadow boxes and collages everywhere—in his bedroom, in crannies behind the stairs, in an abandoned fridge, or in random towering piles in the cellar, and in an open garage, where his best work was exposed to wind and rain. His days and nights with Helen would have been intolerable had it not been for Robert.

Robert had a much sweeter temperament than his gloomy brother, who always dressed in gray; like a delicate, hunched-over homunculus, Robert would operate a whole gallery of electric trains with a series of levers beside his wheelchair at the center of the living room—a little god-invalid with magical levers; later he would have epileptic fits, and Cornell had to feed his brother and care for him. Robert *humanized* Joseph, removed him from his nineteenth-century dreamscapes for a little while; whatever gift of real affection he had came from his love for Robert. But Robert was also an entry point into Joseph's art, and would appear in the shadow boxes in many guises—as a Renaissance prince, a ballerina, or some songbird that could fly in great unbridled leaps.

Still, Cornell was grievously depressed in his workshop-prison on Utopia Parkway, and he would have to "fly" out of there to Manhattan or Main Street, Flushing, where he could sit in his favorite cafeteria, Bickford's, or "Bickie's," scribble notes on a napkin while he gobbled pistachio ice cream, or wander into Woolworth's and watch a "frail teener salesgirl," and perhaps another teener with a "boney frame—emaciated—wan—but real *fée*." Cornell's diaries are filled with these sightings of wan, androgynous girls, but mostly they are about meals and metaphysics.

They record his insatiable hunger for sweets. When he wasn't wolfing Milky Ways, he was brooding about his own strange art, the "metaphysics of ephemera," of recapturing Fanny Cerrito and other lost souls, but always through some perverse, indirect route, where he had "that curiously plaguing phenomenon of purposely not trying to find desired things."

He had to happen upon his treasures, or as Charles Simic writes in *Dime Store Alchemy* (1992), perhaps the most penetrating study of Cornell's fragile, elusive art: "America still waits to be discovered. Its tramps and poets resemble early navigators setting out on journeys of exploration." Cornell was one such poet-tramp, and the America he discovered couldn't have occurred without his involvement in dime-store debris.

But Cornell's America had a European bent—it harked back to the concert halls and opera houses where Fanny Cerrito performed and the negligible hotel rooms where she stayed as she wandered from engagement to engagement, each hotel room a little seedier than the last, and none of them ever giving us a glimpse of the ballerina. He never "sighted" any other nineteenth-century ballerinas in Manhattan, even though Fanny Elssler, the tall, dark-haired Viennese beauty, was much more voluptuous, and her great Swedish-Italian rival, Marie Taglioni, was far more famous than Cerrito. Neither of them could awaken

Cornell from the near slumber he was often in—only Cerrito, who played a sea goddess in *Ondine* (1843), a siren who falls in love with a young Sicilian fisherman and tries to steal him from his fiancée.

He would devote a series of boxes to Cerrito and her favorite ballet; his construction of these boxes happened to coincide with World War II. Cornell tried to enlist, but was turned down by his draft board. He would work at a defense plant with contemporary *mermaids*—housewives and young unmarried women. He would befriend one of the women, write her notes, but nothing ever came of this little one-sided romance. Actor Tony Curtis, a "disciple" of Cornell's who constructed his own boxes, pinpointed Cornell's dilemma: "He adored women, but relationships weren't possible for him. He wasn't able to put two and two together, to go from step to step with a woman—from holding hands, to 'I'll see you later, come back at four, we'll go to the movies,' to sticking your tongue in her mouth."

He must have seemed like a Martian to most women at the plant, this gray man dressed in gray. "He looks like Captain Ahab ashore—irritable, absolute, sensitive, obsessed, but shy," according to artist Robert Motherwell. And cultural impresario Alexander Liberman once said that Cornell, with his hooded eyes, could have been Joan of Arc's inquisitor.

Yet this morose man, this Ahab ashore, who seemed to frighten women away, was the practitioner of a woman's craft most of his adult life. The Surrealists may have done their own assemblages, their "readymades," reliquaries of junk in a box, and their art may have coincided with Cornell's—Marcel Duchamp admired his boxes—but Cornell appropriated very little from the Surrealists. Assemblage was a legitimate American craft, relegated to women in the nineteenth century, since most other forms of art were denied to them. It was a "parlor pastime," a kind of recreation for genteel ladies, who weren't supposed to sculpt or paint, since that might have revealed their ambition to become artists, so in the era right after the Civil War they occupied themselves with "pseudo-arts," such as collecting seashells and seaweed, arranging feathers into flowers, where they wouldn't have to compete with men. Among these pseudo-arts was the shadow box, a three-dimensional, glass-fronted frame lined with black velvet or silk and housing objects that were artfully arranged. These objects often had a sentimental value—they might celebrate the friendship of two women, or record the mementos of a marriage, or remind a mother of a son who had died in the Civil War, with a series of relics from that war.

And Cornell's boxes had much of the same sentiment when he was trying to celebrate Fanny Cerrito, but unlike the assemblages of these Victorian ladies, Cornell's art was about absence rather than presence, about evasion and unconscious desires, bitterness and anger, not against Cerrito, but against himself.

3

THERE WAS ANOTHER NINETEENTH-CENTURY ballerina who was as elusive and mystifying as Cerrito—Emily Dickinson, and Joseph saw her as a ballerina-poet. His favorite Dickinson poem was about her own dream dance as a prima ballerina. He reprinted the poem in a special issue of *Dance Index* (Summer 1944), a twenty-two-page album that he devoted to Fanny Cerrito.

I cannot dance upon my Toes—
No Man instructed me—
But oftentimes, among my mind
A Glee possesseth me,
That had I Ballet knowledge—
Would put itself abroad
In Pirouette to blanch a Troupe—
Or lay a Prima—mad . . .   [Fr381A]

Actually, he discovered Dickinson long before he found Cerrito and the other queens of classical ballet—Dickinson was his first love.

Whatever we think of the poet, and however we compare her electric language with Cerrito's lyrical leaps, Dickinson does become a Prima in the poem, and it's probably one of the most accurate descriptions of what it must have been like for Cerrito to have danced as Ondine in London or Milan, with "One Claw upon the Air," her shape "rolled on Wheels of Snow."

He kept Dickinson's poems beside his monk's cot in his upstairs bedroom on Utopia Parkway and collected whatever he could of her. In 1951, his mother visited Amherst and sent him a postcard with a picture of the Homestead, and now he could conjure up an image of Dickinson's bedroom-workshop. And in Millicent Todd Bingham's introduction to *Bolts of Melody* (1945), he would come across Dickinson's own collection of dime-store debris—poems and fragments written on the backs of discarded paper bags and bills, "on tiny scraps of stationery pinned together. . . . There are pink scraps, blue and yellow, one of them a wrapper of *Chocolate Meunier*," a kind of cooking chocolate made in France. Cornell would store that yellow wrapper in his mind and it would later reappear as a totemic signature to a series of shadow boxes devoted to Dickinson, but he wasn't quite ready to begin. Cornell needed two more "sightings," or "sparks."

In 1952, during one of his expeditions from Flushing to the Fourth Avenue bookshops, he stumbled upon a picture of Emily in Millicent Todd Bingham's *Ancestors' Brocades* (1945), a "cabinet photo" made from the original daguerreotype; the background is gone, and we don't see the poet's hands, and there's a shadow behind the poet, like a gray mountain. But Cornell was overwhelmed. It was, as David Porter suggests in his essay on Dickinson and Cornell, "a transcendent moment"—an *unfoldment*—where the poet's "fragile features from an earlier era" were juxtaposed "with the crowded doings of the modern city." In this *doctored* daguerreotype Cornell had discovered an authentic *fée* from another century—a child-woman looked out at him with the kind of innocence he adored. A strange Renaissance princess—delicately defiant and androgynous—who was as wan as one of the "teeners" he might have found at Woolworth's (medical doctor, poet, and Dickinson scholar Norbert Hirschorn believes she may have been suffering from tuberculosis at the time the daguerreotype was taken).

And then there was Rebecca Patterson's book, with its notion that Dickinson's "lost" romance was with a woman rather than a man; most of her life, Dickinson feared and longed for that "Blue Peninsula," where she could "perish—of Delight" in some dreamt-up Italy, with or without Kate. Cornell could see his own complexion in Dickinson's mirror. She'd become his androgynous bride—this gray man and the poet with red hair were suddenly Marco Polos of the imagination, Baedekers without a bone. If Cornell had his vacant hotel rooms where Fanny Cerrito or another Prima might arrive and depart without leaving much of a clue, Dickinson also traveled like a Prima, could sing and tumble in her corner room, while she danced on her toes—toward the Blue Peninsula that never changed with the seasons, and was like a kind of delicious death.

Cornell had his own particular clues: He would devote a series of eight *Chocolat Meunier* boxes [spelled *Menier* by Cornell] to the poet, where she is often absent and present at the same time, appearing as a hummingbird inside a postage stamp from Ecuador, or as an invisible warbler attached to a "warbling string," a parrot on a perch, or a mouse on a child's block, but we're always trapped with the Prima inside a drab whitewashed room—and the foreign lettering of *Chocolat Menier* invokes Cerrito as much as Dickinson, two ballerinas in the same shadow box.

But the most devastating of all the Dickinson boxes is *Toward the Blue Peninsula (for Emily Dickinson)*, ca.1953, which Cornell must have worked on right after seeing the daguerreotype and reading Patterson's book. It is, according to Christopher Benfey, "the single most trenchant response, in all of American art, to the meaning of her life and art." It is also the most disturbing commentary on Dickinson's double, Joseph Cornell.

The box is a minimalist's dream, with Cornell's usual spare effects: drab white walls, a bird perch (without a bird) that extends across the 10¼-inch box, a wire grid with an opening, and a window, partly framed by the opening, that looks out upon a blue sky. For Cornell, the poet had finally escaped her prison-perch. But that window is no promise of paradise; the blue sky could be as mordant and misleading as Cornell's other clues; and that wire home with its prison-perch could be the core of her creativity. What matters is that haunted house of a box helped conjure up a ghostly dialogue between Cornell and Dickinson, and "their dialogue across a hundred years is yet another Cornell construction: two figures, solitary and unaccountable, brought into correspondence, as he said of the objects he placed in his boxes, to discover what they would say to one another," according to David Porter.

Porter believed they were both "artists of aloneness," who "inhabited self-made realms in which only the fiercely independent can flourish. . . . No generic blueprint sanctioned their art or provided it with coherence. That solitude accounts for the piecemeal, idiosyncratic nature of this singular . . . American genre of small, rickety infinitudes."

Porter wrote about this dazzling encounter between Dickinson and Cornell over twenty years ago, but now their infinitudes no longer seem quite as *rickety*, or quite as small. Cornell talked about his desire to create "white magic," yet he and Dickinson were singular magicians of the dark. A sad lyricism pervades their work, almost a death song. Cornell couldn't recapture Cerrito no matter how hard he tried, yet his art ricochets like that swirl of colors in the entombed pencil he sent to Jay Leyda. He was a master of the unnamed, and the unnamable, a storyteller at a time when stories fell out of fashion—his boxes always tell stories, even if they end in riddles that can't be solved. Dickinson may have fled, but *we* are never absent from her room, and we can feel its merciless power. This is where creation begins, in some vast, solitary confinement, encapsulated in a shadow box that was often not much taller than a hand. Cornell once said that his greatest wish (or "recurrent obsession") was to have his objects move—and his wish was answered in a way. His boxes are filled with an invisible flutter. Cornell was involved all his life with performance, from the time he saw Buffalo Bill at Madison Square Garden and Houdini at the Hippodrome, and the wonders he encountered with his family at Lunar Park, to the *fées* who seemed to perform for him at some delicatessen or department store, to Fanny Cerrito and Emily Dickinson, whose boxes are also minuscule stages; we can *feel* Dickinson's traces in *Toward the Blue Peninsula*, and even if she's fled to her own far country, halfway between nightmare and paradise, Cornell still means us to hear her steps, the absent ballerina, who's put her skills abroad—

> *In Pirouette to blanch a Troupe—*
> *Or lay a Prima—mad . . .*

It's Charles Simic who best articulates the "dime-store alchemy" that binds Dickinson and Cornell. He tells us that somewhere in Cornell's magic city of New York there exist four or five disparate *still-unknown* objects that belong together. And once they're found, they will make a work of art. That's Cornell's metaphysics. And Dickinson's unknown objects are her words that only she can find and place together in that "Whip lash" language of hers. Her poems are like boxes that break the boundaries of conscious thought and lead us toward delusion.

It's almost as if we ourselves have gone with the poet out beyond the furthest reach of language—"opon Circumference"—where every order of coherence, every sequence of words has *ravelled* out of Sound, and dances with some infernal logic, like balls (or objects) bouncing willfully onto a floor with a musical clutter all their own.

Cornell and Dickinson, according to Simic, are both unknowable. "If her poems are like his boxes, a place where secrets are kept, his boxes are like her poems, the place of unlikely things to happen. . . . Voyagers and explorers of their own solitudes, they make them vast, make them cosmic." Neither was a *public* poet, though Dickinson did share her poems, or some version of them, with a few choice recipients, and Cornell did show his work at galleries and museums, though he never traveled to another town whenever his work was shown, nor did he ever keep a clipping related to his work, while he collected mountains of material on Cerrito and his favorite movie stars; Cornell often made boxes for his favorite stars and dismantled them once he discovered that a particular star, such as Greta Garbo, despised the box he had devoted to her. He didn't like to sell his boxes, and would grow angry if a collector revealed too much interest in his work.

Cornell and Dickinson were intensely secretive and private souls. But she wasn't "the eccentric, quivering, overstrung recluse" that Deborah Solomon writes about in her 1997 biography of Cornell, nor was she trapped in her Amherst prison-house, as Rebecca Patterson would have us believe. And Cornell was even less reclusive than Dickinson. He would have parties where he served pumpkin seeds and warm pineapple soda, and he entertained Marcel Duchamp, Tony Curtis, John Ashbery, Andy Warhol, Allegra Kent, and a host of others on Utopia Parkway, even had one of his favorite "teeners," Joyce Hunter, a former cashier at Ripley's Believe It or Not Times Square museum, live with him for several months in 1964, though she was much too sharp for Cornell and sold every "souvenir" collage and box he gave her to collectors she had met through him. Tina, as he called her, had a baby daughter and lived a marginal life of crime; she and two of her boyfriends stole nine shadow boxes from Cornell's garage; they were all arrested, but he refused to press charges against this rather plump and avaricious *fée*. Hunter was as innocent as Robert in his eyes; she would be murdered later that year, stabbed twice in a rickety Harlem hotel room that could have been a replica of a Cornell hotel box. He had her buried in Queens, near his own family plot, and hired detectives to find Hunter's baby girl, while he dreamt of adopting her, but the little girl was never found. Cornell's relationship with Tina continued after her death; he wrote letters to her, collected certain dime-store gifts, as he would do after his mother and Robert died. Cornell was deeply saddened after Robert's death in 1965 and couldn't stop mourning him. He seldom left the house on Utopia Parkway, and had fewer excursions to Flushing and Manhattan.

Cornell's devotion to his invalid brother wasn't that removed from Dickinson's attachment to her own "baby" sister. Dickinson believed that she and Vinnie had come from very different wells in the ground, like two dissimilar mermaids, and most critics would have us believe that Emily was the *invalid*, and that Vinnie watched over her all their lives. But I suspect it was the other way around. Emily was the only one of the Dickinsons who risked her father's wrath, who challenged Edward when he beat his horse, who smashed a piece of crockery out on the lawn after her father complained that it was chipped, and who stopped going to church. She had her own fierce temper, while Vinnie had once been a voluptuous *fée*—with fat arms—who sat in Joseph Lyman's lap and tied him to her with her own strands of hair, like a mermaid. But that mermaid never went back into the sea. She kept to dry land with her narrow, conventional thoughts. The poems she wrote reflected this mundane imagination.

> *The stars kept winking and blinking,*
> *as if they had secrets to tell;*
> *But as nobody asked any questions,*
> *Nobody heard any tales.*

Her poems were as childish as the rabbits Robert loved to draw and paint—Robert was the "artist" of the family, and Joseph would incorporate his brother's rabbits into his own collages, but there was nothing of her sister's that Emily could incorporate into her own verse.

Emily "had to think—she was the only one of us who had that to do," Vinnie noted. "Father believed; and mother loved; and Austin had

Amherst; and I had the family to keep track of." And Emily must have felt a kind of tender concern for that foreign mermaid who often slept in the same bed with her. She was Austin's wild sister, after all. Her basket held "just—Firmaments." [Fr358] And Vinnie's held nothing but banal, everyday fare. So Emily must have taken some measure not to frighten her sister with those thunderous disconnections of hers, those lightning entrechats. Perhaps she pitied Vinnie a little, pitied and loved her and protected her like some forlorn Prima with a pupil who could never have imagined what it was like to dance upon her toes.

Perhaps all great art comes out of a void, and Cornell and Dickinson were the prince and princess of isolation, cosmic dreamers who inhabited some bare space with crumbling whitewashed walls. "In a secret room in a secret house his secret toys sit listening to their own stillness," Charles Simic writes of Cornell. Dickinson's toys weren't quite the same, but her words were also found objects that fit together with a frightening stillness.

Inside all of us, Simic says, there are the same secret rooms. "They're cluttered and the lights are out. There's a bed in which someone is lying with his face to the wall. In his [or her] head there are more rooms," and in these rooms are objects that move in and out of visibility—a broken compass, or perhaps a hairbrush, in Emily's case, a watch spring—"each one of these items is a totem of the self." And orphans that we are, Simic insists, "we make our sibling kin out of anything we can find."

This is why *Toward the Blue Peninsula* is such an original portrait of Dickinson and of ourselves—secret poets with our own secret toys in secret rooms—and is so much a part of the appeal that Dickinson and Cornell have for us. We cannot encapsulate their mystery, find formulas and quotients that will resolve their riddles, and yet we ourselves are soothed somehow by that quiet desolation.

4

T HERE'S A THIRD PRIMA WHO CONNECTS Fanny Cerrito with Joseph Cornell and Emily Dickinson: Allegra Kent. And it's not simply because she was Joseph's friend, and that he had devoted several boxes to her, or that she was Fanny Cerrito in the flesh—she wasn't a classical dancer like Cerrito, but she was a twentieth-century Ondine, who came pirouetting out of the water for a little while to delight us in a way that few other Primas have ever done.

She was eleven when she took her first ballet class with Bronislava Nijinska, the younger sister of Vaslav Nijinsky, the greatest male dancer of his time. It was Nijinska who told her, "We are born originals, we die copies," and she never forgot that lesson— no amount of technique or training could get in the way of her wildness. She also studied with Carmelita Maracci, who loved to push her students beyond their physical boundaries into some demonic dreamscape of their own. She told Allegra stories about Fanny Cerrito and the other queens of classical ballet, whose costumes of misty tulle helped catch the elusive quality of the sylphs and sirens they portrayed. "Their beauty was ethereal and unearthly, but their technique was achieved by endless work. . . . Carmelita believed that even if you had never done a step correctly before, if you got excited enough you might just do it in class." It was Carmelita who sent her off to study at George Balanchine's School of American Ballet. At fifteen, she was the youngest member of Balanchine's company, and would become a Prima of the New York City Ballet at nineteen. Allegra was an autodidact who read and learned on her own and would have a certain shyness about language all her life. "I wished to speak in a different way, soundlessly," and ballet permitted her to do so.

Balanchine taught her that greed was important to a dancer, akin to desire, and that her arabesques, in reach and desire, should be like creating "gold and ice cream." She was more petite than many modern Primas, but she had long legs and a very long neck. And she was the most acrobatic dancer, male or female, in the company. Allegra had her own private sense of gravity, where "the gyroscopic laws of tops took over, stretching the limits. . . . I wanted to have the untiring, springing, elastic muscles of a grasshopper for my leaps, and the pneumatic knees of a swamp mangrove," and she did.

The ballets Balanchine choreographed for Allegra Kent were unlike anything he had ever choreographed, as if he, too, wanted to defy natural laws for his very own Ondine. In *Bugaku* (1963), he creates a siren in a Japanese ceremonial dance, where Kent portrays the concubine-wife of a young samurai prince (Edward Villella), and they have their own highly stylized mating ceremony in the most erotic pas de deux ever performed at the New York City Ballet.

That was my introduction to Allegra Kent. It was the first time I had ever seen her dance upon her toes. She appears like a wraith in a gossamer kimono with a long transparent white train that seemed to float to the edge of the world—and beyond that, into infinity; underneath the gossamer, she had on a chrysanthemum tutu, tights, and a white-flowered bikini bottom and bra. When her four female attendants "disrobe" her for her pas de deux with the samurai prince, she has an absent, ethereal look that I might have imagined on Cerrito herself. "I decided that more should happen in the eye and body and less on the face, that a perfectly simple ritualistic movement could be rich with currents under the surface," Kent noted about her performance.

Villella was a perfect partner, gentle and brutal at the same time, and as Kent weaves her body around his like a woman in a trance, her limbs performing their own ritualistic wonder, I felt that she had an instinctive poetry in these limbs—controlled and abandoned—that no other dancer had. She'd taken us outside the contours and limits of dance, and into another realm, where she was inventing her own trancelike language—her persona was onstage with Villella and with us in the audience, while her limbs were somewhere else, in a wild country of their own. And I thought of Dickinson, of her psychic split, that perverse ability to be elsewhere within her poems:

I heard a Fly buzz—when I died—
The Stillness in the Room
Was like the Stillness in the Air—
Between the Heaves of Storm—   [Fr591]

We are also "Between the Heaves of Storm" as we watch Kent in her pas de deux, surrounded by the white expanse of the set; lost in her strange agility, she's like a feline *fée,* boyish and feminine, fragile and fierce. I doubt that Joseph Cornell ever saw her in *Bugaku.* He grew more and more claustrophobic, and would have found it difficult to attend a performance all the while Balanchine was creating roles for Allegra Kent. But he did sense that quality of a catlike *fée* in a photograph that appeared in *Newsweek*; it was of the Prima rehearsing her role in "The Unanswered Question," one of the episodes in *Ivesiana* (1954), where Allegra is held aloft by four men. Cornell was intrigued by the photo and filed it away; he'd been making short films with the help of Stan Brakhage—Cornell himself was utterly unmechanical; he never learned to drive a car or operate any kind of camera, but he wanted to make a short film on the Ondine motif, set in modern-day Manhattan, and he was looking for a *fée* who wandered from thrift shop to thrift shop. And in 1956, he got in touch with Allegra through a friend at the New York City Ballet. She recalled meeting him in the studio apartment she shared with her sister on East Sixty-first Street. "His hands [from shellacking all his boxes] were kind of yellowish. He looked creepy. . . . And he really seemed to like me, which I found scary. I felt he liked me too much." He told her about the film he intended to make. "'I want a girl who haunts thrift shops.'"

Allegra wondered if he were prescient, since she did haunt thrift shops. But she refused to take part in his film, didn't want to be his Ondine. "He was a little too engaged in his disengaged manner." After that interview, she began receiving letters from him that entertained Allegra and aroused her interest. He'd included her in his "sendings," his letter-collages, like captured butterflies.

She looked forward to these letters from Joseph. "My favorite form of entertainment was receiving letters in a mailbox . . . a kind of little square present," as it was for Dickinson, who fed like a voracious hawk on the letters she received, and thrived on the "pictorial letters" she herself created, her own constructivist art, which Jay Leyda talked about to Cornell.

"He saw someone," Allegra recalled in my interview with her, "and created a story about them, put them in a box, a setting. Cornell set little stages. . . . Balanchine did that, too."

"Maybe he was another box maker," I said.

Allegra wrinkled her nose. "The stage was his box."

I wondered if it was a form of entrapment, if Balanchine collected butterflies, like Nabokov (and Cornell), and put his human butterflies inside a box. But Allegra didn't agree. "Mr. B. saw something in you, put you in an ethereal atmosphere," as if he were looking for some ideal woman.

Balanchine, she said, "could fall in love with the drop of a leotard," and so could Cornell, who was also a master choreographer in his own way. And in 1969, he saw his favorite living ballerina again. She was in an odd state at the time. "I'd had an operation to get rid of stretch marks on my stomach, so I could do *Bugaku* again [in her white-flowered bikini bottom]. But they cut too much, and I had nerve damage." And thus she couldn't dance. So she went out to Utopia Parkway as an invalid, like Cornell's brother. He asked her to bring a book of erotic art and a mocha cake, as if she were about to plunge through the looking glass with an androgynous, grown-up Alice who loved *fées* and had a sweet tooth.

"He was very gentle . . . he'd stopped making boxes after his brother died. It was hot in his garden so I made a paper hat," her own piece of constructivist art. "The house was in a great mess, but his cellar workshop had its own internal order. He showed her box after box.

He did quite a few collages for Allegra after that visit. And when he fell ill with prostate cancer in 1972, he wrote her letters from the hospital. "One I ripped up—it was too sexual [about his nurse]. I don't think he wanted that to exist."

And then she ruminated about her own career. She's probably the one Prima on the planet who had three children in her twenties and still managed to dance for Balanchine. "I loved being pregnant," she said, almost as if she were defying Mr. B. and his own mercurial laws as a dancing master. "I was married to a madman, a drug addict [photographer Bert Stern]. And I wasn't the most stable person."

But I wondered if some of the power she had as a ballerina had come from that same instability. "The way Mr. B. communicated with me was almost the way a human relates to wildlife. Some people are good with untamed animals. They don't startle the creatures," Kent declared in her autobiography. She intuited her own raw grip over the audience when she wrote, "Some excellent technicians were so used to being perfect that they didn't astonish themselves. They might astonish the audience, but it wasn't quite the presentation of the unknown."

And I realized how much she resembled Dickinson, who also sought to present the unknown.

> *He fumbles at your Soul*
> *As players at the Keys*
> *Before they drop full Music on—*
> *He stuns you by degrees—*   [Fr477A]

Dickinson may be addressing the Prince of Death here, but she's also talking about the nature of her art, the "One—imperial—Thunderbolt—/That scalps your naked Soul—" And Allegra danced with the same imperial fire. She's brutally shy, frightened of people, she says, and so was Dickinson, who fled from strangers. Their art, like Cornell's, leaps into the unknown.

SIX

Phantom Lady

1

I T WAS A RUDE PROCESS THAT FRACTURED the face, revealed your mirror image, so that your cheeks were reversed on the silvered copper plate, and your left eye was where your right eye ought to be— the daguerreotype, invented by some French lunatic in 1839. And still Emily sat for her *Mold* as she called the making of the image. Emerson had called it a kind of rigor mortis when he was *daguerreotyped* in 1841, keeping "every finger in place with such energy that your hands became clenched for fight or despair, and in your resolution to keep your face still, did you feel every muscle becoming every moment more rigid, the brows contracted into a Tartarean frown, and the eyes fixed in a fit, in madness, or in death?"

She wasn't enthralled by the tinted ghostly double that stared back at her from the copper plate, and neither was anyone else among the Dickinsons. "It was too solemn, too heavy. It had none of the play of light and shade in Emily's face," the future poet's brother and sister believed. "To capture the flow of movement and grace in a single photograph of the dance" [would be no less impossible] "than it was to produce by any means then known a satisfactory likeness of Emily Dickinson," according to Millicent Todd Bingham. Dickinson posed for the daguerreotype in 1847; she was sixteen years old, an adolescent with a long neck and beautiful long hands. She looks serious and slightly cockeyed, and reminds me of Emmeline Grangerford, the graveyard poet in *The Adventures of Huckleberry Finn*. "The young woman in the picture had a kind of a nice sweet face, but there were so many arms it made her look spidery, seemed to me," Huck tells us in his own sympathetic and bemused portrait of Emmeline.

Dickinson has no extra arms in the daguerreotype, but she does have a spidery design in her dark cotton dress and her ribbon bracelets and the dark ribbon around her neck. We can imagine how uncomfortable she must have been before this "Daguerrian Artist," whoever he was. Polly Longsworth and most other critics believe he was Otis H. Cooley, who had his own studio in Springfield, Massachusetts, from 1844 to 1855, whereas Millicent Todd Bingham informed her loyal readers in *Emily Dickinson's Home* (1955) that the daguerreotype had been taken by some unremembered wisp of an itinerant photographer who visited Mount Holyoke near the end of 1847 and photographed as many seminarians as he could. But Dickinson declined his overtures—*possibly*. "With Dickinson the story is never finished," writes Polly Longsworth.

And Mary Elizabeth Kromer Bernhard, in "Lost and Found: Emily Dickinson's Unknown Daguerreotypist," has another story to tell. She's convinced that the two Emilys—the poet and her mother—sat for William C. North, "Daguerrian Artist," at Amherst House sometime between December 1846 and March 1847. Advertising in the *Hampshire and Franklin Express*, North noted that he had taken rooms at the Amherst House for the sole purpose of executing "Daguerreotype Miniatures" in his superior and substantial style. "Secure the Shadow ere the substance fades," he warned his potential clients.

We might never really know the identity of the phantom photographer who posed Dickinson and prepared the silvered copper plate. But it has become one of the most iconic portraits in American history, even though it was despised by the Dickinsons themselves and was later dismissed as "flat, itinerant work." The daguerreotype had a subterranean journey through the nineteenth century and the first half of the twentieth—misplaced by the poet, who denied it had ever existed, it was "found" by Maggie Maher, returned to Vinnie, who had a Boston miniaturist, Laura C. Hills, repaint a "cabinet photograph" of the original daguerreotype, correcting the poet's astigmatic eye, and giving her a white dress and ruffled collar, so that she was part angel and part circus clown (this is the face we see on the cover of Rebecca Patterson's book); then, in cavalier fashion, she gave the daguerreotype away and it didn't surface again until it fell into Millicent's hands, like some magical quotient.

And now it's *everywhere,* whether it's fastened to the poet's mythic white dress and appears as a giant-size balloon in *Being John Malkovich* (1999), Spike Jonze's zany, surreal film that moves with the "spasmodic gait" Colonel Higginson once saw in the volcanic lines of his half-cracked poet and could almost be an elliptical reconstruction of "I started early—took my dog" [Fr656], where we are all taken on some interior voyage, with mermaids swimming at our feet, and where our waking life is never as memorial as our moments inside the mind of Emily Dickinson (or John Malkovich); or her own image is cleaved in two, with Nefertiti on the left and Dickinson on the right, wearing bold red lipstick, on the cover of Camille Paglia's *Sexual Persona* (1990), or else we can catch her on dozens of other book jackets in the daguerreotype's original chaste form; and she's the first face that appears, in her gussied-up clown's collar, whenever I light up my Kindle.

The daguerreotype can also be seen in some kind of pale Technicolor in Topps 2008 American Heritage Baseball Trading Card # 6, as if her image is as much a piece of American folklore as Babe Ruth's flaring nostrils and Shoeless Joe Jackson's mystical bat, Black Betsy. Dickinson—and her picture as an adolescent—have become "a cultural palimpsest of our emotions, desires, opinions, and literary histories," according to scholar Martha Nell Smith, who launched the Dickinson Electronic Archives in 1994. Dickinson's daguerreotype has entered our world in a way that few images ever have. And, says Polly Longsworth, its tantalizing power "has played a role in shaping the iconography of and critical thinking about the poet," as it offers us a glimpse into the poet's almost invisible life. "Her face is as familiar as a mask and holds the mask's elusive promise that if we knew what she really looked like, underneath it, we could have the key to her enigmatic poetry."

There is no such key, as we have all come to learn. But one of the most poignant meditations on the daguerreotype and the doll-like power it has provoked is Joyce Carol Oates' futuristic tale, "EDickinsonRepliLuxe," in *Wild Nights!* (2008), her own brutally etched portraits concerning the last days of Dickinson and four other iconic American writers—Hemingway, Poe, Mark Twain, and Henry James.

The title of the collection comes from one of Dickinson's most enigmatic poems.

> *Wild Nights—Wild Nights!*
> *Were I with thee*
> *Wild Nights should be*
> *Our luxury!*
>
> *Futile—the winds—*
> *To a Heart in port—*
> *Done with the Compass—*
> *Done with the Chart!*
>
> *Rowing in Eden—*
> *Ah—the Sea!*
> *Might I but moor—tonight—*
> *In Thee!*   [Fr269]

Oates, who came *late* to Dickinson (in her twenties), has turned this "love poem" into a crazy, passionate, and cruel dance with the sirens of love *and* death. And they're often the very same sirens. Harold and

Madelyn Krim are a loveless couple who live in the suburban village of Golders Green, New York, and have been married for what seems to be nineteen years, yet is only nine. Maddie feels as if she'd never been kissed. Harold's a tax accountant and she's a housewife who had once wanted to become a poet. They decide to purchase a pet—not a cat or dog—but a RepliLuxe, a computerized replicant of some fabulous cultural icon. And this quasi-human pet will cost only a fraction of what it would cost to raise a *real* human child. Maddie has her heart set on a poet, but *Sylvia Plath* and *Robert Frost* are not yet in the public domain. And like a sleepwalker she suddenly says, "Emily Dickinson!"

EDickinsonRepliLuxe has certain restrictions. She's programmed from age thirty to fifty-five (when Dickinson died). But the Krims, who own all rights to the "Emily" mannequin, can accelerate those last twenty-five years of the poet's life however they wish. The RepliLuxe is a brilliant distillation of Dickinson, as if her soul had been sucked out and reinstalled in a replicant without intestines or sexual organs or blood. But the Dickinson doll can talk, write poetry, and bake brown bread with molasses. Yet the Krims are deeply disappointed when the mannequin arrives and is unpacked. She looks like a malnourished girl of ten, rather than the brilliant poet of thirty they had paid for. The RepliLuxe is an almost exact model of the 1847 daguerreotype.

> *Her eyes were large, dark, and oddly lashless, her skin was ivory-pale, smooth as paper. Her eyebrows were wider than you'd expect, heavier and more defined, like a boy's. . . . Her dark hair had been severely parted in the center of her head and pulled back flatly and tightly into a knot of a bun, covering most of her unusually small ears like a cap. In a dark cotton dress . . .with an impossibly tiny waist,* EDickinsonRepliLuxe *more resembled the wizened corpse of a child-nun than a woman-poet of thirty.*

The Krims are woefully disappointed in this mannequin (and they mirror the reaction of some Dickinson devotees to the 1847 daguerreotype, feeling that it offers a very pale glimpse of the future poet and her radiant red hair). Madelyn had raided antique stores to find replicas of the furnishings in the poet's mythic bedroom on Main Street; she comes up with an authentic sleigh bed of the 1850s that looks like a child's crib, a milk-glass kerosene lamp, a maple bureau, and an impossibly small writing desk. Madelyn could be Joseph Cornell, assembling a giant-size shadow box that will serve as a kind of prison for Emily, who is forbidden by law to leave the Krimses' house, since these mannequins might run amuck, and the world could have entire teams of *'Babe Ruth'* and poetry slams filled with EDickinsonRepliLuxe.

Madelyn is a bit more sympathetic to her Dickinson doll. "Emily could have no idea where she was, who the Krims were, if she was awake or dreaming or if there was any distinction between wakefulness and dreaming in her transmogrified state." Curious about the workings of her RepliLuxe, who flutters through the house like a forest animal and scribbles words on scraps of paper, she clicks off *activate* on her remote control and Emily tumbles into the *sleep mode.* Madelyn summons up the courage to touch the mannequin, with its papery skin and metallic smell. She's aroused by Emily, has the urge to kiss her on the lips, and realizes that it's been a very long time since she's kissed anyone or anyone has kissed her. Madelyn resists the urge, but she removes one of the scraps of paper from Emily's pocket and reads the poem written on it, replete with Dickinson's signature dashes.

> *Why am—I—*
> *Where am—I—*
> *When am—I—*
> *And—You?—*

It's the lament of an amnesiac, or is it? She shows it to Harold, who's enraged. "It's some sort of computer printout, words arranged like poetry to tease and to torment."

Harold has imprisoned the RepliLuxe but feels like a prisoner in his own house. Meanwhile, the poet begins to wear a white dress "that looked like a bridal gown, smelling of must, mothballs, melancholy."

He's even more enraged, with a deluxe doll haunting *his* house in her ghostly gown. And one starry midnight, he burgles his way into her bedroom, with its antique hurricane lamp and candles in wooden holders that flare up like firelight. He looms over the doll like a grotesque swaying bear, kisses Emily on the mouth, rips away her nightgown, pawing at her flattened breasts, fumbles between her legs, sees "a shallow indentation where a vagina should have been," and excited and repelled at the same time by a doll woman without a hint of pubic hair, he slaps Emily, and has to flee this room, "where flames fluttered as in an anteroom of Hell."

Later, when Madelyn shyly enters the bedroom, it feels as if a tornado had visited it, and she finds the poet all disheveled. The Repli-Luxe begs for her own freedom.

"*Accelerate,* Mistress. Lift the wand and—there's freedom."

The *accelerate mode* on the remote control will push her beyond the doll-like look of the daguerreotype and deeper into the wildness of her poetry.

The husband comes home from his Manhattan office—Madelyn and Emily are gone. In his study, he discovers two lines written in a strange, slanted hand, in purple ink that has the look of an "antique."

Bright Knots of Apparitions
Salute us, with their wings—

These two lines are from another of Dickinson's enigmatic poems, this one about ghosts who are far more vivid than we are.

Of nearness to her Sundered Things
The Soul has special times . . .

The Shapes we buried, dwell about,
Familiar, in the Rooms . . .

The Grave yields back her Robberies—
The Years, our pilfered Things—
Bright Knots of Apparitions
Salute us, with their wings—   [Fr337]

The dead welcome the living, as Helen Vendler reminds us, "as if we were the ones who had perished. . . . The ghosts, like a *corps de ballet,* move in and out of their 'Knots'" . . . and perform for us, while they pity us, since they are the mourners and we are the mourned.

Oates' tale is as puzzling and apocalyptic as some of Dickinson's best poems; no one is spared— not the reader, not the author and her characters, not the 1847 daguerreotype, not Dickinson and all her hagiographers and devotees (including myself), and not our modern culture, with its desire to rouse the dead and make us immortal with one gadget after the other. It's the poems that survive in *EDickinsonRepliLuxe;* they are the "Bright Knots of Apparitions" that continually haunt our heads. And Oates has fashioned a brutal tale about the mystery that surrounds the poet and the one image we have of her; she's become a doll in a culture that worships dolls. And if "EDickinsonRepliLuxe" represents the way popular culture has come to *read* the poet and all the apocryphal tales about her—the consumptive adolescent who morphs into a wraith in a white dress—then this doll with flat breasts and a metallic smell is the monster we have made of Emily Dickinson.

2

THERE HAVE BEEN OTHER "SIGHTINGS," of course, discoveries of daguerreotypes that would supposedly *revolutionize* Dickinson scholarship and offer us a brand-new Emily. Two recent sightings caused quite a stir. One was a 3″ by 1¾″ photograph purchased at an undisclosed date by Mr. Herman Abromson from a Greenwich Village bookseller; "Emily Dickinson 1860" is scribbled on the back of the photograph. The other is an albumen print of a daguerreotype discovered in 2000 by Professor Philip Gura of the University of North

Carolina at Chapel Hill. Neither of these prints has any real "provenance," and after much research, most scholars do not consider them authentic images of the poet. But in some disturbing way, their authenticity doesn't matter, since the face that stares out at us in both images has the bland, dollish demean of a RepliLuxe. And artist-photographer Nancy Burson (born in 1948) used her own computer-morphing technology to "age" the poet in the 1847 daguerreotype and create her own silver print, *Emily Dickinson at age 52* (1995). Nancy Burson's Age Machine might be a miraculous rendering of the poet in her fifties, but her prunelike look reminds me of the mannequin in Oates' tale near the end of EDickinsonRepliLuxe's twenty-five year life span. Yet, as Polly Longsworth tells us, Dickinson's *polar privacy* helped create "a vortex of compelling mystery, which, with all the energy of a black hole, draws the public into a quest for her identity."

And at a meeting of the Emily Dickinson International Society in Cleveland on August 3, 2012, Martha Nell Smith revealed the existence of a new daguerreotype, *possibly* of the poet, taken around 1859, where for the first time she doesn't have that undernourished, wizened look of a replicant, and also for the first time she's posing with another woman, possibly Kate Scott. Martha Nell Smith makes no extravagant claims, nor does she insist upon any miraculous discovery. "Whether this picture turns out to represent Emily Dickinson or not," she says, "it has enabled audiences to imagine her as an adult Emily."

And this is the critical point. The other *resurrections* of the poet—Gura's or Abromson's or Burson's computerized metamorphosis—reveal nothing new; they cannot take us into the poet's "Wild Nights" of creativity; and we cannot glimpse the outlaw who invented her own linguistic logic, who twisted language around like some forlorn female Prometheus (as Susan Howe suggests), who would not melt away and dissolve into the silly conventions of her own time; and most of all, these images tell us nothing about her sexual and poetic powers. But the daguerreotype uncovered by a photography collector at a Springfield junk sale in 1995 does offer us a glimpse of what a *mature* Emily might have looked like. She defies all our expectations in the daguerreotype, all our stereotypes, all our myths, often perpetrated by Dickinson herself. The poet was, as Rebecca Patterson says in *The Riddle of Emily Dickinson,* "undeniably plain," and "suffered morbidly on account of her plainness." So we have been led to believe. That is how Higginson saw her, and that is the sense we often have of Miss Emily in her own letters.

She's the only Kangaroo among the Beauty, as she tells the colonel. She provides her own verbal *daguerreotype,* enlisting herself as small, like the Wren, etc. This is the Emily we have found comfort in for almost 125 years—the Kangaroo no man could ever want. And that's why she remained a spinster. Of course, Sue's daughter, Martha Dickinson Bianchi, talked about Emily's myriad suitors, but this was one more of Martha's *mangled* memories.

The new daguerreotype, first published in the *Guardian,* on September 5, 2012, "depicts two women seated side by side." Both are staring into the camera. The woman at the left has a tight, enigmatic smile; she almost looks like some kind of predator, or at least a woman with a fierce will and a sharpshooter's *Yellow Eye,* as we picture her composing "My life had stood a loaded gun" and a hundred other apocalyptic poems. The other woman seems much more vulnerable and severe; her hands are folded upon her lap, like a schoolmarm. She's dressed in a widow's black garb. The anonymous collector who has assigned himself a code name—Sam Carlo—believes that the daguerreotype may have been taken by a certain J. C. Spooner, who flourished as a photographer in Springfield at the time.

The poet is wearing a dress that's out of fashion, and dates from the 1840s, when she sat for the earlier daguerreotype. But that doesn't disrupt the authenticity of her portrait in Springfield. Dickinson liked to describe herself as old-fashioned; it was one of the masks she wore when she wanted to avoid seeing someone. "I'm so old fashioned, Darling, that all your friends would stare," she wrote to a former schoolmate,

Abiah Root, declining an invitation to visit. [Letter 166] She often clung to old friends, but could also be reckless in her abandonment of them when they failed to amuse her or provide a decent mirror for her own words. And the old-fashioned dress that the Dickinson figure wears in the new daguerreotype is remarkably similar to a swatch of blue-checked cloth found in the collections at the Emily Dickinson Museum. This in itself is no "provenance."

But other evidence has been uncovered since "Sam Carlo" first surmised that the figure on the left might be Emily Dickinson. He concentrated on the other figure in the daguerreotype, and after several years of research into the poet's life, he settled on Kate Scott, identifying two moles, one more prominent than the other, on her chin in the new daguerreotype and in an earlier portrait of Kate. There was also a question of Emily's astigmatism. Dr. Susan Pepin, director of neuro-ophthalmology at Dartmouth School of Medicine, who had long been fascinated by the poet's eye problems, studied the distinct characteristics of the poet's astigmatic eye in both daguerreotypes and concluded that the woman in the 1859 portrait was the same woman identified in the Dickinson daguerreotype of 1847. But as Dr. Pepin noted, so much in her own report to determine Dickinson's own peculiar facial asymmetries was limited by image resolution and variation in lighting of the measurements she took, and the idiosyncratic nature of the daguerreotypes themselves. Even with twenty-first-century magical tricks, there may never be a perfect fit. Still, for the first time in over 150 years, we have what may be an image of Dickinson in her own prime as a poet, and with some sexual heat, rather than a recluse and a nun in white, or the RepliLuxe doll that our own mass culture has made of her.

3

EVEN JAY LEYDA, PROBABLY THE MOST enlightened student of Emily Dickinson we've ever had, felt that Dickinson's relation to Kate Scott had been obscured by Rebecca Patterson's construction of a "fictitious set of sexual circumstances." But what are we to make of Patterson's book in light of the 1859 daguerreotype? Emily holding her right arm around Kate (in the daguerreotype's own mirror image), coveting her, protecting her perhaps from the camera's prying eye. Whatever Patterson might have told us about Kate as the dark-eyed seductress of Cooperstown, Dickinson is in control here, Dickinson is in delight, and Kate is the widow with a vacant look.

Perhaps now we can comprehend Sue's mercurial behavior—her cooling off to Emily—once the widow came to town. Sue was more involved with Kate than she herself might have realized. Androgynous in her own secretive fashion, Sue may have been as much in love with Kate as Dickinson would ever be, though she had married Dickinson's brother and presided over the Evergreens as a kind of prisoner-queen. The most intense involvement the three women ever had was probably with one another. I suspect Sue never really loved Austin and never cared much for his or any "man's requirements." And she couldn't have felt much joy when she watched Emily and Kate fall in love in her own parlor, as if she had pulled them together and played some willful, unconscious Cupid.

How will we ever know whether Kate and Emily spent one or more "Wild Nights" in Emily's corner room at the Homestead, that Pearl Jail where the poet perfected her craft? Patterson is much too willing to seize upon particular poems to narrate the stations of their romance—Dickinson wasn't serving out her biography on a silver plate, she was lashing at herself and others with her own language, writing about volcanoes, deserts, rape, as Adrienne Rich reminds us in "Vesuvius at Home," about madness, suicide, murder, angels, wild beasts, the end of the world, and the tender violence of love and hate. And yet we can feel the presence of Kate, or some other female siren, like a maddened whisper, in a few of the poems.

When I hoped, I recollect
Just the place I stood—

At a window facing West—
Roughest Air—was good—

Not a Sleet could bite me—
Not a frost could cool—
Hope it was that kept me warm—
Not Merino shawl—

When I feared—I recollect
Just the Day it was—
Worlds were lying out to Sun—
Yet how the Nature froze—

Icicles opon my soul
Prickled Blue and cool—
Bird went praising everywhere—
Only Me—was still—

And the day that I despaired—
This—if I forget
Nature will—that it be Night
After Sun has set—
Darkness intersect her face—
And put out her eye—
Nature hesitate—before
Memory and I—   [Fr493]

Patterson limbs this poem into an unforeseen encounter with Kate in mid-March 1859. "Unquestionably she was standing in her bedroom, when something occurred, so unexpected, so exciting, that it engraved on her memory every detail of the weather and even of the spot where she had stood."

The problem here is that Patterson is *partially* right. Something did happen "At a Window facing West," but the psychic landscape shifts so rapidly that it's hard to locate the speaker or where we can locate ourselves in the poem. The speaker moves with a whiplike recall from hope to anxiety to deep despair—from a Sleet that cannot bite her to a soul that's Prickled Blue—from all the lure and possibility of love to a kind of eternal night that will maim and obliterate all memory of her beloved.

There's a much clearer signal of Dickinson's devotion to Kate in her letters. Sometime during the summer of 1860, she wrote to her Condor Kate, who had been long gone from Amherst, pleading for her to come from her crags again in Cooperstown. "You do not yet 'dislimn,' Kate . . ." [Letter 222] *Dislimn* might utterly baffle us here were she not echoing *Antony and Cleopatra,* her favorite among all of Shakespeare's plays (she loved to see herself as Antony, wooing her own Cleopatra—whether Sue or Condor Kate).

In act 4, scene 14 of the play, Antony dwells upon his own *captivity* to Cleopatra and wonders if he himself has disappeared into the clouds.

> *Sometime we see a cloud that's dragonish,*
> *A vapour sometime like a bear or lion . . .*
> *That which is now a horse, even with a thought*
> *The rack dislimns and makes it indistinct*
> *As water is to water.*

And the *second* daguerreotype helps clarify one of the little secrets of Dickinson's life—that no matter what crag Condor Kate is on, or where she travels from Blue Peninsula to Blue Peninsula, she will never *dislimn.*

In one of her later poems, circa 1877, Dickinson speaks to us, as she often does, from heaven:

> *I shall not murmur if at last*
> *The ones I loved below*
> *Permission have to understand*
> *For what I shunned them so—*
> *Divulging it would rest my Heart*

But it would ravage their's—
Why, Katie, Treason has a Voice—
But mine—dispels—in Tears. [Fr1429]

Nothing in this poem is clear. If it is about "erotic loss or betrayal undergone," as Helen Vendler suggests, it's still hard to determine the difference between the ravaged and the ravager. Is Kate's "Treason" that she married for a second time, in 1866? Or is Dickinson herself the "Treasoner?" As usual, the ground shifts so rapidly from line to line that the speaker sounds like some ventriloquist hurling her voice right from heaven.

Kate, it seems, was still gnawing at her mind. Did Dickinson shun Katie, or was it Katie who ended whatever bits of passion they once shared? Dickinson might have had five or six years of fury on account of Kate, where poem followed poem, like an endless avalanche, but there's scant evidence that Kate's constant wanderlust ruined Dickinson's life, whether or not it filled her with "Infinites of Nought" [Fr693] and "that White Sustenance—/Despair—"[Fr706]. She was writing poems before Kate arrived in Amherst and continued to scratch other poems in her Pearl Jail long after Kate had fled to her Blue Peninsula.

Still, whatever happened between Kate and Emily may have been more than Sue Dickinson could bear. She grew more and more mercurial. She adored her children but was cold to Austin in his copperish wig, and her relations with Emily no longer had the same ebullient charm; she was now mistress of the Evergreens, a woman who entertained Bret Harte and Harriet Beecher Stowe. The eroticism of Emily's poems must have disturbed her, aroused her own dormant—and ambiguous—sexuality. She seems utterly asexual in her later photographs. Yet Sue was much more sensual than either Emily or Kate in the images we have of her as an adolescent, with luminous dark eyes and a ripe mouth.

An orphan from another social caste—her father was a ne'er-do-well who owned a tavern—she struggled in a way that Emily never had to struggle. Sue was voluptuous, moody, brilliant, and bisexual, which wasn't all that uncommon in nineteenth-century America, where women had deep emotional ties among themselves, and men were often like extraterrestrials, as Carroll Smith-Rosenberg has pointed out in "The Female World of Love and Ritual." It's likely that a woman's first sexual experience in a middle-class culture was with another woman, since women often slept in the same bed as adolescents, kissed, and fondled one another freely. A woman knew more about another woman's body than a man ever would, unless he visited the town brothel or read the Marquis de Sade.

Sue arrived in Amherst almost like an indentured servant, lived with a married sister and a brother-in-law who never really appreciated her. Unlike the local belles, she didn't have an abundance of clothes. But she was cultivated and also as dark as a Gypsy. Emily fell in love with Sue—they were poets in a land of prose, but Sue didn't have the time or the means to luxuriate in language. Austin pursued her for years like a patient, bumbling hawk. And when Sue finally succumbed, she married the whole tribe of Dickinsons—she sorely needed a tribe of her own. Austin couldn't fathom the Cleopatra he had on his hands, but Emily could. If she herself was Vesuvius, then there was an even greater volcano living right next door.

And we have to imagine the jealous rage Sue might have hidden, perhaps even from herself, when she realized how drawn Emily and Kate were to each other, as if Sue were harboring a kind of criminal in her own house, someone who could upset her tranquil borders at the Evergreens. I suspect she scared Katie off. Condor Kate's visits grew less and less frequent, until Emily felt like a mermaid stranded in her own private sea.

Sue was visited with much the same dilemma after Dickinson's death. Vinnie, whom she considered a fool, wanted her to gather up Emily's *scratchings* and find a publisher for them. And Sue procrastinated. She planned to publish the poems for a private circle of friends, thus burying them forever. She must have felt a kind of erotic pull toward Kate in every other line. And she now had entered a danger zone; Emily's poems had become live bombs dancing abroad, and might reveal Sue's bisexual past. But Vinnie, who had her own volcanic will, took back the poems and gave them to Sue's one great rival in Amherst, Mabel Loomis Todd. Sue held on to her own stash of letter-poems and did her best to neuter Emily, present her sister-in-law as Amherst's asexual genius. Also, she now had someone else to promote—her daughter, Mattie, had become a pianist and a poet, as if the creativity Sue has suppressed all these years could now *breathe* through Mattie's loins. But there were too many ghosts in her closets at the Evergreens, too much hidden heat that would rise up right out of the past. And like some stubborn, half-mad chancellor, she tried to eradicate all knowledge of the real or imagined liaison between two friends she loved most in the world, but all her machinations would spill onto her daughter's lap. Martha Dickinson Bianchi spent half her life manufacturing her own myths about Aunt Emily, nonsense about the poet's seductive charms. "Nothing would be more delicious to me than to repeat by name the list of those whom she bewitched. It included college boys, tutors, law students, the brothers of her girl friends,—several times their affianced bridegrooms even; and then the maturer friendships,—literary, Platonic, Plutonic; passages varying in intensity, and at least one passionate attachment whose tragedy was due to the integrity of the Lovers, who scrupled to take their bliss at another's cost," she wrote in her introduction to *The Single Hound* (1914).

Whole industries have been built around that "passionate attachment," with novels, plays, and scholarly tomes identifying one candidate after the other as her phantom male lover—starting with her brother's Amherst classmate George Gould, moving on to her father's law apprentice, Ben Newton, continuing with the hypnotic Philadelphia preacher, Charles Wadsworth, whom some would like to identify as the Master in those three poignant, self-effacing, exuberant, and sadly comic letters that are among her greatest works of art. And there's also the seductive editor of the *Springfield Republican*, Sam Bowles, or perhaps Colonel Higginson himself, or Thomas Niles, the Boston editor who first published Dickinson's poems with an almost shameful reluctance, or some unknown aeronaut, when all the time that one monumental attachment wasn't with a man at all, but with an obscure woman from Cooperstown, a wanderer whom Martha and her mother had wanted so desperately to hide.

4

AND SO WE'RE LEFT WITH ONE DAGUERREOTYPE whose provenance we may never ascertain, which could be the deluded dream of some junk dealer in Massachusetts, but which, nonetheless, rides us right into the twenty-first century with Emily Dickinson, not so much because of the revelations about her and Condor Kate, but because of the *enchantment* of the daguerreotype itself, and the persona it reveals to us, Dickinson as a carnivore, a huntress, much taller than we had ever imagined: the record book of the funeral director who buried Dickinson notes that she was five feet six inches. She protects Kate in the daguerreotype, stares at us with a slight astigmatism in her *Yellow Eye,* sits in her old-fashioned dress, with a confidant half smile, with the long fingers of a pianist—a hunter's hand.

"Abyss has no Biographer—," Dickinson wrote to Sue's sister, Martha Gilbert Smith, in 1884. [Letter 899] But perhaps it does, since the daguerreotype takes us into the landscape of "My life had stood a loaded gun." [Fr764] And we now can stare into the "Abyss" of the poem. It's darker than we might ever have imagined. The Master and his Loaded Gun share the same persona. The Doe they hunt is for a different kind of winter meat—sexual prey. They're a couple of cavaliers. The speaker identifies with the cruelty of her Master, with his sense of sexual play. To seduce is to plunder, to feel the mindless joy of a Loaded Gun. And isn't Condor Kate Dickinson's "prey" in the daguerreotype, her conquest, whom she's sharing with the camera and with us? And this is what is so disturbing about the image: Dickinson feels more contemporary than we are, even in her fluffed-out clothes. Kate is somewhere back in another time, tentative, forlorn, frightened of a shadow box that can capture her image and suck at her soul. But Dickinson is much more comfortable with the black magic of technology. We can only see four of her fingers; the "emphatic Thumb" of her hunter-killer's hand is hidden. She's no picture out of the poem. She is the Loaded Gun.

SEVEN

Within a Magic Prison

1

I F A SINGLE DAGUERREOTYPE PLUCKED OUT of a scavenger sale in Springfield can twist our imagination so and reveal Dickinson as a huntress rather than a shy Kangaroo, then we might have to admit that the more we learn about the Belle of Amherst, the more mysterious and ungovernable she becomes. What do we really know about her after gathering all her texts and every variant—the letters, sent and unsent, the anthologies of her poems that she stitched together like some seamstress of mind and soul, the fragments that suddenly appeared on the backs of envelopes and bits of brown paper bags in her last two decades and were largely ignored by her earliest editors, since *all* of them believed that protean as she was, Dickinson was well beyond the "White Heat" of her most productive period? And if we pin together the details of her life, as she often pinned the lines of one poem onto the lines of another, or examine every pinning or poem like some celestial jeweler, can we discover a significant shape for Dickinson other than the ragged outline of one iconic lie after the other? We cannot really determine *why* she began to wear a white dress, or when she began her subterranean existence as a mermaid-poet in that frigate of hers on the second floor, or even if Vinnie slept with her in the same narrow sleigh bed? And can we speak of a

Dickinson *canon* when each poem (or letter) with all its variants, is utterly isolated, a canon all its own?

"Except for Shakespeare," Harold Bloom tells us, "Dickinson manifests more cognitive originality than any other Western poet since Dante." Like Shakespeare, her language is "dragonish," shifting shapes while it *dislimns*, as words fly out of nowhere—little dragons that caress and kill at the same time. But I doubt that Dickinson would ever have believed in a "Western Canon," even if it commenced with her beloved Shakespeare and included George Eliot, a novelist she adored. She would have said that language began in Arctic bliss, with icicles under her tongue, that all words were "Zero at the Bone." Dickinson believed in violent shifts of landscapes and language—the volcano was her natural home, with all its molten lava and centuries of sleep. If Lear represents the unraveling of civilization, the wild ravages of an old man's heart, Dickinson would never have sided with him, but with the Fool, who asks, "Can you make no use of nothing, nuncle?" And Lear answers with all the canonical pomp of kings: "Why, no, boy; nothing can be made out of nothing."

But Dickinson knew otherwise. Language came from the abyss; hers was a dragon's lair. And she composed, almost until the very end, with that mordant humor of hers, like a bird in mid-flight. To her favorites, Fanny and Loo, she wrote just before her death, in May of 1886.

> *Little Cousins,*
> *Called back.*
> *Emily.* [Letter 1046]

It was the very last missive she would ever send.

But there were also poems and fragments, scraps she wrote on the sly, and might pin to a poem, or use to accompany some doodle, as if she were liberated from the strictness of meter or the imprisonment of a page. They were like the excretions of a snail, a few words on the back of some recipe, or the strip of a used envelope, or a handbill, on every kind of colored paper, like a fortune-teller's cards, with words spilling onto an envelope with her very own slant or some other inscrutable design, as if she were building her own *rickety* enterprise, as David Porter might say, or examining words as a carpenter would, with every curve and mark. And I suspect that these markings, often written with a pencil she carried at her side like some gunslinger, offer as much of an entry point as we will ever have to the silent music and constant chaos of her life and her work.

2

D ICKINSON SCHOLAR MARTA L. WERNER has devoted a good portion of her own life to these fragments, or "radical scatters," as she calls them. And the archive she has assembled about these fugitive scraps has migrated from one electronic library to the next, like isolated, lonely birds that Dickinson herself might have coveted. Werner reveals how she happened upon the name for her electronic archive of the poet's late fragments—it was in a book by British ornithologist G. V. Matthews about the strange and irregular migratory patterns of birds. While trying to determine the flight paths and homing instincts of certain birds, Werner tells us, an expert—called a *liberator*—"throws several birds into the air one at a time" in different directions. "The birds are then watched until they are out of sight, and the points at which they disappear from view are recorded." A "scatter diagram" is then drawn up. And for reasons that are still unclear, "some birds on the outward course drift widely across the migration axis"—that is, their moves are utterly unexpected. "These drifts, called 'radical scatters,' both solicit and resist interpretation." And Werner is convinced that Dickinson's late fragments "are textual counterparts of the scattered migrants"—they often migrate from text to text, appear and disappear, and fly beyond their own limits, where readers can no longer capture them.

I saw several of these "fugitives' in the archives of the Robert Frost Library at Amherst College; and nothing else I had ever seen of

Dickinson's—the fascicles, the 1847 daguerreotype, which was much tinier and more fragile than the icon I had imagined, or the letters with their different scrawls, some careful, others chaotic—excited and disturbed me as much as these fugitive fragments, with their crosshatches, their lines that could spill in every direction, their erasures, the wiggle marks of the poet trying out a new pen, the ascending and descending dashes, like private musical notes that no army of scholars could ever interpret, the words that broke the *tyranny* of a line and seemed to shimmer in front of your eyes, or stared out at you with the boldest pen strokes on a tiny strip of paper:

Grasped   by
God   —   [PF 76; manuscript: "A 169"]

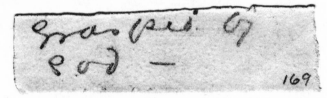

Credit: PF 76; manuscript: "A 169," Amherst College Archives and Special Collections.

It was as if we were watching the poet in the act of creation, in some eternal present tense, with not a soul to step between us and mediate. I felt like that "liberator" flinging birds with a blind abandon, and knowing that no two flight patterns would ever be the same, that Dickinson would always startle, always run rampant.

These fragments were mostly ignored when Thomas H. Johnson first published some of them over sixty years ago as a kind of *appendage* to his collection of Dickinson's letters. He called them "Prose Fragments" and "Aphorisms." It was, Johnson insisted, impossible to say very much about Dickinson's "unformed, worksheet jottings." They must have unnerved him a little with their almost accidental, anarchic appearance, and their bold declarations, like some wild telegraphic operator tapping at his keys:

> *I don't keep the Moth part of the House—I keep the Butterfly
> part* [PF 80]
>
> *A something overtakes the mind—we do not hear it coming*
> [Like her own cataclysmic acts of creation].   [PF 119]
>
> *What Lethargies of Loneliness*   [PF 120]
>
> *With the sincere spite of a* Woman   [PF 124]

Johnson tells us that the final "Aphorism" above, composed on a
scrap of stationery, was unique among all the fragments "in that it is
in the ink and in the handwriting of about 1850." She could have been
talking about Sue here, or some unfaithful friend, but since all discus-
sions about the *evolution* of Dickinson's handwriting are imprecise, she
might also have been talking, ten years later, about some sudden lurch
in her love affair with Condor Kate.

Perhaps I misread Dickinson's purpose and intent in this fragment,
and it has nothing to do with Kate. Still, what's important is that Johnson assigned all such fragments to oblivion, and they "disappeared
from view almost in the very moment they had first appeared in print."

Werner doesn't blame Johnson; she blames it on the "Cold War"
mentality of the 1950s, when our own hysteria over national borders
also enclosed us within "textual borders—a need to define and contain texts," so that we were blinded to the originality of fragments that
seemed "an embarrassing excess." But this *blinding* occurred long before
Johnson; there had been a "Cold War" in relation to Dickinson's texts
from the moment they were discovered in the poet's mahogany drawer.
Perhaps Sue was the only one who understood the poet's subversive
powers, but her secretiveness pushed her away from shepherding the
poems into print; and Dickinson's first "discoverers," Higginson and
Mabel Loomis Todd, who felt that half her poems were fugitives, frag-
mented the poet's voice and created their own borders.

Even Johnson's monumental editing of the poems and the letters
couldn't really repair a misconception that had haunted us for over
half a century, that overriding image of the Queen Recluse. But at

least we had her own full closet of poems, without fake titles and "improvements" upon her syntax, and letters that revealed a complex tapestry of purpose we had never seen before. Their riches dazzled and overwhelmed, and perhaps none of us, including Johnson, was prepared to examine the outer edges of that tapestry, where her own narrative seemed to unravel into a tatter of words. And then came Jay Leyda's *The Years and Hours of Emily Dickinson* (1960), which talked about "the omitted center" of Dickinson's design, that elusive short-hand of her letters and poems, where she had her own elliptical language with certain recipients, such as Sue.

Leyda and the poet were a perfect fit. His entire life was elliptical. It's not even certain where he was born, or what name he was born with. He grew up in Dayton, Ohio. His father was a circus performer, and he was raised by a grandmother who pretended to be his mother. He went to Moscow to study with Sergei Eisenstein, returned to the United States, was an assistant curator of film at the Museum of Modern Art (it was here that he probably met Joseph Cornell); accused of being a Soviet secret agent, Leyda was driven out of the museum in 1940, but he still went to Hollywood in 1942, where he served as a technical adviser at Warner Bros. and MGM on films about the Soviet Union, such as *Mission to Moscow* (1943), and later landed at the Folger Library in Washington, D.C., and up at Amherst, working as an archivist on the chaotic collection of Dickinson papers and poems that Millicent Todd Bingham had inherited from her mother and given to Amherst College—he'd already written *The Melville Log*, a compilation of the days and hours of Herman Melville, originally intended as a birthday present for Eisenstein. And Leyda was one of the first to examine Dickinson's late fragments; he shared some of his thoughts with Joseph Cornell, and wrote to literary critic Alfred Kazin (and others) about his adventures of wandering through the Homestead, of standing in the poet's room, dreaming of her vistas. And he did his own Dickinson log, gathering the minutiae around her life like a pile of compost that he could sift through, but even Leyda—the ultimate Dickinson detective—couldn't intuit the relationship of the fragments to the rest of her work.

It took another kind of detective, Marta Werner, searching for migrations rather than minutiae, to reexamine the fragments almost forty years after Leyda. And she has bolted us into a recognition of Dickinson's habits as a huntress of words that we might never have had without her own electronic archive. These "radical scatters," she tells us, were never meant to be seen by anyone but the scriptor herself, and "are not so much 'works' as symptoms of the processes of composition." And her discoveries were no accident. These fragments could not become *visible* until a brand-new century, when our notions of stability have changed, and we are all nomads in a sense. "Homelessness is our inheritance and our condition," according to Marta Werner. "A poetics of exile, of the margin, is our rejoinder."

Yet "homelessness" was not only the condition of the poet's fugitive fragments but of Dickinson herself, a nomad within her father's house, and within the nineteenth century, with its wholesale prescriptions upon her sex—no woman could deny her husband the rights to her body—and its pinch upon her purchasing power that kept her a child, as Susan Howe suggests. She was "voiceless" within a male hierarchy, and therefore had to create a coded voice of her own. Dickinson became the master of this voice, and if there is a secret motor to her very best verses, it is the lyrical lash of rebellion. She needed to inflict pain, often upon herself, but also upon the culture that had created her. And for Dickinson, it was a culture of words. If her Lexicon was her only friend, it was also her chief adversary, the historical script of her bondage to males that was packed into every epigram, every narrative, every word. There were no female narrators in the Bible, and no Judith Shakespeare to lend a voice to Elizabethan drama. And that's why she idolized Barrett Browning and the Brontës, and devoured the novels of George Eliot, who had to hide her ferocious intelligence under a male mask, or her own writing might never have been taken seriously. Women were toys, the playthings of Victorian plutocrats, as Dickinson knew in her bones.

3

YET ONE OF THE KEYS TO *deconstructing* Dickinson (as much as we will ever be able to dislodge her codes) lies at the peripheries, where we don't have scripted books, but scatterings, where we have to try and fathom her radically flying birds. Dickinson's fragments, Werner tells us, "depict the beauties of transition and isolation at once." They might stand *positionless* or migrate to another text, appear in a letter or as variant lines in another poem. "Belonging to a chronology of the instant, vulnerability is the mark of their existence." They are here and nowhere, like wandering ghosts, leaving their trace upon a particular text, "as if poems, letters, and fragments communicated tele-pathically, a line or phrase from a fragment re-appears, often altered, in the body of a poem, a message, or even another fragment." But such ghosts are almost impossible to define—"neither residents nor aliens, neither lost nor found . . . they require that we attend to the mystery of the encounters between fragments, poems, and letters," and these radical scatters can suddenly take asylum in a text, and then pull away into some boundless space and time.

And this is where our study of the poet ought to begin—at the edges and outer borders, Werner insists. Her scatterings "are the latest and furthest affirmation of a centrifugal impulse, a gravitation away from the center, that is expressed at every level of her work." And perhaps we even have to abandon the traditional notion of a poet's "work," in Dickinson's case—her poems, her letters, and manuscript books—and consider a new definition, without beginnings or endings, "a work in throes." This is why Dickinson seems so different from any other poet, because her writing is in constant crisis, where contradictions abound from line to line, or within a line, like sonar booms that hurt the ear as we try to listen to each bolt of melody. Werner reminds us again and again of the unhomeliness of her poetic condition—"as well, of course, as our own." And perhaps that is why we are addicted to Dickinson and can never seem to get enough of her. We cannot locate who we are or where we are in relation to her poems, since the speaker can be male and female, or some glacially sexless creature, murderer or angel, Goliath or gnome, as we move from line to line. Allen Tate scoffed at her as a lyric poet who could never have written a novel. "She cannot reason at all. She can only *see*. It is impossible to imagine what she might have done with drama or fiction." Well, he's wrong. Reading the best of Dickinson is like being stuck inside *Gulliver's Travels* and *Alice in Wonderland* at the same time, where our psyche seems to spill into some wonderland of "noiseless noise" as we follow the speaker's traces, that deceptive *I* who can ride on a carriage to an eternity that's limbed with the little houses of hell, or cast her *Yellow Eye* upon us all, her uninvited guests, who have intruded upon her hunting grounds, the private sanctuary of her poems, where we have little purchase and will never be able to "unriddle" her.

But most of all, Dickinson's "radical scatters," with their "turbulence of mind"—those mysterious angled dashes, pen tests and other scratchings, and question marks that seem to float across a particular scrap of paper—offer us a glimpse of something we could never have in a *finished* poem, our own secret desire "to register the progress of the hand/mind across the page." We have rendered her naked for a moment, have caught her in the act of writing, as if we could shatter time and had some kinetic power to catch that pencil in her hand, and that "emphatic Thumb" as it moves with the terrible lightning of thought. Or, as Werner tells us, all the wanderings and deletions, and the additional scrawls that move like some magnificent crab across the very borders of a page, seem to mirror "the hand in the present tense of writing."

4

ONE OF THE MOST PUZZLING PIECES of "work in throes" is a fragment that appears on a scrap of brown wrapping paper.

A   *Woe*

of   *Ecstasy*   [Fr1599A: manuscript: "A 112"]

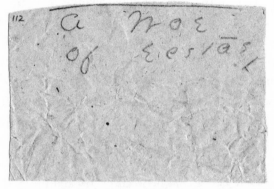

Credit: Fr1599A; manuscript: "A 112," Amherst College Archives and Special Collections.

We could crush an entire universe into those four words, and consider all of Dickinson's writing "A Woe/of Ecstasy." But the fragment exists both "as an autonomous lyric throe" and as a variant to the final line of a particular poem:

> *A Sloop of Amber slips away*
> *Upon an Ether Sea,*
> *And wrecks in Peace a Purple Tar,*
> *The Son of Ecstasy—*   [Fr1599C]

"Please accept a Sunset," she wrote coyly to the poem's possible recipient, Edward Tuckerman, professor of botany at Amherst College. She is, of course, describing that elusive and violent sinking of the sun, and she captures the moment in a deeply lyrical portrait that no one else could ever have painted. And her last line, "The Son of Ecstasy," in the version she may have sent to Tuckerman, lends the poem a

Christ-like sense of awe, and a playfulness about the repetitive patter of "Son" and "sun." But the variant of "A Woe/of Ecstasy" changes the discourse as it migrates into the poem, and it holds us and the poem "spellbound" for an instant, as Werner suggests. Suddenly that "Sloop of Amber" is a bit more ominous as it "slips away." And we now have a poem about Apocalypse; Dickinson's "Sloop of Amber" might well be the poet's craft, with its delicate and delightful color, as it ripples, or "wrecks [the] Peace," of that "Purple Tar," and drops the poet into the nothingness of eternal night—hence, "A Woe/of Ecstasy," as if beauty and destruction arrive in the same breath, like some irritable angel, and leave without one last trace of awe.

Dickinson's fragments are "solitary outriders" that often gallop right into the middle of a letter, and "may at any moment revolt against the sovereignty of singular address," so that the letters of her last two decades are as "undomesticatable" as the scraps themselves, and live in some borderland between poetry and prose. In one particular draft of an 1885 letter to Helen Hunt Jackson, we have all the beats and line breaks of a poem.

> *Who   could   be*
> *ill   in   March—*
> *that   Month   of*
> *proclamation?*
> * Sleigh   Bells   and*
> *Jays   contend   in*
> *my   Matinee,   and*
> *the   North   surren—*
> *ders   instead   of*
> *the   South,   a*
> *reverse   of   Bugles—*   [Letter 976; manuscript: "A 976"]

And one of her *crafted* poems migrates right into the shivering lines of the letter like some magnificent fugitive that barely creates a rift.

Of God we ask one favor, that we may be forgiven—
For what he is presumed to know—
The Crime, from us, is hidden—
Immured the whole of Life
Within a magic Prison
We reprimand the happiness—
That too competes with Heaven—   [Fr1675B]

Jackson herself was a kind of fugitive—a female author—who begged Dickinson to publish her poems. A writer with little suppleness of her own, and a clubfooted gait, she still understood Dickinson's angular style and relentless music. And why, we would have to ask again, didn't the poet have any genuine male preceptors, even if she liked to pretend that Colonel Higginson posed as one? None of the males around her, neither Higginson nor Sam Bowles, had the least clue of what her poetry was about. Both were prominent editors who championed women's causes, yet they'd never have recognized that rage within the poet, or the Vesuvius she had become. They couldn't sift through her volcanic ash. Sue had become her part-time preceptor, had dealt with this ash and some of her "Snow," but Helen Hunt Jackson was a *huntress* with her own Yellow Eye, searching for other poets, and would have made Dickinson dance and sing in public—she who was only a Prima within the shadow box of her mind. And that's why those two lines—"Immured the whole of Life/ Within a magic Prison"—flew into her letter like some strange missile, torn from a poem about human guilt, and some hidden Crime, as she must have seen herself as a criminal in that undecorated room with its minuscule desk and sleigh bed, where she became an alchemist of sorts, firing her Woe of Words, like pellets that weren't meant for public consumption, but to wound herself perhaps, or to shatter her Lexicon, to break and break and break, though her violence went unseen, sequestered as she was, a homebound waif in a white dress, sentencing herself to" a magic Prison."

"Agoraphobia was her alibi," Werner reminds us in *Emily Dickinson's Open Folios*, " 'I' was her alias." She had many personas, more than one. And we, like ghouls, try to toy with her biography, to link her language with her life. We cannot master her, never will, as if her own words skate on some torrid ice that is permanently beyond our pale, yet we seek and seek, as if somehow that soothes us, as if we might crack a certain code, when all we will ever have is "A Woe/of Ecstasy."

5

THE DEFIANT ONES, SUCH AS MARTA WERNER, match fire with fire, as if some of their own sparks will bring us a little closer to Dickinson—language is the one witchery we have at our disposal to deal with a witch. And this is what Marta Werner does in *Radical Scatters*. She has found a lexicon to examine the Lexicon of Dickinson's late fragments, and has revealed the radical heart of Dickinson's writing: This poet was not a *finisher*; everything she wrote was always involved in its own entangled process and growth, like one of her perennials, and she moved with such a nimble violence between poetry and prose, until their lashing rhythms were almost identical.

"Having abandoned the institution of 'authorship' early in her writing life," Werner insists, "Dickinson was able to set in motion a work without beginning or ending. . . . The fragments—the work in throes—scatter in all directions at once." And, what is most critical, "[e]verything must be redefined in their wake."

We now have to reconsider the poet's workshop—both early and late—as an alchemist's laboratory, where she was in constant agitation, and where "pandemonium" reigned—"the spectacular turbulence and commotion . . . that attended the act of composition." She seemed much more interested in the outreaches of her mind than in the notion of a finished text—everything was in flight, and in flux, in that laboratory, where lines could migrate from text to text like wild, astonishing birds. And it's no simple conceit that her narrators often spoke to us from the other side of the grave, or that she seemed so involved with the dead in her poems.

Like Men and Women Shadows walk
Opon the Hills Today . . .   [Fr964]

She communed with us, like some clairvoyant, as if she had found a melody and a cadence to speak for the dead—and inhabited a necropolis all her own. But it was no high-wire act, no ventriloquism, even though she had the artist's power to mimic.

We can never outgrow her "radical scatters"—each time, we discover a different trajectory, another dip and arc, and we approach her with a certain peril. We all want our own Miss Emily, a RepliLuxe we might fathom and control, and that's one of the reasons we're so obsessed with her biography. To *know* Dickinson is to contain her. Even if we found a certain "provenance" for that 1859 daguerreotype, genuine proof that she loved Condor Kate, it might utterly destroy that stale image of a sexless, reclusive mouse, but we still couldn't solve the great riddle of her art.

What if there were a host of Condor Kates? And she devoured one Kate after another with her wildness and her will? And what if we found the recipient of the "Master Letters"? Or could prove that she had more than an epistolary romance with Judge Lord? None of this could give us much purchase into her mind. She lived the life of a *privileged* spinster in a nineteenth-century New England cow town with its own college. Her father was a tyrannical man who beat his horses and was captain of his own fire company. But his elder daughter was as tyrannical as he was. She built a whirlwind around her and lived within its walls. I doubt he was ever aware that Miss Emily was an alchemist, and creator of her own recondite language. We know she never married, whether or not she was "The Wife— without the Sign." She might never have slept with a woman, or with a man. And she never traveled beyond Boston or the nation's capital.

"To shut our eyes is Travel" [Letter 354], she wrote, and she traveled everywhere she required in the shifting harbors of her poems, where she could search for her "Blue Peninsula." She had her "Wild Nights" and who are we to question them? Whether they were with Condor Kate or with the *ravelments* of her pen while everyone else was asleep at the Homestead, she brought the English language to the very borders of possibility and then pushed beyond these borders. Her move from word to word was so rapid that we can barely keep up with her transcriptions and marks on the page. Perhaps her various dashes are internal whispers of the mind trying to keep pace with the *violence* of thought, where the melodies *atomize* the words, shove them at us like broken teeth.

6

BEHIND ALL HER ARIAS THERE SEEMS TO BE a black hole. It's Roland Barthes who said *In Writing Degree Zero* that modern language has moved outside history, into dream and menace. And that's one reason why there's so little reward in studying the poet within the context of her times. She's larger than her Lexicon. And nineteenth-century manners and dominions cannot explain her. She tore some of her vocabulary from Shakespeare, but what she must have sensed most was the menace that lurked behind every speech in *Hamlet*, as the doomed prince of Denmark chased ghosts in the dark. "Hamlet wavered for all of us—," she wrote in 1877. [Letter 512] And like Hamlet, she ran after these ghosts, the living and the dead, witness and illusion, with the one rapier she had. "Words, words, words." She could inhabit the psyche of all her favorite characters at once—Hamlet, Antony, Cleopatra, Enobarbus, Ophelia, Lady Macbeth—enchantress and doomster, wrapped in a succulent caprice, fat with pity and fear and a glorious spite, she whirls around us and wounds us with her seductions and the jagged edges of her lines—

She dealt her pretty words like Blades—
How glittering they shone—
And every One unbared a Nerve
Or wantoned with a Bone— [Fr458]

With all her Blades and Loaded Guns of language, she endured a deep *ontological* fear, that dread of being alive, yet this is only one more mark of her warlike contradictions, where that same fear is often coupled with a kind of *Ecstasy,* as she floats all by herself in some "syllableless Sea." [Fr1689] She devoured Sam Bowles' *Springfield Republican* every day of her life, knew all about Whig politics, silver mines in Potosí, sea disasters, the eruptions of Mount Etna, butcheries of the Civil War, and even wrote about them, but what she feared most, what obsessed Emily Dickinson and filled her with demons, was Nature's own civil war—the change of seasons. She could delight in the robin's first call, and dread that it might also be the last, as if the signs of some cold spell might be the signature of an eternal ice age.

I dreaded that first Robin, so . . .

I thought if I could only live
Till that first Shout got by—
Not all Pianos in the Woods
Had power to mangle me—   [Fr347]

If she could crack through that morbid catacomb of winter, and wake—with a certain dread—to the robin's "first Shout," none of Nature's other calls could disrupt her own call to music. But the dread *always* returns. It's not only Death that calls in his comfortable carriage, that freezes at the bone, and "Dresses each House in Crepe, and Icicle" [Fr556], but the winter frost paralyzes us and impairs our sense of sound.

When they begin, if Robins may,
I always had a fear
I did not tell, it was their last Experiment
Last Year . . . [Fr1042]

What if she herself became mute, could no longer sing, and had to suffer through her own "Last Experiment"? Would she really drown in a "syllableless Sea"? "The Soul has Bandaged moments," when Dickinson cannot sing, and—

She feels some ghastly Fright come up
And stop to look at her . . .

Caress her freezing hair—

And then, like "the Bee—delirious borne," she dances, "a Bomb, abroad," and her song is in full sway again. But nothing lasts. That listlessness comes back, and she's now a "Felon"—

With shackles on the plumed feet
And staples, in the song.

The Horror welcomes her, again
These, are not brayed of Tongue— [Fr360]

And thus she went through a series of crises, from silence to sound, from powerlessness, where her Feathers were plucked, to rampant song, where all her Feathers preened and she could bray her head off. What caused these crises, like a peristaltic crunch that could freeze her hair, remains a matter of conjecture—and concern. Was it the constant swerve in her relationship with Sue, a volcano every bit as volatile as the poet?

That those who know her know her less
The nearer her they get— [Fr1433C]

Or was it Kate, who also had the power to wound, and could stun the poet into silence? Or some unknown suitor, with a history tucked

away in letters we will newer find? And a hundred other disappointments, a whole catalogue of deaths? How will we ever know?

And with all her sense of "homelessness," she felt at home in the
land of Abyss. That's why she was so drawn to the secret gift of wells—a
well could suck up her own reflection in its damp, dark plummetless
bottom, could *annihilate* whatever outline she had.

> *What mystery pervades a well!*
> *The water lives so far—*
> *A neighbor from another world*
> *Residing in a jar*
>
> *Whose limit none has ever seen,*
> *But just his lid of glass—*
> *Like looking every time you please*
> *Into an abyss's face!* [Fr1433A]

Her own language was like that damp abyss, with its deceptive lid of
glass and plummetless bottom, where words could migrate from well to
well. But not all scholars believe in the authority of Dickinson's magic
wells. In *This Republic of Suffering*, a poignant study of the Civil War's
visible and invisible casualties, Drew Gilpin Faust, historian and president of Harvard University, talks about the discontinuities in Dickinson's
poetry, her smashing of syntax and her questioning of Christian myths:
The poet is at war with language itself, as if she had moved beyond sound
and sense, beyond heaven and hell, and the crisis of language she has
provoked "is about not just whether there is a God and we can know him
but whether we can know or communicate anything at all."

Faust isn't wrong about the poet's quixotic quest—to tear apart the
order and hierarchy of all things. And Dickinson never doubts her ability to do so, even if her music should fail her.

> *The Definition of Melody—is—*
> *That Definition is none—* [Fr849]

It's the world that seems so tentative to her, with all its rumblings. If Higginson *abandons* the poet, runs off to South Carolina to command his own Negro regiment, his "Scholar" says in her own testy voice: "I should have liked to see you, before you became improbable. War feels to me an oblique place—" [Letter 280, February 1863]

And Lincoln himself is just as improbable and oblique. Right after his reelection in 1864, she scribbles a note to Vinnie while exiled in a Cambridge boardinghouse with her own eye troubles, and she must have *witnessed* the full panoply of the torchlight parades of Lincoln Clubs through Cambridge:

The Drums keep on for the still Man . . . [Letter 297]

And not another word about Lincoln in her letters, oblique or otherwise, as if there's no room for him in her eschatology—she might have also held a grudge against Lincoln, since her father was an old-line Whig, who never had a real place in the Republican Party. And yet she was able to create her own little *daguerreotype* of Lincoln, a portrait in three words that captures his one essential feature. Lincoln was "the still Man," who held a nation together with his own silent glue.

And "the still Man" did remain in her imagination long after he was shot. In a letter-poem to Sue right after Gib's death, she wrote:

The Tent is listening,
But the Troops are gone! [Fr1625]

She could have been talking about Lincoln, and her own silent life as a poet— that Bird of Dissolution she had become. Perhaps her own sense of the Apocalypse came from the Civil War. Drew Gilpin Faust reminds us how much greater and more *personal* the carnage was than we could ever have imagined—"infantry engagements, even as they grew to involve tens of thousands of men, remained essentially intimate; soldiers were often able to see each other's faces and to know whom they had killed." She tells us about all the shallow graves, where hogs rooted relentlessly for whatever human parts they could unearth, while souvenir seekers roamed the battlefields robbing the dead. And in April 1865, when Union soldiers entered the burning capital of Richmond (the rebels had set their own fortress on fire), they found almost all the women dressed in black—the war had created a necropolis of widows and ghosts. That sort of necropolis must have whirled around in Dickinson's brain—ghosts loomed everywhere in that haunted house of hers. Never a Civil War poet, she did record the carnage in her own fashion; the *amputations* she wrote about related to the Lord. She was, like Jacob, "Pugilist and Poet" [Letter 1042]; she boxed with God and all His angels in her poems, and according to Dr. Norbert Hirschhorn, "it's not clear that God won."

She never had her own cosmology of angels and devils, unlike William Blake. Whatever she watched was mostly from her windowsill. This was how she framed the world. The circuses she saw passed beneath her window.

> *Friday I tasted life. It was a vast morsel. A circus passed the house—still I feel the red in my mind though the drums are out.* [Letter 318, early May 1866]

That *red* was palpable enough, and was like a lasting streak that colored her "little workmanships" [Fr640], the monumental tinkering she did with the help of her pen and little black pot in the tiny drawer of her tiny desk. She gardened, she baked, attended a mother who had become more and more of an invalid, and spun her startling web of words like the spider-artist she had become.

> *A Spider sewed at Night*
> *Without a Light*
> *Opon an Arc of White—* [Fr1163A]

That Arc of White was a danger zone, where none but the poet herself could thrive. She often had to dance at the very edge of madness, a

Prima of her own design. That daring design could rip and plunge her into nothingness, as she danced *opon* a thread.

> *The Spider holds a Silver Ball*
> *In unperceived Hands—*
> *And dancing softly to Himself . . .*
>
> *He plies from nought to nought—*   [Fr513]

There was always that danger of disappearing into her own web of words, and never climbing out. It was "Illocality" [Fr824] that frightened her, the loss of logic, where she could not place herself in any landscape, and everything shrank around her in that spider's design.

> *The Earth has seemed to me a Drum,*
> *Pursued of little Boys*   [Fr1095]

She had no equal as a poet, has no equal now. No one took the same risks. No one could build so suddenly and then *disrobe* and plunge into disrepair. She was a celestial knife thrower, hurling her blades at our heads. One of her favorite weapons was the *oxymoron*, for want of a better word—a compact ripple of contradictions that twisted language with a metallurgical skill: "Dirks of Melody," "a Maelstrom, with a notch," "A Battlement—of Straw," "An Everywhere of Silver," "An Overcoat of Clay," and "the sweet Assault, " almost always with a combative tone, as the Pugilist and Poet struggled "Like a Panther in the Glove—" [Fr242].

There was a price to pay, as if all the sewing of silver had left her with little else, and she began to disappear within her own texts. I can only think of one other nineteenth-century writer who suffered from the same *sickness*—Gustave Flaubert, an alchemist of his own; the spaces between his sentences in *L'Education sentimentale* almost serve like Dickinson's dashes, creating enormous white holes in the text, bald islands that allow every single sentence to drift as a tiny, disjointed novel. Voyaging across these bald islands is like living in Emily Dickinson's universe, where we have an immediate sense of vertigo, and might disappear at any moment.

I stepped from Plank to Plank . . .
I knew not but the next
Would be my final inch—   [Fr926]

Flaubert's novel *seems* to be about Frédéric Moreau, a young law student from the provinces who goes to Paris and falls in love with an older woman, Madame Arnoux. But Frédéric has no real persona; he wanders into the middle of a revolution and wanders right out; nothing ever happens to Frédéric, nothing touches him. He unravels right in front of our eyes, until he plunges into that white expanse of space and we're left with a walking ghost.

Henry James, who despised the novel, wrote in a little chapter on Flaubert in *French Poets and Novelists* (1904) that "the book is in a single word a *dead* one," and that reading *L'Education sentimentale* was like "masticating ashes and sawdust." The entire novel, he said, was "elaborately and massively dreary." James, our Master, the great modernist, didn't understand a word of Flaubert, who wove his own tale of dissolution in *L'Education sentimentale*, and was the same artist-spider as Emily Dickinson.

French critics were even less kind to Flaubert, the hermit of Croisset, who invented the modern novel from within the walls of his country estate. He was another celestial knife thrower, who wielded language like a scalpel—the son of a surgeon, Flaubert watched his father perform operations as a boy; he removed all the "excess fat" from his prose, until Frédéric Moreau inhabited a land without primitive psychology and all decorative detail.

He traveled.
Chilly awakenings under canvas; dreary mail-packets; the dizzy kaleidoscope of landscapes and ruins; the bitter taste of friendships nipped in the bud: such was the pattern of his life.
He came home . . .

We step from Plank to Plank with Frédéric—and Flaubert—and as readers, we unravel like a Silver Ball. There's no place to hide. We're left with a kind of dread. And we feel the same with that ultimate Spider, Miss Emily. We risk our lives—and our sanity—as we read her. She takes us deep within our psyches, a world of terror and wounds, and reminds the timid not to go there.

> *There is no second War*
> *In that Campaign inscrutable*
> *Of the Interior.*   [Fr1230]

And still we go.

EIGHT

Nothing

1

THE ARCHIVIST DELIVERS A BOX TO YOUR TABLE. It's not one of Cornell's, with the shadow of some nineteenth-century dancer trapped within a wall of glass; this box has a hint of beige, like the portfolio you once had as a high school student, with its worn wraparound string that protected your entire oeuvre, drawings you did from the age of five. You're a bit distracted. You open the box. There's a strange, frazzled treasure trove inside, and you soon discover that the archivist has brought you a perverse portfolio, a "warehouse" containing the near-perfect facsimiles of Dickinson's envelope-poems with their transcriptions printed in blue, plus a visual index, and other material by Marta Werner and artist Jen Bervin, who, like a pair of postmodern sorceresses, have found a way into the labyrinth of Dickinson's deeply puzzling "word paintings" with a puzzle all their own. None of us can match Dickinson's "synesthesia of sight and sound," but Werner and Bervin have come as close as they can, and we realize soon enough that this is the most radical rendering of Dickinson we have ever seen, because it tries to replicate the visual dynamics of her work without intruding upon the mysteries of creation.

There are only sixty such boxes, all designed by Jen Bervin; the box at my library table has come from within the bowels of the Dickinson archives at Amherst College, where I had been looking at the pencil marks of her letter-poems with both devilment and delight, as if these marks were the lashings of some strange music that I might decode one day and keep for myself. But it's only a delusion. None of us will ever get near enough to Emily.

Marta Werner's own initiation into this project may have begun at Amherst, when one of Dickinson's envelope-poems fell—or *rose*—out of its acid-free envelope by pure chance and she discovered the curious construction of a halved envelope that mimics the velocity and disturbance of flight itself, an envelope with its own hinged wings and wing texts that seem to stir the atmosphere. As Werner tells us, the right and left wing may once have been folded, "perhaps even pinned close; at rest, the manuscript has yet to be transformed into a fully living figure."

On the right wing, slanting west, are the lines "Afternoon and / the West and / the gorgeous nothings / which /compose / the sunset / keep," written upside down. [A 821] And on the left wing, slanting east, and with much more space between every word, are the lines "Clogged / only with/ Music, like / the Wheels of Birds." [A 821a] Werner believes that this envelope-poem remains unborn until we ourselves "launch" it and mimic the act of flight.

That first act of flight just before migration is painful, almost unbearable, for a bird, as ornithologist W. H. Hudson—author of *Green Mansions*—once noted: Nothing can rid the bird of such pain but the rapid flight of its wings. And this is what Dickinson's envelope-poems are about—"the isolate, piercing notes of a bird" as it is about to take flight. But we cannot remain passive observers; we must help this bird-poem take flight with our very own hands. As we rotate the fragment, point by point, we seem to put into motion "a whir of words." And for a second or two we've become the poet's accomplice, as if Werner and Bervin have conspired with the Devil to bring us a bit closer to Dickinson's art with a boxful of fragments.

Suddenly we have to deal with texture as well as song, with the perversity of addresses and postage stamps, the ragged borders of a telegram, the art of folding and cutting an envelope, so that we can feel the shiver of a bird in the pinning and unpinning of some fragment with lines penciled along its crease. We have to think of such fragments as Dickinson's own "small fabric," according to Jen Bervin.

> *Excuse Emily and her Atoms—The "North Star" is of small fabric, but it denotes much—*   [Letter 774 to Susan Dickinson, October 1882]

"When we say *small,* we often mean less," Bervin reminds us. "When Dickinson says *small,* she means fabric, Atoms, the North Star." And Dickinson's most artful fabric was an envelope of every sort: the pocket of her white wrapper where she kept her pencil stubs and scraps of paper; the letter she folded into thirds and pinned together into a "pocket," with a pencil stub enclosed inside, as a reminder to Mr. and Mrs. Sam Bowles that they ought to write to their *Emily*; and the envelope scraps she coveted like some great hoarder. "These envelopes have been opened well beyond the point needed to merely extract a letter; they have been torn, cut, and opened out completely flat, rendered into new shapes," so that they breathe and fly and whisper as much as the words scribbled on their flaps and seals.

Dickinson's entire life seemed to whirl around envelopes, as if each contained a ghostly marking. "What a Hazard a Letter is!" she wrote to Colonel Higginson in 1885. [Letter 1007] This is perhaps the central theme of *The Gorgeous Nothings*—the risk that the poet took with every scratch of her pencil. "A message enclosed in an envelope," Werner tells us, "a poem inscribed upon it and prepared for sending over miles or years is not a bit or byte of information but an archive of longings." That was her *telos,* if she ever had one—to inscribe in fire, as if the envelope were her own skin, and language some kind of infernal tattoo. We know little about her except this archive of longings. Her own life was *reportless,* a word she invented and that no one else ever used.

In many and reportless places
We feel a Joy . . .
It comes, without a consternation—
Dissolves—the same—
But leaves a sumptuous Destitution—
Without a Name— [Fr1404]

That "sumptuous Destitution" was her own craft—solid and invisible at the same time, a language and a Lexicon she could never share. No matter where these envelopes might fly, they always encased an archive of longings; this had little to do with her love for Sister Sue or Condor Kate, or some mysterious Master; she may have been "Jumbo" to Judge Lord, and Higginson's perfect Gnome, but none of them could parse the strings of her intellect: Dickinson was all alone.

"The envelope is the repository of damages it cannot heal or even contain; slit open, it functions not as a soothing bandage, but rather, as a second and almost simultaneous site of rupture," the site of an ever-deepening wound. There is no *suture* in the art of Emily Dickinson, and very few sentimental journeys. And her last writings have their own rough texture, their own mournful music. "The inaudible *whirring* of the envelopes is part of the message they are sending. Slit open, unfolded, written across, and handed over to chance, they reject the asylum offered by the lyric to probe the last privacies of our existence," Marta Werner writes, as if she were willing to share that endless isolation of the cosmos with Emily Dickinson.

2

"MY FATHER FIRST READ HER POEMS TO ME when I was very young," Marta told me in June of 2013. "I'm not sure why he did this. He was an extraordinary man, but not a man intensely drawn to literature. He loved nature and science. I learned about the layers of the Earth and the lives of the stars from him. I'm not sure what it was in Dickinson that drew him. But I think it might have had something to do with [her] stark questions about origins and ends."

Perhaps there was also another reason. Marta's father was a kind of itinerant teacher in love with anthropology. "He taught everywhere—elementary school, high school, and college," where he was always an adjunct. He remained at the periphery, like Emily Dickinson, had his own ragged edge.

"It was summertime when he read her poems to me, and we were in a remote place in the mountains of New Hampshire. It was something we did alone, without my sisters or brother." And a year before her father died, "he suddenly proposed that we read Dickinson together again. He would send me a letter with nothing but numbers"—the numbers of Dickinson's poems in the Thomas. H. Johnson edition—"and I would send a letter back—also just a list of numbers—no explanations. The lists were records of Dickinson poems we loved, but they were also a kind of code of love we had for each other. . . . My father followed my work on Dickinson until he died. I was writing an essay on 'In many and reportless places' when he took the fall that would lead to his death, and I've been looking for him in those reportless places ever since."

But those "reportless places" are also Dickinson's private hunting grounds, and that's why it's so hard to find her and equally hard to let go. No matter where Marta turns, no matter what writer she seizes upon, she always comes back to Emily, as if Dickinson's ghost were imbedded in everything she writes.

Marta also had another mentor.

"The poet Susan Howe was my teacher, and I could not have had a greater guide to Dickinson. . . . It's impossible to describe the power of her lectures. I once read of the poet Anna Akhmatova that she was always alert and watchful because she was always waiting for words. Susan Howe strikes one as similarly vigilant. At times, Howe seemed almost to fall into a trance herself. . . . She was in contact with language in a very profound way. She taught me that language has a life of its own, and that words carry their histories—their desires and disappointments—with them." And their shadows, I wanted to say, because Dickinson was constantly shifting shadows in her very own box, or Lexicon.

Marta attributes much of her own work on *The Gorgeous Nothings* to Susan Howe, whose own "shadow" was deep within the Dickinson archives, with Marta and Jen Bervin, helping them sift the documents and deal with that great puzzler, Emily Dickinson.

"We came from different worlds," Marta said about herself and Bervin, "she from an art world, and I from the world of textual scholarship—and we met on the margins of Dickinson's poetry. But we were both drawn to the problem of how best to represent the conditions of Dickinson's late works . . . and we were both committed to finding a form for her fragments that might gather and scatter them at once.

"The best textual home for the late work seemed to us to be a temporary, perhaps even makeshift, shelter, where Dickinson's works might momentarily gather before dispersing again. Thus the contents of *The Gorgeous Nothings* arrive not between two covers but in an archival box, and they must be unpacked, unfolded, and slowly sifted," making each one of us an archivist, an explorer entering territories where only Dickinson herself had gone.

And when we sift any one of those unbound color facsimiles with our own hands, we're transported to a very private place, where the facsimiles assume their own luminous fabric and "also seem to dilate before our very eyes. The painstaking erasure of every bit of shadow from around the edges of the images allow the facsimiles to float on the paper—to appear as if they are suspended in air. In a perpetual paradox, they flicker between presence and absence and appear very close and very far away at once. For as we hope to suggest, the manuscript is the text's 'other scene,' the record, only partly discursive, of a vision that cannot ever be completely decoded or encoded."

3

THERE'S A KIND OF RAPTURE AS WE SIFT through *The Gorgeous Nothings*, boxes within a box, and that sense of serious play does remind me of Cornell, but Cornell's parchments and bird cages and barren walls are all entombed in glass and wood, and we are passive participants in the drama, voyeurs of a sort, safe in our admiration and despair of never finding Emily Dickinson within these walls; she's flown to her "Blue Peninsula" and left us in the lurch.

While alive, Cornell was the only active player in the drama. He could unscrew the lid, find other escape routes for Dickinson, and we might even escape with her to some "reportless land"—in our voyeuristic dreams. But there are no escape routes within *The Gorgeous Nothings*—an open box is also an open wound.

As I unpack the portfolio, sift through all these *Nothings*—the language and the material of the letter-poems, the different pencil strokes and scraps, I also feel a little spooked, as if I've come a bit too near the village Prometheus with the mirroring techniques of the twenty-first century and might get scorched.

> *We*
> *talked with*
> *each other*
> *about each*
> *other*
> *Though neither*
> *of us spoke—*
> *We were + too*
> *engrossed with*
> *the Seconds Races*
> *And the Hoofs of*
> *The Clock—*
> *Pausing in front*

> *of our* + *Sentenced*
>   *Faces*
>   *Time's Decision*
> *shook—*
>   *Arks of Reprieve*   [Fr1506; manuscript "A 514"]

I have no "Arks of Reprieve." I marvel at what Marta Werner and Jen Bervin have done; they've captured the violence of Emily Dickinson, that scratch of sound, that profusion of indecipherable scrapings— the floating plus signs and flying crosses and question marks—and sculpted Dickinson's "gorgeous nothings" into an astounding visual field; but even after *The Gorgeous Nothings* was taken out of its archival box and published between covers in 2013, with a preface by Susan Howe, I began to fear that we may all be caught up in a Swiftian satire, where textual scholars battle readers bound to the contours of the printed page. I myself still cling to Thomas H. Johnson's old, worn version of Dickinson's poems, that musty antique with all its errors, where the Promethean poet might be ripped right out of her alchemist's shop, but where I can still relish in the constant syncopations, and read the poems as a relentless series of jagged lines that shatter like bombs on the page, though much of this syncopation, I admit, comes from Johnson's own artifice as an editor.

Susan Howe is correct, of course, when she says that even R. W. Franklin in his variorum edition of *The Collected Poems* (1998) was blind to the visual and acoustic fireworks of all the poems and, in particular, the late fragments, while Marta Werner and Jen Bervin, among a few other scholar-artist-poets, "have dared to show us the ways in which what we thought we saw was not really what was there."

Howe talks about the sense of chance. "Viewing these 'envelopes' as visual objects, while at the same time reading her words for sound and sense, one needs to seize upon luck and accident—slips on paper slips." And that's what Marta and Jen Bervin have recorded, the mind in pure motion, Dickinson's conscious and unconscious struggles to find the right *envelope* for her desires.

Dickinson scholar Jerome McGann insists that we must respect the "regular irregularities" of these texts, where each scrap becomes "an unrhymed shard of verse." Or, as Marta Werner says, Dickinson displays an "astonishing recklessness" in these letter-poems and subverts all our expectations "by the snapping or short-circuiting of lyrical cables. In place of melody and measure come suddenness and syncope."

Dickinson has her own magical eye and hand that map out the territory of the slit-open envelope as if she were a mountain climber creating ridge after ridge, sculpting each little mountain of words with her pencil, while she hears whatever she wants in a willful way. She hints at this in a letter to Higginson.

> . . . *The Ear is the last Face.*
> *We hear after we see.*   [Letter 405, January 1874]

Marta and Jen Bervin have gone through the looking glass and brought us a very perverse Alice with a pencil in her hand. Dickinson's pencil strokes, "often slanting to the right, give the impression of a hand pressed forward by some force external to it." That rhythmic arrangement of words in a white field "promotes a curiously hypnotic effect, tranquil, without ever being still, and invites both eye and mind toward a prolonged act of gazing. . . . At last, these manuscripts function like mirages: The small squares of paper seem to dilate in space large enough to walk around in—or vanish through."

"Nothing," Bervin says, was a totemic—and defiant—word for Dickinson.

> *By homely gifts and hindered words*
> *The human heart is told*
> *Of nothing—*
> *"Nothing" is the force*
> *That renovates the World—*   [Fr1611]

Nothingness was her own divine condition in her manuscripts, both early and late; we can all imagine ourselves vanishing deep within her texts. That's the hold she has on us. It's dangerous to read Emily Dickinson, and it's always been, even in the nineteenth century, when "The Snake" ("A narrow fellow in the grass"), was robbed from her and published in the *Springfield Republican* in 1866, without her knowledge or her punctuation and a title "pinned" to the text; the *Republican*'s readers must have been mesmerized a little, and some, at least, left "Zero at the Bone." They had their own taste of *nothing*, and we still have it after 150 years.

4

IF THERE'S A MAGICAL MUSE BEHIND *The Gorgeous Nothings*, as Marta Werner suggests, and a battling scholar who has helped bleach out that reductive portrait of Dickinson as a spinster genius decked in white, it's Susan Howe, a poet and critic who has dared with Emily Dickinson to dance at the edge of communicability in her own writing. Howe admires Melville and James Joyce, who shaped her sensibility, and who, like Dickinson, went to extremes and "worked away from audience. Sometimes they're so far ahead of their times, they're just nowhere—they're out there . . . and there's always a danger that you break off communication" and land in some cosmic space that's akin to madness, Howe told me in 2013. But we both agreed that this risk was necessary, and that there would have been no Emily Dickinson—or Melville—without such risk.

"We were born the same year," Howe reminded me. "We were born into the war." Both of us grew up amid the rumble of World War II, with all its uncertainties and fears, and mythical demons and heroes. But Howe was from Boston, Cambridge, and Beacon Hill, and I was from the Bronx. Her father, Mark DeWolfe Howe, was a historian and Harvard law professor who went away to war. So she barely knew him when she was a little girl. "I was about nine when my father came back from the war. He was by then almost a stranger and his reading to me at bedtime took such a hold on me that I never lost the sense of awe and bedazzlement with his reading of Charles Dickens," Howe told Tom Gardner in an earlier interview. And her own experience of *sharing* literature with her father wasn't so different from Marta's—"my father and I were undemonstrative shy New Englanders; the way we could best express affection was through reading aloud the words of others."

Howe graduated from the Boston Museum School of Fine Arts in 1961, with Dickinson already in her blood. Her maternal grandfather knew Colonel Higginson, had letters from him, and the New England side of her family was steeped in Dickinson lore. Howe was seduced by Dickinson when she began to incorporate words into her own paintings, and sensed how palpable and tactile Dickinson's images were, as if the poet had scratched words upon her own skin. She would come to Dickinson once again through another act of reading, many years later. It was 1974, and she was living on Christopher Street in Greenwich Village as an artist who had begun to shift from painting to poetry. Her aunt, Helen, who lived uptown, on the corner of Fifth Avenue and Ninety-seventh Street, was bedridden and about to die. Sewall's biography of Dickinson had just been published, and Aunt Helen was much too feeble to read the book on her own. "I felt vividly how tiny and birdlike she was in that solid Manhattan building," as birdlike, perhaps, as Emily Dickinson.

So Howe immersed herself in Sewall and felt "called" to the Dickinson clan; her own father could have been Edward Dickinson—"not only was he a lawyer, but he was a representative of the old New England type. . . . I understood her sense of awe and devotion in relation to him. I understood why she couldn't leave home."

But it was still hard for me to grasp that Howe, who had done so much to revitalize the poet and deflect that image of the "spidery recluse" spun by so many other critics, still believed in the catchword of Dickinson's crippling agoraphobia.

"I'm slightly agoraphobic," she said in protest. "So I sympathize. But I really have a problem. I can hardly travel." She smiled and we wondered if all Dickinson *inebriates,* including Marta and myself, were turning into recluses, like that Prometheus on the second floor.

I asked her about the 1859 daguerreotype of a possible Dickinson sitting beside a possible Condor Kate.

Howe had a devilish grin. "I hope it's her. I love the old one! But I hope it's her, because she kind of looks powerful. She doesn't look like this grim thing."

And that is the "daguerreotype" of Dickinson that Howe has projected in her own work about a riddling poet of ruthless and mysterious power. "She isn't comforting." Dickinson never holds our hand. We have to leap into the dark with her. "She is a robber, as all great writers are. She read and read and read." She stole from Emerson, Dickens, the Brontë sisters, Shakespeare, the Bible, and her dictionary. "Noah Webster's pages bristle with brackets, dots, dashes, and slashes," she told Tom Gardner. Yet, I had to admit—there was no Lexicon for song, at least none that I knew of.

Her music and her topography were utterly her own. We'll never fathom why she wrote on one surface or another. "Did she simply grab something at hand to write an idea down as it flashed through her mind?" Did she choose to write her riddles on brown wrapping paper by pure chance? "Or is there something about the surface that matches the thought?"

All we will ever have are her strokes and her murmurs on the back of some envelope or other paper missile. "Every mark on a page is acoustic," Howe insists. The relationship "between sound, sense, and sight" is absolute. "She pushes that, so we cannot separate them." And what are we left with as readers? "The sound of what you say sings in your head at the moment you read. I don't care what the cognitive scientists say—the mind is theatre."

And that is the deepest delight we will ever have—with Dickinson.

"Emily Dickinson in a sense had a happy life. To accomplish that amount of work, at that fever pitch, you must have privacy, you must have shelter," Howe insisted. And she used every stratagem she had to protect that privacy. She was an artist "with ink on her hands. And fierce. A Calvinist." And a warrior.

The three "Master Letters" were a turning point for her, according to Susan Howe. She perfected her craft while writing them, that bewildering, satanic sense of play. "They're erotic," but there never was any *identifiable* suitor, any suitor at all. These letters were a supreme act of willfulness, where she finally "admitted to herself that she was Versuvian. It was like a conversion experience. Once she crossed that crisis, she was off. She was one with the Muse." And her poems flourished in that marvelous theater of her mind. "She went underground—or she took off and flew." And we've been looking for signs of her ever since.

NINE

—⊸∞⊶—

Cleopatra's Company

1

I'D FOUND THE BOOK IN A GARBAGE BARREL, with its battered green cover and gaudy gilt edges, like some mischievous archive or heirloom that dated right back to Dickinson. It seems that in 1869 one of the most celebrated authors on the planet, Harriet Beecher Stowe, had published with her sister Catherine a self-help book for women of a certain caste. The two sisters considered their book a compendium of household truths, born out of their own experiences as genteel ladies from one of New England's most brilliant clans—the Beechers, a brood of educators, ministers, abolitionists, writers, and editors.

The American Woman's Home represents the dreams and desires of the two sisters' social class. They warn their readers to be on guard against Irish servants, since these "daughters of Erin" can establish such "a reign of Chaos" in the kitchen that nothing will ever be restored.

The worst sin of all in creatures of good breeding is the "excessive exercise of the intellect and feelings," which can lead to derangement, idiocy, and an early grave. Beware of constant mental stimulus, such as novel reading, the sisters warn.

Emily Dickinson may have shared some of the sisters' prejudices—she also had problems with the Irish until Maggie Maher came along—but she could never have fit inside their cosmology. She was much too closeted, a witch of the Imagination obsessed with words, though she did bake her father's bread—"& people must have their puddings." [Letter 342a] Yet it's odd to hear Harriet Beecher Stowe rail against novel reading, when she herself wrote *Uncle Tom's Cabin* (1852), the most popular novel of the nineteenth century. She met Lincoln at the White House ten years later, and it's become part of America's string of myths that he bowed to her, took her hand in his paws, and said, "So this is the little lady who made this big war."

It no longer matters whether Lincoln actually uttered that remark. Harriet Beecher Stowe did help fire up the Civil War. She had moved in 1832 with all her clan to Cincinnati, Ohio, where her father, Lyman Beecher, was appointed head of Lane Theological Seminary. She was twenty-one at the time, and would meet her future husband, a widower, Calvin Stowe, who taught with Lyman Beecher at Lane. Cincinnati had become a providential place for Harriet Beecher Stowe. It was on the Ohio River, right across from Kentucky, a slave state; and for a while it seemed as if Kentucky and Ohio, a free state, would have their own civil war, as fugitive slaves fled across the river and seemed to melt right into the atmosphere. But not all Ohioans were abolitionists, and Harriet witnessed several race riots in Cincinnati, where black men were beaten to death. And then, in 1850, the Fugitive Slave Act was passed, which made a criminal of any man or woman who harbored such fugitives. Harriet felt outraged and decided to write her own antislavery novel.

Personal tragedy would weave itself into the fabric of the novel. Her eighteen-month old child, Charley, had died of cholera in the summer of 1849. "It was at his dying bed and at his grave that I learned what a poor slave may feel when a child is torn away from her. . . . I allude to this here because I have often felt that much that is in that book [*Uncle Tom's Cabin*] had at its root in the awful scenes and bitter sorrow of that summer," she wrote in 1852.

Edmund Wilson was one of the first literary critics to *resurrect* Harriet Beecher Stowe in his book about Civil War writing, *Patriotic Gore*

(1962). Wilson admits that Harriet had no interest in literature. "Her writings flowed onto the paper with little more punctuation than Molly Bloom's meditations in *Ulysses*." But *Uncle Tom's Cabin* had its own special lament and fierce, electric charge, as if God had written the book, said Harriet Beecher Stowe, and she was some silent witness to His power while in her own trance. And most of her characters seem under that same spell. "They come before us arguing and struggling," Wilson says, "like real people who cannot be quiet." Beecher Stowe hurls at us, under enormous compression, "a flock of lamenting and ranting, prattling and preaching characters, in a drama that demands to be played to the end."

2

FOR ALL HIS ASTUTENESS ABOUT Harriet Beecher Stowe, Wilson was deaf, dumb, and blind to Emily Dickinson, convinced that she's "the tragic case of a poet who was never allowed to emerge." He bought into every conventional and clichéd notion we have of her, perhaps encouraged by the poet herself, who preferred her subterranean existence in Amherst, the woman in white who conspired in her own vanishing act.

She's been a moving target from the moment she was first published in 1890 by Colonel Higginson and Mabel Loomis Todd. The colonel couldn't make up his mind about Dickinson and the "fossil bird-tracks" she left on the page in that peculiar script of hers, and the piecemeal publication of her poems also resembles prehistoric bird tracks, with every sort of mystery and mutilation of texts. Even in 1955, when Thomas H. Johnson gathered all her poems in three volumes, not as a combatant in the Dickinson wars, but as a renowned scholar, he left us with his own "imprint" of partial truths.

"Emily Dickinson," he writes in his foreword, "was born to her talent but she felt no dedication to her art until she was about twenty-eight years old, in 1858. By 1862, her creative impulse was at flood tide, and by 1865 the greater part of her poetic energies were spent."

I suspect she was honing her craft long before 1858; we can feel this preening art in her early letters to Sue. And we shouldn't be misled by the fascicles as the mark of her seriousness and devotion. No one can really tell us why she copied out her poems on gilt-edged paper, in her fairest hand, and "stabbed" them together into little booklets. The forty fascicles, Marta Werner reminds us, are "like forty locked doors." And Martha Nell Smith writes in *Rowing in Eden*: "The primary project of the fascicles may well be to expose the failure of any narrative to sustain that which is outside itself." They could have been Dickinson's own desperate desire to hermetically seal herself inside her poems and create some semblance of order. And they could have been written *long* before she began to encapsulate and embalm them with her needle and thread. We have this flurry of fascicles, this "flood tide," as Johnson says, and then a waning of her powers, according to him. But after her second trip to Cambridge, in 1865, and her suspicions that she might go blind, and after Carlo died, her writing went underground. There were fewer fair copies, fewer and fewer poems, yet greater flourishes with the pen. "The handwriting is fierce," according to poet Amy Clampitt. It is also more and more insular and secretive, as if, suggests Martha Nell Smith, these flourishes had little to do with the "expectations created by type-face" and "practically qualify as a new form of spelling," and perhaps even a new, protean language and form of art. Dickinson herself gives us a hint of this *inversion* in one of her "radical scatters," swooped up by Johnson as PF 30:

> *Did you ever read one of her Poems backward, because the plunge from the front overturned you? I sometimes (often have, many times) have—A something overtakes the Mind—*

The "her" referred to in this fragment is tantalizing and disturbingly ambiguous. Such a prescription couldn't apply to Dickinson's favorite female poet—that Dark Lady, Elizabeth Barrett Browning, whose meter was regular enough and who wouldn't have to be read topsy-turvy. Dickinson could only be talking about herself. She was her own Dark Lady with brilliant red hair.

—*A something overtakes the Mind*—

That was the single mark of her composition; she had no other—the Mind moving at its own miraculous and irregular pace, even if she may have revised each poem to the end of her life. But she worked with her own sense of abandon, and we must shut our eyes and abandon ourselves to Dickinson's votive powers, follow "the trajectory of her desire to inscribe herself outside all institutional accounts of order," as Marta Werner herself has done in *Emily Dickinson's Open Folios.* Like Susan Howe, Werner has entered that void where Dickinson seemed to thrive as a poet—

> *Emerging from an Abyss and entering it again—that is Life, is it not?* [PF 32]

Poetry is precarious, Howe reminds us. "If you follow the word to a certain extent, you may never come back." And that's why none of us can claim her, and so few theories about her time or her gender reveal very much about her art. "I think she may have chosen to enter the space of silence, where power is no longer an issue, gender is no longer an issue, voice is no longer an issue, where the idea of a printed book appears as a trap."

Dickinson was an outlaw from the day she began to scribble those strange, elliptical songs and scatterings. "One note from/One Bird," she wrote in pencil on the torn seal of an envelope. [PF 97; manuscript: "A 320"] She was that bird, singing to herself and a select society—Sue, of course, and her Norcross cousins, Condor Kate for a little while, Sam Bowles. . . . But even her most intimate recipients may never have been part of the same ruthless voyaging with words—flights from her pencil or pen—where she was testing her plumage and the purposeful stutter of her songs, with each flight "a dart that returns immediately to the sender," as Marta Werner warns us.

She was a hunter of words—with her Yellow Eye, her emphatic Thumb, lost somewhere in language, with a killer's instinct. "Freedom to roam poetically means freedom to hunt," says Susan Howe. "The poet is an intermediary hunting form beyond form, truth beyond theme through woods of words tangled and tremendous." It also means that the Loaded Gun of Dickinson's ruthless, aggressive art had to stare right back at "the aggression in God's yellow eye of Creation" without blinking once. Yellow was a fearsome color for Dickinson, a color that could freeze the bones. And she lived with it much longer than most writers did.

Her apprenticeship was lifelong. That's why she's unlike any other poet. She never really left her workshop. And why should she? Never mind the oddities of her script—"in holograph," says Martha Nell Smith, "Dickinson's poems visually control the page, while in print the white space of the page practically consumes the poems, minimizing them," and emasculating the words and her line breaks. She wasn't her own printer, unlike William Blake. Nor was she her own editor—the variants were part of her poetic stream. The fascicles were a *strategy,* not a form of self-publication. She had no need for that. They were a poet's private catalogue, her inventory, her stock. Perhaps she had to halt her own "yellow eye of Creation" to *codify* her poems in what Martha Nell Smith calls her "presentation script." But that flourish was for no one but herself. She never shared these packets of poems with her sister, her brother, or with Sue, her closest collaborator. There's a hint of this deep isolation in a poem of hers that Franklin attributes to the second half of 1863. It's found in Fascicle 32:

The Tint I cannot take—is best—
The Color too remote
That I could show it in Bazaar—
A Guinea at a sight—

The fine—impalpable Array—
That swaggers on the eye
Like Cleopatra's Company—
Repeated—in the sky . . .　　[Fr696]

We could juggle the meaning of these lines forever as we assemble Dickinson's clueless clues. Art versus Nature, or the soul's "Moments of Dominion" that fracture the poet and leave *her* soul "with a Discontent/Too exquisite—to tell—"?

But the *Tint* she cannot take is the public avowal of her poetry, with its "impalpable Array" that she could show "A Guinea at a sight." Her tint of color would swagger in the eye "Like Cleopatra's Company"—the retinue of a queen—"Repeated—in the sky," until it fades and disappears into the dark; or mutates, as Helen Vendler suggests, "into the blank and unfeeling 'Prank' of Snow." Cleopatra is the poet's catchword for Sue, as we know. And Dickinson often becomes a cross-dresser in her letters and poems, a forlorn Antony, wooing an implacable queen with words as her only device. But she isn't wooing Cleopatra in the poem. She'd distancing herself from the public retinue of publishers and queens.

Like some meticulous truant and weaver of webs, she was building her own labyrinth, with the finest silken cords. She wasn't looking for illumination, but for something else. "Writing traces the way to get lost: in the aftermath of logic, on the moor-body of imagination," writes Marta Werner, who has followed these illusive, contradictory traces as best she can. We must enter the labyrinth with Emily Dickinson, which means we can never really trust the dating of her untitled and undated poems, or have a definitive reading of her script, as Theodora Ward attempts to do in "Characteristics of the Handwriting." Ward gives a year-by-year account of the changes in her script from 1850 to 1886, the year of Dickinson's death. For example:

> 1861: "Noticeable change in appearance: letters elongated and uneven, as if written with excess of nervous energy . . .
> 1871: "Capitals are larger. Fewer ligations . . .

1874: "Writing in ink reaches maximum size—sometimes only one word on a line.

1885: "Further exaggeration of all characteristics described in 1884; letters further apart and irregular.

1886: "Large, loose, and badly formed, showing physical weakness."

We could be hovering over Dickinson, watching her flourish and watching her die with a brutal, regular logic. But, as Werner reminds us, there's a music to the poet's script that defies any logic: poems morph into "word-paintings" that cannot be so easily categorized; her alphabet is like "a drift of birds" out of a dream, where "dashes become waved or wandlike, the streaming ascenders and descenders of the *ds* and *ys* resemble lighted wicks," and we are far removed from a world where Dickinson is trying to mimic pages of print, as Ward seems to suggest. Graphologist Susanne Shapiro believes that Ward was on "a dangerous mission" the moment she attempted to date the poems in terms of the size and slant of Dickinson's script, that she's utterly in the dark when confronted with an unusual trait and doesn't know how to interpret the "non script"—that is, the spacing between individual letters and words.

Shapiro is no foreign intruder or neophyte in regard to the poet. She delivered a paper—"Secrets of the Pen: Emily Dickinson's Handwriting"—before a conference of the Emily Dickinson International Society at Mount Holyoke College, in August 1999, in which she analyzes a late letter-poem to Sue [Letter 910, about 1884] where "the spaces between the words often exceed the size of the words themselves."

B a n q u e t s   h a v e
n o   Seed,   or
B e g g a r s   w o u l d
s o w   them —   [Letter 910; manuscript: "HCL B 88"]

The graphologist's term for this peculiar spacing is "*rivers.*" And such rivers reveal a drifting away, as if each letter were its own private

cosmos, or, as Shapiro says, "an island of its own." According to Shapiro, "She was like a wounded animal." This has nothing to do with
her precarious mental state, as Shapiro believes, but with the almost
aggressive joy of her *wound* as a writer. Her own words had sundered
her. "You cannot solder an Abyss/With Air—" [Fr647] She was rampant, as she strove through that private domain of her calligraphy, her
Sahara of endless patches, where the world of print and pagination had
no meaning and no place.

It isn't clear when she got into the habit of scratching her little
syncopations on slivers of paper, slit-open envelopes, etc. Dickinson's
earliest "envelope-poem" dates from around 1864, the year she ended
her habit of "stabbing" her poems into little booklets, and embarked
on less ambitious projects. But I suspect the reverse was true, that
her mind was taking her along another route, toward a different kind
of rapture—the dissolution of language, as if her mind was much
too quick for the trappings of meter, for poetry itself, and all she
could encode was the stuttering of words. "The cometary pace of her
thought determines her choice of materials—whatever lies close by—
and is registered in the disturbance of the scribal hand," as if writing
itself had become a form of stutter—and she was ripping the notion
of the lyrical into shreds.

In several scraps that may have been meant for Judge Lord, she
writes:

[Antony's remark]
to a friend , " since
Cleopatra   died   "
is   said   to   be
the   saddest   ever
lain   in   Language —
That   engulfing
'Since "   — [Letter 791, about 1882; manuscript: "A 741b"]

Dickinson is referring to her favorite Shakespearian duet, the saga of Antony and Cleopatra that keeps knocking around in her head. Enraged, fearing that Cleopatra has betrayed him, Antony vows to kill her. Cleverer than he is, Cleopatra pretends to have slain herself. And Antony cannot recover.

> *Since Cleopatra died*
> *I have lived in such dishonour that the gods*
> *Detest my baseness. I, that with my sword*
> *Quarter's the world, and o'er green Neptune's back*
> *With ships made cities, condemn myself to lack*
> *The courage of a woman . . .*

After a bit of flamboyant posturing, he falls upon his sword, *womanish* in his own way, only to learn that Cleopatra is still alive. And all we can do is ponder how Dickinson, the Antony of her own isolated court, must have identified with his lines:

> **That   engulfing**
> **'Since   "** . . .

What were the circumstances around this "radical scatter"? Was she feeling slighted by her own Cleopatra—Sue? Or had Language itself become "Cleopatra's Company," a kind of hopeless retinue, and she herself engulfed within its snares? So she had to disembowel her own Lexicon, sing with stutters like that lone songbird "in the centre of Dissolution." She was the new queen of Pompeii, her staccato arias falling into a void.

> *Pompeii—All its (the) occupations crystallized—Everybody gone*
> *away.* [PF 100]

3

B UT THERE WAS STILL SUE, a most enigmatic queen of Amherst, the commissar of culture, who enraptured and puzzled Emily Dickinson for over thirty years.

Susan knows she is a Siren—and that at a word from her, Emily would forfeit Righteousness . . .   [Letter 554, mid-June, 1878]

Susan was restless her entire life. She may have had a "fling" with Kate Scott at Utica Female Academy, may have been in love with Sam Bowles, who was some kind of secret Lothario, and at times she was like Dickinson's own dominatrix, with the poet pleading for whatever little affection she could get (at least in the deep chill of Dickinson's letters and poems). Sue was a greater riddle than Emily or Kate, because we do not have any tickets to her wants and desires. She's "a dead spot," undecipherable, according to Christopher Benfey. It's as if she disappeared inside her own mantle as housewife, mother, and mistress of the arts, and seems like a somnambulist going through her traces, trapped in some hypnotic spell.

In "Annals of the Evergreens," the chronicle of her *adventures* as Amherst's ruling matron, she summons up Harriet Beecher Stowe's visit to Amherst in the summer of 1872; the novelist was benumbed, in a kind of perpetual shock; not only had she lost a son to cholera in 1849 but her daughter Georgiana had become a morphine addict, and her own favorite, her son Fred, an alcoholic captain who had been wounded at Gettysburg, sailed to California in 1871 on a ship bound for the Far East "and vanished into thin air."

So she'd come to Amherst to spend the summer and fall with Georgiana, who was married to the town's new Episcopal rector, and still addicted to morphine. And, of course, the mistress of the Evergreens swooped up Harriet Beecher Stowe. "I remember her distinctly as the light from the chandelier [fell] upon her mobile face, her eyes twinkling with fun and merriment, her forehead covered with soft brown curls, confined with a band of black velvet, as seen in her pictures."

Harriet Beecher Stowe must have had Fred and Georgiana on her mind. "I knew she was taciturn at times," Sue recalls, and invites Harriet on a carriage ride into the country. But there's no mention of that other *writer* in town, Sue's sister-in-law, the supposed agoraphobic who lived right across the lawn. And it's hard to imagine that Harriet Beecher Stowe and the Queen Recluse ever met. What did they have in common other than their social caste? One had written a novel that was a tinderbox full of inflamed caricatures and operatic escapades that millions could recite, and the other was utterly unknown and unremarked, with a tinderbox inside her head. But Dickinson's little cousin Loo found some resemblance between the two women. In 1904, after her own dead cousin had become a "public poet," Loo would declare in a letter to the editors of the Boston *Woman's Journal:*

> *Mrs. Harriet Beecher Stowe wrote her most wonderful sentences on slips of paper held against the kitchen wall while she was hovering over culinary formations. And I know that Emily Dickinson wrote most emphatic things in the pantry, so cool and quiet, while she skimmed the milk; because I sat on the footstool behind the door, in delight, as she read them to me. The blinds were closed, but through the green slats she saw all those fascinating ups and downs going on outside that she wrote about.*

It almost sounds like a recital, the way Dickinson had once invented tunes on the piano for Kate and Sue, at the Evergreens. And considering her own sensitivity to sunlight, she would have skimmed the milk within that little dark wall of green slats, and scrawled a few lines on a scrap of paper, tapped them out like a timpanist to Loo, though her little cousin didn't have an inkling of that staccato rage in her lines—no one did.

Yet it was 1904, long past the furor over Harriet Beecher Stowe and her antislavery novel, and suddenly she was as subterranean as Emily

Dickinson—more of a renegade and less of a Christian lady than we might have imagined. Her novel was practically out of print. She'd been so successful in 1852 because she appealed to a female audience of Christian mothers, who had suffered and lost children of their own, and could identify with Eliza Harris, a black Jane Eyre with "bright" skin, who leapt across the ice of the Ohio River with her son Harry in her arms, while the slave catchers pursued them with their dogs, always a couple of *wrinkles* behind in the plot. They all belong to a land of half-forgotten ghosts—the murderous and comic slave-catchers, the little Christian saints, and the evil plantation owners, such as Simon Legree. "The Lord never visits these parts," says Cassy, the mysterious stranger who rises out of this heart of darkness.

Legree is a nineteenth-century gargoyle, with his bullet head and hairy arms, but Cassy, his slave mistress, a refugee from a New Orleans brothel, is a much more modern ghost, and she haunts the novel in a way that none of the other characters ever can. Cassy's lament wasn't "written" by God, but by Harriet Beecher Stowe; it is her "work in throes," and it contains a lexicon and a music that is absent from the rest of the novel, as if she had entered into that sumptuous and sexually charged world of New Orleans, with its quadroon balls, and gives us its splendor and degraded stink.

Cassy is already used up when we first meet her at the plantation, with her gaunt body and dark eyes. But her mystery and her musk pervade Legree's mansion. Harriet Beecher Stowe paints her as a wild woman, bewitched, half mad, but reveals her own witchery, her own mad song, as if she has inhabited Cassy's demons, Cassy's pain, not as a ventriloquist, or an adept puppeteer, but as someone who has found that soft, violent poetry at the edge of madness. Cassy had to "rescue" her own little boy from the torment of slavery by suckling him to death with laudanum. And I wonder how much of Harriet's own unconscious despair was compressed into Cassy's tale, with a murderous rage she would never reveal again.

That rage reminds me of Dickinson, where language explodes like terrifying splinters. It's as if Miss Emily, the patrician poet from a privileged and protected New England town, were Cassy's secret sister. She was no quadroon, of course, never visited New Orleans and its midnight balls, never had any children to lose, and she had freckles, rather than Cassy's creamy white complexion, but both seemed to erupt out of a similar void. Simon Legree can descend into hell, but Cassy has nowhere to go. She's lost in the maelstrom, like that defiant Belle of Amherst with her amber eyes. And Cassy is much too defiant in her strange absence-presence to be just another victim in a novel about victimization. She's outside Harriet's evangelical reach. She's a poet-witch who's as violent and mercurial as history. And we, as readers, are caught between her outbursts and her moody withdrawals.

Dickinson was another poet of outbursts. "Why don't we talk about Dickinson and violence?" Christopher Benfey asked while I was with him at Mount Holyoke. "What does she say? 'I measure every Grief I meet/With narrow, probing eyes' [Fr550]—it's all violence, all the time." But there's a contradiction, a rupture in all that agony. "She is the great poet of pauses, the great poet of rest, the great poet of silence. . . . She knows what silence is."

We cannot imagine Dickinson as another Julia Ward Howe, going to sleep one night in November of 1861 at Washington's Willard Hotel and waking up with the "Battle Hymn of the Republic" bouncing inside her brain.

"Unto the Dead/There's no Geography—"[Fr476], Dickinson sings in her own battle hymn of apocalyptic thunder. There's no redemption, no healing, only a world of tin behind God's "terrible swift sword." We've all sunk into "Miles on Miles of Nought—" [Fr522] And she herself "Went out upon Circumference," where no one could listen, no one else could see. She was all alone, "too proud—for Pride." [Fr705] Suddenly the world itself has vanished, with all its battles and its watch fires.

"He lived the Life of Ambush" [Fr1571B], she wrote, talking about herself and the "Yellow Whip" [Fr1248] of her own words. And finally we come back to the most apocalyptic of all her poems. "My life had stood a loaded gun" may be a woman's war cry, a chant about Dickinson own aggression, her own sexuality, but it's also a poem about the end of the world, masquerading as a fairy tale about a huntsman who carries off a bride he's never even met—his Loaded Gun—on a honeymoon that's also a massacre, a shooting spree in those "Sovereign Woods" the Master owns. We can call him God or the Devil. It's of no real consequence—it's a godless world, fraught with evil, a slaughterhouse, ruled by the Master and his surrogate, the speaker's "Sovreign" Yellow Eye.

And Dickinson's "Whip lash" music, the violence of her images, her ability to stun us with "A perfect—paralyzing Bliss—" [Fr767], and with sounds "Soft as the massacre of Suns" [Fr1146]—seem outside morality, untamed, untouched. She may have seen "New Englandly" [Fr256], but with a wilder heart.

TEN

The Witch's Hour

1

ADRIENNE RICH COMES CLOSEST to understanding the dilemma that Dickinson faced most of her life in a village where any female without the "Title divine" of marriage and motherhood was looked upon with suspicion and deep distrust. "For motherhood," Rich tell us, "is the great mesh in which all human relations are entangled, in which lurk our most elemental assumptions about love and power." But that entanglement comes at a great risk, as Dickinson must have known. Women who were neither wives nor mothers in nineteenth-century Amherst fell afoul of the quasi-religious belief that female creativity could only exist "within the mothering role." Everything else was considered mere decoration or some kind of witch's work. Once Dickinson lost Carlo, and morphed into an old maid, she was often mocked as the half-cracked village muse, and had to pay a price for that unholy power in the pencil at her side.

Forced to become Amherst's first secret agent, she hid herself in that white dress, masked her bisexuality, while her language molted like feathers and could make her words liquefy. She was an enchantress, whose intellect and imagination had utterly isolated her. She could serenade Susan, share some of her poems, but never her *tradecraft*. She shared that with no one. She may have scribbled poems in the pantry, recited them to her little cousin Loo, but she really wrote in stealth at her lozengelike desk upstairs. She was her own prisoner of war, who pulled lightning from the chaos in her head, danced on her toes, broke down syntax like bits of crockery, and then reassembled the broken bits in a way no one had ever done before.

2

"TALENT HITS A TARGET NO ONE ELSE CAN HIT; genius hits a target no one else can see," said Arthur Schopenhauer, the German philosopher of doomed desires. And how can we ever explain the riddle of Emily Dickinson's genius?

I kept probing Christopher Benfey while I was with him at Mount Holyoke, on Dickinson's *grounds*. Benfey believes he has found some clues in the idiot savant twins that British-American author and neurologist Oliver Sacks describes in his book of essays, *The Man Who Mistook His Wife for a Hat* (1985), about the poetic world of patients with neurological disorders. The twins savored numbers in much the same manner that Dickinson savored words, according to Benfey. "Every number has a kind of taste and a character and a face."

Like clouds, I said, that could shift their shape in Hamlet's mind as he taunts Polonius, one more of his adversaries, real or imagined.

> HAMLET: *Do you see yonder cloud that's almost in shape of a camel?*
>
> POLONIUS: *By th'mass, and 'tis like a camel indeed.*
>
> HAMLET: *Methinks it is like a weasel.*
>
> POLONIUS: *It is backed like a weasel.*
>
> HAMLET: *Or like a whale.*
>
> POLONIUS: *Very like a whale.*

"And for Dickinson," Benfey says, "every word looks like a weasel or it looks like an ocean or it looks like death, or you go inside it and it smells a certain way. It may be that certain poets—Shakespeare,

Rimbaud, Dickinson—had that kind of gift. So Rimbaud has to go to North Africa to get away . . ."

"From words, like one of Oliver Sacks' idiot savants," I said.

Sacks had worked with those twins for eighteen years, and in all that time he could never unravel their mystery—diagnosed as autistic and retarded, they could still document "the tiniest visual details of their own experience . . . as if they were unrolling or scrutinizing an inner landscape, a mental calendar." John and Michael had their own kind of "absolute pitch" for numbers, "could hold in their minds . . . an immense mnemonic tapestry." Numbers had become their harmony, their musical scales. Sacks wondered if "the need to find or feel some ultimate harmony or order is universal of the mind," and the twins were only the rarest example of this need. "Numbers for them are holy," and also friends—"perhaps the only friends they have known in their isolated, autistic lives."

They live in their own heaven of numbers the way Dickinson lived in a heaven—and hell—of words. And the neural pattern of words in her mind may have been as limitless as the patterning of numbers was to the twins. I suspect that's why she seemed so strange. She was always somewhere else, in her own "thought-scape," like the twins. But she wasn't an idiot savant locked away in an asylum. She was born in a college town with its own religious fervor and little else. So where did her genius come from? She didn't ride out of some cradle of creativity. Her maternal grandfather was reckless and melancholic and died in disgrace. Her father was a failed congressman who had no intellectual pursuits. He would buy his poet daughter novels and forbid her to read them. And Austin, her beloved brother, did his best to mutilate her legacy, as he scissored Sue, his embattled wife, out of whatever fragments and letters he could lay his hands on. And yet Dickinson thrived with that cosmic sense of hers, in some hot cauldron at the edge of chaos.

I think of something John Updike said when he was a young man, about to begin his career as a novelist, poet, and satirist. "There is no danger of my eking out an existence in a garret"—and Emily's room was like the garret of a privileged prisoner. "If all I have is talent, industry and intelligence, I should be able to please enough people to make money at it."

But he was much more ambitious than that. "We do not need men like Proust and Joyce; men like that are a luxury, an added fillip that an abundant culture can produce only after the more basic literary need has been filled," he wrote to his parents in 1951, while a freshman at Harvard who would become editor of the *Lampoon*, the college's mythic humor magazine, and would graduate ninth in his class. "We need great artists who are willing to accept restrictions, and who love their environments with such vitality that they can produce an epic out of the Protestant ethic. . . . Whatever the failings of my work, let it stand as a manifesto of my love for the time in which I was born."

He would produce such an epic in his Rabbit Angstrom novels, with their melodious and tactile verve, but I can't imagine Dickinson with the same lucid drive or vision of her place on the planet; she was little more than a patrician chattel a hundred years earlier, in 1851; even then she was an outlaw, who had defied Mary Lyon at Mount Holyoke, and couldn't have been in love with the time she was born in, a bisexual woman in a town where most other belles had to take part in that passive hunt for husbands, or be maligned as old maids.

And what an old maid she was, on her own sexual prowl, and perhaps she was a pointillist of her own time, talking about her apocalyptic rage as a woman in a culture that didn't permit female lust and female power. And so she smashed the pillars of that Protestant ethos, like some Samson in a white dress, and she went through the looking glass in a way that would have frightened Updike and most other men, and dealt in dreams and hallucinations, with all the tradecraft of a witch.

3

ALWAYS FELT LIKE A DETECTIVE in regard to Emily Dickinson, that I could map her genius somehow. I was convinced she was left-handed, and that her brain had its own unusual nodes, as left-handers sometimes do, that she was wired in a different way. Yet there's no evidence that Dickinson was left-handed, alas, or even a crypto-lefty trained to scratch around with her right hand—not a word in her chatty letters to Abiah Root, her childhood friend, not a word from Vinnie, the sister who sometimes slept at her side, and nothing at all in the *remembrances* and mythic lies of Martha Dickinson Bianchi about her mysterious aunt; the white housedress we have at the Dickinson museum tells us nothing, and the two daguerreotypes with their mirror images show her favoring her right hand, but suppose Dickinson was a righty with the crossed wires of a left-hander. Her brain had to have had extra plugs. Her poems read like Shakespeare's soliloquies crammed into one polyphonic voice, like a great rush of wind that leaves us breathless, the blood beating in our brains. How did she compose? "Letters are scrawls, turnabouts, astonishments, strokes, cuts, masks," writes Susan Howe in *The Birth-mark*. Deaf to rules of composition, as Howe suggests, she invents her own rules. "Spaces between letters, dashes, apostrophes, commas, crosses form networks of signs"—like synapses in the brain—"and discontinuities. . . . Who knows what needs she has?"

Certainly they weren't about recognition, and some meteoric rise to fame, or she would have ridden on Higginson's back to wherever she had to go. How did she survive as long as she did, a woman with perfect pitch, like those autistic twins, who lived in a world of the deaf, where no one but they themselves had the music of numbers in their ears? And so they *dueled* with themselves, caught in a colossal word of infinities. And that, I think, is how Dickinson survived, within the dueling hemispheres of her brain. What other project could she have had but to please herself—and stun herself at the same time. It was play so serious that she risked her own sanity.

And yet she played. And perhaps she did falter, did break down. And she reported her mental state like some cosmologist of the soul. At a time "So terrible," she tells her soul to sing, but the strings have "snapt," and her brain begins to laugh, "keeps giggling—still."

Could it be Madness—this? [Fr423]

There's nothing quite like that intensity of hers, as if she's burning from within. And it's curious how modern her lament is, how it even fits in with the Marine Corps and its latest advertisement campaign, attracting young men and women to dance deftly "Toward the Sound of Chaos." That could be Dickinson's very own dream song—and war cry.

Yet Oliver Sacks' idiot savants, with their wealth of numbers and mysterious inner lyricism, tell us more about creativity than all the miracles of brain research in the twenty-first century. "The Brain is just the weight of God—" [Fr598], Dickinson noted 150 years ago, like some neurologist in advance of her time. It's the most intricate *creature* in the universe, with synapses far more complex than the solar system.

Neuroscientist Nancy Andreasen suggests that during the act of creating, "the brain begins by *disorganizing*, making links between shadowy forms of objects or symbols or words or remembered experiences that have not previously been linked." When this happens, "associative links run wild," and the poet drifts into a dreamlike mental state, where "words, images, and ideas collide." It would be the witch's hour, where Dickinson danced closer and closer to the sound of chaos in her brain.

And so her isolation was essential, that "Scarlet prison" of hers upstairs [Fr411], where she was a female Jekyll and Hyde—she didn't garden or bake in her Scarlet prison, may not even have worn her white dress; she dreamt of blood, roaming in the "Sovreign Woods" of her mind, hunting, trapping words, while she searched for some infinity of her own, perhaps at the end of a carriage ride with the Angel of Death. She never really had to leave her room, since, as she told her Tutor, Colonel Higginson:

> It is solemn to remember that Vastness—is but the Shadow of the Brain which casts it—
> > All things swept sole away
> > This—is immensity—   [Fr1548]

And she longed to live in that immensity—she reached for the infinite whenever she scribbled a line. And she would have felt at home among modern philosophers and physicists, who believe more and more that there's no one *implacable* infinity. Instead, there's a grab bag of infinities, for mathematicians, cosmologists, theologians. There are flat infinities, hunchback infinities, etc. Recent studies of "the cosmic microwave afterglow of the Big Bang," where the universe began 13.7 billion years ago, suggest that *our* universe is just a tiny patch "embedded in a greater universal fabric that is, in a profound sense, infinite." Either it's a "monoverse," or "an infinite bubble bath of infinitely budding and inflating multiverses."

The implications have startled a number of modern physicists. If we have an infinite universe, where we can sample finite physical systems in an infinite way, we will get duplicates of everything, says Anthony Aquirre, an associate professor of physics at the University of California, Vera Cruz, whose field is theoretical cosmology.

"If I ask, will there be a planet like Earth with a person in Santa Cruz sitting at this colored desk, with every atom, every wave function exactly the same, if the universe is infinite the answer has to be yes."

This wouldn't have stunned Emily Dickinson, who would have stared out her window overlooking the Dickinson meadow and waited for her doppelgänger to arrive. There may be variants as well, an idiot savant who can play Bach like Glenn Gould, an Oliver Sacks who has become his own patient, or an Emily Dickinson who married a church warden, had five daughters, and never wrote a line in her life.

As science writer Natalie Angier reminds us, "The finite is nested within the infinite, and somewhere across the glittering, howling universal sample space of Buddha Field or Babel, your doppelgänger is hard at the keyboard, playing a Bach toccata."

We're almost back in Joyce Carol Oates' world of EDickinson-RepliLuxe, of variants and replicants, of a doll with a suede vagina and a relentless human heart. And if Dickinson's *immensity* is still out there, and we inhabit one finite speck of that "infinite bubble bath," then the poet may still be at her desk. And how shall we imagine her, writing poems that we still puzzle over, and she the greatest puzzle of all: an apprentice who was a master of her art. She had no vanity, no smallness of mind.

I'm tempted to compare her with van Gogh, who may have his doppelgänger in the heavens with the same missing ear. Like Dickinson, he was a master and a student at the same time. But he had a much shorter apprenticeship, and painted most of his masterpieces in the last year and a half of his life, often while he was locked away in the madhouse at Saint-Rémy.

He'd gone to Arles in 1888 to paint in the sun. He invited Gauguin to stay with him in the Yellow House, which he'd rented in hope of forming a little fraternity of painters. They quarreled, and in a drunken stupor, Vincent cut off his own ear. That wouldn't have seemed strange to Emily Dickinson, who often wrote about acts of self-mutilation, in order to sculpt herself as a man.

After his confinement at Saint-Rémy, he packed up and moved to a humdrum hotel, the Auberge Ravoux, in Auvers-sur-Oise, outside Paris. I went on a pilgrimage to Auvers-sur-Oise several years ago. The humdrum hotel is still there, much more pretentious now, and one can eat in the same café where Vincent ate, perhaps even sit at his table in the back. And for the price of a few euros, collected by a ticket taker at a little kiosk in the rear yard, I climbed upstairs and visited van Gogh's room. It was barren, with a tiny skylight and a cane-back chair; the walls were full of crust, the floor was made of barren boards, and I couldn't stop crying. I imagined him alone in that room, his mind whirling with colors, and his psychic space as primitive and forlorn as a lunatic's world. He might as well have remained in Saint-Rémy. He'd written to his sister Willemien while he was still in the madhouse. He mentioned his lost years, and his isolation, as hard to bear as exile—he was always alone.

And yet he completed seventy paintings in the seventy days he was in Auvers-sur-Oise. And the paintings he did in the fields beyond his tiny room and at the madhouse have an illumination, a wild rush of color, we had never seen before. They're like visual songs that could accompany Dickinson's lyrics on the page.

Adam Gopnik sees a kind of lesson in van Gogh's fate. "It is the moral luck of making something that no one wants in the belief that someone someday will." It is a long shot in a society of sure things. But this "moral luck" of van Gogh remains at odds with our own liberal civilization "that always, and usually intelligently, prefers compromise to courage."

And isn't it also the lesson of Emily Dickinson, that she was the longest of long shots, a poet who was thrust out of obscurity in spite of herself? Would we love her as much, revere her, if we hadn't encountered her first as the reclusive waif in the white dress, with tales of renunciation and unrequited romance, with butchered, bowdlerized versions of her poems that transformed her into an asexual nymph? We cannot dislodge or *dislimn* her from her own history, or the history of her poems, how they arrived, when they arrived, with all their accompanying myths. Perhaps we wouldn't summon her up in the same way without all those accoutrements that few other creators have. Van Gogh had his missing ear, the madhouse in Saint-Rémy, his claustrophobic room upstairs at the auberge in Auvers-sur-Oise, his brother

Theo, who lies next to him in a little boneyard beside the fields where Vincent's colors ran rampant, while the *limbs* of his suffering stick to us like Stations of the Cross.

And the Queen of Calvary? We have the Scarlet prison where she worked, now a shrine that's the main attraction of a museum devoted to her memory, but isn't it just as terrifying as Vincent's room, *barren* in its own way, with its bureau and sleigh bed? It was here, alone, in the turbulence of her own mind, she created poems and pictograms that are works of art, like some cave dweller of the nineteenth century with her own hieroglyphics. However unstable she might have been, moment by moment, she was fearless in her own work, or investigations, as we might call them, since she was as much an explorer as a poet, delving into landscapes where no one else had gone. And it's futile to define Dickinson in terms of gender or social station, or the topography of her own time. She was male and female, as we all are, at least in our dreams and acts of creation, and that's why her poems resonate with such force. She will continue to fuel our hunger and to baffle us, no matter how many portraits of her we uncover, or how many interpretations we have of every image. She's still out there "opon Circumference," where she'll always be hard to find.

CODA

—❦—

Sam Carlo

I'D BEEN TRYING TO TRACK DOWN SAM CARLO for the past several years, but I didn't have Dickinson's Yellow Eye or her Loaded Gun, and of course I failed. I wanted to know more about the second daguerreotype, how Sam Carlo had happened upon it. At least I could smile at the very mask of his name: Sam obviously stood for Sam Bowles, and what Carlo could he have had in mind other than Dickinson's dog? I liked his playful bent, but that didn't get me any closer to Sam.

Then, in January 2015, I wrote to Mimi Dakin, archivist at Amherst College, asking her permission to reproduce several items in the Dickinson collection for *A Loaded Gun*. Since a copy of the second *dag* was also housed in the same collection, I asked Mimi if she could put me in touch with Sam, the owner of the daguerreotype. I wanted to interview him. Mimi tried. The answer came back swiftly, like some damaging angel. Sam said no to my request, and his answer was irrevocable—he wanted nothing to do with me or my book. I wondered why. I e-mailed Mimi, saying that the second *dag* was critical to my argument about Dickinson's apocalyptic powers as a poet, that I coveted the second *dag*, and looked favorably upon Sam. Mimi passed my message on to him. He sent a message back that he *might* be willing to talk. And thus our elliptical dialogue began, with its own staccato rhythm.

He'd been burnt so many times, he said, ridiculed, told that the *dag* was a fake, and that he was a fraud. He called himself "partially cracked." Again I smiled, and knew I was entering that country of the Queen Recluse, as her "Tutor," Thomas Wentworth Higginson, had called Emily his half-cracked poetess. Finally Sam and I did talk on the phone one Friday morning. I was surprised to learn that he'd had no interest at all in Emily Dickinson before 1995. He was a daguerreotype collector who lived in the wilds of Vermont. His background was in economics and finance. He was sixty years old, he said.

He'd found the daguerreotype at a junk shop outside Great Barrington, Massachusetts. The junk shop's owner would buy "big house lots," clean out a place, and auction off an entire lot. "I wasn't out looking for Emily Dickinson stuff," Sam said. For him it was always a question of "trash and treasure," and often he could hardly tell the difference. He bought the *dag* for twenty-five bucks, found it at the back of a shelf. "Bingo!" Because he was involved in the nineteenth century in his daguerreotype hunts, he had a hunch that the woman on the left might be Dickinson. "The similarities were there. . . . She did look just like her to me. I'd seen the earlier daguerreotype. I'd devoured all my research books," Sam told me.

He quizzed the junk dealer about the new daguerreotype. "Where did you get this?"

"I got it from a house clean-out over by Springfield."

That's all the junkman would reveal.

"I ain't no writer," Sam would later declare in an e-mail. "I'm a detective basically," and he did a lot of detecting: He dove into Dickinson's archives, studied the 1847 daguerreotype, and compared it to his own. He scanned both images, and the deformity in her right eye seemed a bit too similar. The young, almost tubercular Emily of 1847 and the older, powerful woman on the left in the 1859 daguerreotype have a misshapen, flattish cornea, "and the dot of the ocular reflection to the light is way up and to the right" in both images.

"I spent a lot of time with an eye surgeon at Dartmouth," Sam said, and that surgeon, Dr. Susan Pepin, director of Neuro-Ophthalmology at the Dartmouth School of Medicine, who has an abiding interest in Emily and her eye problems, seemed to support Sam's thesis that the woman in the 1859 portrait bears startling similarities to the woman in the 1847 daguerreotype—both have a similar astigmatism and a similar corneal curvature.

"I've got Emily! I've got her eyes," he said.

But now Sam Carlo had a deeper problem—to identify the *other* woman in the *dag*. "For ten years I was stymied. It just gnawed at me. It was eating at my insides." And one night in 2005, while having a glass of wine, he opened Sewall's biography of Dickinson and landed right on a picture of Kate Anthon (i.e., Kate Scott). "I glanced down at the chin—that lady's got two moles on the side of the chin." Kate Anthon and the dark lady of the daguerreotype "had two of the exact same moles." This was "the bingo moment!" He now had a complete tale—Emily and Kate—even if he had no real provenance. He poured through Emily's letters and discovered that in an 1862 letter to Sam Bowles, Emily spoke about a mysterious image:

> *When you come to Amherst, please God it were* Today—*I will tell you about the picture—if I* can, *I will*— [Letter 252]

Sam believes that this "picture" was the second daguerreotype, taken when the young widow, Kate Anthon, arrived in Amherst in 1859 to visit Sue and fell in love with the poet. But now it's 1862; Kate has abandoned Emily, who writes to Bowles in Springfield "about a picture that's upsetting her tremendously." We get a glimpse of this anguish, according to Sam, in the penciled lines on the outside folded surface of an 1873 poem she had written to Kate but never sent:

> *We shun because we prize her Face*
> *Lest sight's ineffable disgrace*
> *Our Adoration stain* [Fr1430A]

"Sam Bowles was gaga over Kate Anthon," and would have prized the daguerreotype, but he couldn't reveal its existence to his children or his wife. "It goes into a box." Enter Sam Carlo, 133 years later. Sam is convinced that the *dag* he had snatched up, almost by accident, had come from a drawer in the Bowles' family house in Springfield, which the junkman from Great Barrington had cleaned out in 1995. And in a way, Sam's been sorry ever since. The *dag* has been driving him "fairly insane—I told Mimi [Dakin] it was a curse that I found it, really. A curse." But that didn't dampen his detective work.

Sam believes that the Dickinson clan—Austin, Sue, and Mattie— plotted to hide the poet's affection for Kate, but the chief culprit was Mabel Todd's daughter, Millicent, who in *Bolts of Melody* did hint at Emily's "disappointment in a too-much-loved woman friend." Yet after Rebecca Patterson published her book about the "riddle" of Emily's romance with another woman, Millicent cobbled together *Emily Dickinson: A Revelation* (1954), about Judge Otis Lord's courtship of Emily Dickinson. Lord was only one more in a very long line of mysterious and not so mysterious male suitors. Whether or not Emily's letters to Lord, which were never sent, may have been spliced together from bits and pieces, I still liked the idea of Emily manipulating that thunderous man, and used it in my own novel about Dickinson (I had not read Patterson's book at the time, since it had virtually disappeared, and the second *dag* had not surfaced yet.)

Still, my own fondness for Lord doesn't weaken Sam's argument. Otis Lord may have indeed been a "beard," used to cover up Emily's fling with Kate. How will we ever find out? So much of Dickinson's life has been redressed, like the first daguerreotype. We know her through her letters, poems, and fragments, which are every bit as deceptive as the deceptions that have been built around her. The fabric always tears as we try to approach her life through her lines. She's already gone by the time we get near. That's why Joseph Cornell's boxes on Dickinson are so revealing. They leave us with all the sadness of an empty room, all the scratches and violent pull of flight. Dickinson has not only fled; she's taken our entrails with her.

Almost none of us recover from reading Dickinson, Sam Carlo included. And I'm grateful that he's gone deep into the well, like some merman, and dredged up the second *dag*, which has its own miraculous provenance. Dickinson is a predator, and poor Kate seems to fall into some private infinity as she sits near the Loaded Gun.

Endnotes

EDITOR'S NOTE: The Selected Bibliography on pages 235–44 includes full references with all bibliographic details pertaining to the abbreviated citations used within this endnote section with the exception of the works of Shakespeare, which have been cited here in full. Each endnote starts with the page number on which the cited text begins.

Author's Note

8   "People like us": Overbye.

ONE: Zero at the Bone

17   "But always, from his polite replies": Luce, p. 63.

17   "But I'll have you know": ibid., p. 70.

18   "His voice haunted me": ibid., p. 71.

20   "For months, for years": Rich, p. 158.

20   "Narrowed-down by her early": ibid., pp. 159–60.

20   "I have come to imagine": ibid., p. 160.

21   "Here I became again": ibid., p. 161.

22   "the corseting of women's bodies": ibid.

22   "It is always what is under pressure": ibid., p. 162.

24   "I think it is a poem": ibid., pp. 172–73.

24   "If there is a female consciousness": ibid., p. 174.

25   "an extremely painful and dangerous": ibid., p. 175.

26   "wrote for the relief of": Higginson, "An Open Portfolio," p. 392.

27   "My Dear Mr. Higginson": Bingham, *Ancestors' Brocades,*
      pp. 169–70.

29   "the deliberate skirting of the obvious": Leyda, *Years and Hours,* vol.
      I, p. xxi.

29   "*isolates* her": ibid., p. xx.

29   "she wrote more *in time*": ibid., p. xx.

30   "rag-picking method": ibid., p. xxiii.

30   "riddling ellipsis": Paglia, p. 624.

31   "When Katie walks": Leyda, *Years and Hours,* vol. I, p. 367.

31   "with her dog, & Lantern!": ibid., p. 367.

32   "a helpless agoraphobic": Gilbert and Gubar, p. 583.

34   "Cotton Mather would have burned her": Tate, p. 27.

34   "We did an archaeological dig": Benfey, Interview.

34   "We know of no new friends": Habegger, p. 193.

Two: The Two Emilys—and the Earl

40   "One exaggerates, but it sometimes seems": Blackmur, p. 80.

40   "the playful ambiguity of a kitten": ibid., p. 86.

43   "shallow, self-centered, ineffectual": Cody, p. 42.

43   "*infantile* dependence": ibid., p. 47.

43   "one is led to conclude": ibid.

43   "great genius is not to be distinguished": Habegger, p. 622.

43   "truly a madwoman": Gilbert and Gubar, p. 583.

44   "hated her peculiarities": Bingham, *Ancestors' Brocades*, p. 86.

45   "too uncertain of her attractiveness": Cody, p. 96.

45   "suffered the tormenting paralysis": Howe, *My Emily Dickinson,*
      p. 60.

45   "with Promethean ambition": ibid., p. 18.

46   *"though I've always had a great aversion"*: Bingham, *Emily
      Dickinson's Home*, p. 89.

47   "*The fire-flies hold their lanterns high*": Sewall, *Life of Emily Dickinson*, p. 251.

48   "did not form an isolated and oppressed": Smith-Rosenberg, pp. 9–10.

48   "Girls routinely slept together": ibid., p. 22.

48   "but a shadowy appearance": ibid., p. 2.

48   "Women of Dickinson's class and century": Howe, *My Emily Dickinson*, p. 84.

50   *"for, I think, if you intend to be seen"*: Dickinson and Norcross, p. 172.

51   *"I cannot tell when I shall visit you again"*: ibid., p. 152.

51   "I know not what is in store for us": ibid., p. 137.

51   "the lawful promoter": ibid., p. 24.

51   "not to send another of such": ibid., p. 20.

51   "Pleasant dreams to you dear Edward": ibid., p. 134.

51   "My education is my inheritance": ibid., p. 58.

52   "I have many friends call upon me": ibid., p. 206.

52   "Have I not reason to fear": ibid., p. 173.

52   "with as little noise as possible": ibid., p. 206.

53   *"Sister! Why that burning tear"*: Habeggger, p.67.

53   "Language is first made": Murray, p. 116.

53   "No language acquisition": ibid.

54   *"I know of no one that I should prefer"*: Leyda, *Years and Hours*, vol.1, pp. 15–16.

54   "A warmer relationship with her mother": Cody, p. 103.

55   "between the abrupt ending": Bianchi, *Face to Face*, p. 103.

56   *"Just after we passed Mr Clapps"*: Leyda, *Years and Hours*, vol. 1, pp. 20–21.

56   "she calls it the *moosic*": ibid., p. 21.

57   *"She speaks of her father & mother"*: ibid., pp. 21–22.

57   *"Emily— no wonder you are astonished to hear"*: ibid., p. 23.

58   *"I cant tell you how lonely I was"*: ibid., p. 22.

59   "relatively inelastic spirit": Habegger, p. 32.

59   "this fluttery, timid woman": Sewall, *Life of Emily Dickinson*, p. 89.

59   "the mother, the usual provider": Gordon, p. 27.

59   *"Even Mrs. Dickinson's distaste for writing"*: Sewall, Letter to Leyda.

59   "went secretly to the paper hanger": Leyda, *Years and Hours*, vol. 1, p. 16.

60   "I attended church all day": Wolff, p. 63.

60   *"And I do indeed truly rejoice"*: Leyda, *Years and Hours*, vol. 1, p. 42.

60   "primitive, complex, and continuous": Murray, p. 62.

60   "key silent texts": Murray, p. 100.

62   "will wear away": Vendler, p. 353.

64   "complained about boils, dizziness": Habegger, p. 106.

65   *"Oh! Dear! Father is killing the horse"*: ibid., p. 252.

66   "boundaries within boundaries": Murray, p. 154.

66   "she explored the implications": Howe, *My Emily Dickinson*, p. 11.

68   *"Father says in fugitive moments"*: Sewall, *Life of Emily Dickinson*, p. 66.

68   "We cannot say of this woman": Blackmur, p. 85.

Three: Daemon Dog

69   "huge dog stalked solemnly beside them": Leyda, *Years and Hours*, vol. 2, p. 21.

69   "carelessness of form": Wineapple, p. 275.

70   *"Major Hunt interested her more"*: Leyda, *Years and Hours*, vol. 2, p. 14.

71   "Carlo seems to have accompanied Emily": Cody, p. 360.

71   "Dogs began as allies": Gopnik, "Dog Story," p. 49.

71   "tamer, man-friendly wolves": ibid.

71   "The dog will bark at a burglar": ibid., p. 51.

73   "Silent not merely for want of encouragement": Sontag, p. 142.

74   "all too common reality of a woman": ibid.

74   "as an unfortunate eccentricity": Sewall, *Life of Emily Dickinson,* p. 89.

74   "her backbone made of steel": Wineapple, p. 184.

74   "seems to exist outside of time": ibid., p. 101.

75   *"I sometimes shudder"*: Bingham, *Ancestors' Brocades,* p. 86.

76   "are the only creatures that have learned": Gopnik, "Dog Story," p. 51.

76   "tramping abroad with her dog": Murray, p. 97.

79   "prophetic vision of intergalactic nothingness": Paglia, p. 655.

82   "abattoir": ibid., p. 650.

83   "had a pretended version": Gopnik, "Dog Story," pp. 49–50.

85   "All power . . . including the power of love": Howe, *My Emily Dickinson,* p. 116.

85   "only mystery beyond mystery": ibid.

Four: Judith Shakespeare and Margaret Maher

87   "For it is a perennial puzzle": Woolf, p. 41.

87   "Imaginatively she is of the highest importance": ibid., pp. 43–44.

88   "as agog to see the world": ibid., p. 47.

88   "a gift like her brother's": ibid., p. 48.

88   "the heat and violence of the poet's heart": ibid.

88   "would certainly have gone crazed": ibid., p. 49.

88   "That refuge she would have sought": ibid., p. 50.

89   "spine crib": Adams, p. 7.

91   *"Stimulating and boring"*: Browning, p. xxxv.

91   "a cage-bird life": Leyda, *Years and Hours,* vol. 2, p. 388.

91   *"The works of women are symbolical"*: ibid.

94   "and is one of the oddest": Benfey, *Summer of Hummingbirds,* p. 244.

94   "a bird with wings outstretched": ibid., p. 245.

95   "streaming from its pyramidal smokestack": ibid., p. 247.

95   "suprising poems": Leyda, "Miss Emily's Maggie," p. 150.

96   "Every fence was employed to isolate": ibid., p. 164.

96   *"Maggie's brother is killed in the mines"*: ibid., p. 160.

97   *"I don't know whether it is day or night"*: ibid., pp. 156–57.

97   "The Dickinsons didn't like strangers": ibid., p. 153.

97   *"Mr. Dicksom said he would"*: ibid., p. 157.

98   "the North Wind of the family": ibid., p. 160.

98   "There was an invisible story": Murray, p. 18.

98   "a cacophonous tumbling kitchen": ibid.

98   "the most creative room in the house": ibid., p. 99.

98   "architecture of the unseen": ibid., p. 153.

98   "a seamlessness between the motions": ibid., p. 120.

99   "provide a halting": ibid., p. 123.

102   "balloons embody her imagination's pilgrimages": Snively, "Myself endued Balloon,", p. 1.

102   "Vehicles of beauty and danger": ibid.

102   "Surely Emily intuited that her maid would": Murray, p. 203.

102   "muse, lookout, and beckoner": ibid., p. 218.

103   "like the Wren": ibid.

103   "most interesting & most startling": Bingham, *Ancestors' Brocades*, p. 225.

103   "She had a Boston miniaturist create": Bernhard, p. 600.

103   "your unworth but true Maggie": Murray, p. 213.

104   "with aplomb": ibid.

104   "Little hussy": Gordon, p. 160.

104   "the most dangerous type of alien": Leyda, "Miss Emily's Maggie," p. 159.

104   "madness was one of the gentler": ibid.

105   *"one grate trouble that I have"*: ibid., p. 158.

Five: Ballerinas in a Box

107 "Most of us are half in love": Sewall, *Life of Emily Dickinson*, p. 150.

107 "spinsterly angularity": ibid., p. 15.

107 "wasted in the desert of her crudities": ibid., p. 40.

108 "Her life was one of the richest": Tate, pp. 19–20.

108 "probably the worst book on Emily": Porter, p. 200.

109 *"Dear, dear Sue, I have loved you"*: Patterson, p. 49.

109 *"On a day of early March"*: ibid., p. 116.

109 "Upon the dead, and somewhat desolate": ibid., p. 57.

110 "Having spent her entire capital": ibid., p. 395.

111 "stirred to poetry": ibid., p. 395.

112 "She was no happier than Emily": ibid., p. 332.

114 "I've never called myself an artist": Ashton, p. 4.

116 "The figure of the young danseuse": Deborah Solomon, p. 111.

117 "His greeting was joyous and happy": ibid., p. 351.

118 "frail teener salesgirl": Cornell, *Theater of the Mind*, p. 243.

118 "metaphysics of ephemera": ibid., p. 394.

118 "that curiously plaguing phenomenon": ibid., p. 417.

118 "America still waits to be discovered": Simic, p. 15.

119 "He adored women, but relationships weren't": Deborah Solomon, p. 283.

119 "He looks like Captain Ahab ashore": Cornell, *Theater of the Mind*, p. 15.

119 "Alexander Liberman once said": Deborah Solomon, p. 168.

120 "Among these pseudo-arts": ibid., pp. 82–83.

121 "on tiny scraps of stationary pinned together": Emily Dickinson, *Bolts of Melody*, pp. xii–xvi.

121 "a transcendent moment": Porter, p. 203.

122 "the single most trenchant response": Benfey, *Summer of Hummingbirds*, p. 258.

123 "their dialogue across a hundred years": Porter, p. 199.

123   "artists of aloneness": ibid., p. 220.

124   "recurrent obsession": Cornell, *Theater of the Mind*, p. 256.

124   *"still-unknown* objects": Simic, p. 14.

124   "If her poems are like his boxes": ibid., p. 75.

125   "the eccentric, quivering, overstrung recluse": Deborah Solomon, p. 214.

125   "He would have parties where he served": ibid., p. 357.

126   *"The stars kept winking and blinking"*: Sewall, *Life of Emily Dickinson*, p. 250.

126   "Father believed; and mother loved": ibid., p. 128.

127   "In a secret room in a secret house": Simic, p. 48.

127   "we make our sibling kin": ibid., p. 64.

128   "We are born originals": Kent, *Once a Dancer*, p. 31.

128   "Their beauty was ethereal and unearthly": ibid., p. 32.

128   "I wished to speak in a different way": ibid., p. 39.

128   "gold and ice cream": ibid., p. 58.

128   "the gyroscopic laws of tops": ibid., p. 47.

129   "I decided that more should happen": ibid., p. 180.

130   "His hands were kind of yellowish": Kent, interview.

130   "He was a little too engaged": ibid.

130   "My favorite form of entertainment": ibid.

132   "The way Mr. B communicated with me": Kent, *Once a Dancer*, p. 78.

132   "Some excellent technicians": ibid., p. 158.

Six: Phantom Lady

133   "every finger in place with such energy": Danly, p. 35.

133   "It was too solemn, too heavy": Bingham, *Ancestors' Brocades*, p. 224.

133   "To capture the flow of movement": ibid., p. 224–225.

134   "With Dickinson the story": Danly, p. 40.

134   "Secure the Shadow ere the substance": Bernhard, p. 595.

134   "flat, itinerant work": ibid., p. 596.

135   "a cultural palimpsest of our emotions": Smith, "Iconic Power . . ."

135   "has played a role": Danly, p. 35.

135   "Her face is as familiar as a mask": ibid.

137   "Her eyes were large, dark, and oddly lashless": Oates, p. 46.

138   "Emily could have no idea": ibid., p. 48.

138   "Why am—I—": ibid., p. 55.

138   "It's some sort of computer printout": ibid., p. 56.

139   "that looked like a bridal gown": ibid., p. 59.

139   "a shallow indentation": ibid., p. 69.

139   "where flames fluttered as in an anteroom": ibid., p. 70.

139   *"Accelerate,* Mistress": ibid., p. 71.

139   "antique": ibid., p. 73.

139   *"Bright Knots"*: ibid.

140   "as if we were the ones who had perished": Vendler, p. 139.

141   "a vortex of compelling mystery": Danly, p. 39.

141   "Whether this picture turns out to represent": Smith, "A New Daguerreotype," pp. 4–5.

142   "undeniably plain": Patterson, p. 75.

144   "fictitious set of sexual circumstances": Leyda, *Years and Hours,* vol. I, p. lxix.

145   "Unquestioningly she was standing": Patterson, p. 117.

147   "erotic loss or betrayal": Vendler, p. 51.

149   "Nothing would be more delicious to me": Emily Dickinson, *Single Hound,* p.xvii.

150   "the record book of the funeral director": Longsworth, *World of Emily Dickinson,* p. 112.

SEVEN: Within a Magic Prison

153   "Except for Shakespeare": Bloom, *The Western Canon*, p. 272.

154   "throws several birds": Werner, "A Woe of Ecstasy," p. 46.

155   "unformed, worksheet jottings": Emily Dickinson, *Letters of* . . . , p. 914.

156   "in that it is in the ink and in the handwriting": ibid., p. 929.

156   "disappeared from view": Werner, "A Woe of Ecstasy," p. 27.

156   "textual borders": ibid., p. 28.

158   "are not so much 'works' as symptoms": ibid., p. 27.

158   "Homelessness is our inheritance": ibid., p. 28.

159   "depict the beauty": ibid., p. 29.

159   "as if poems, letters": ibid., pp. 29–30.

159   "are the latest and furthest affirmation": ibid., p. 31.

159   "a work in the throes": ibid., p. 31.

160   "as well, of course, as our own": ibid., p. 31.

160   "She cannot reason at all": Tate, p. 21.

160   "turbulence of mind": Werner, "Woe of Ecstacy," p. 33.

160   "to register the progress": ibid., p. 38.

160   "the hand in the present tense": ibid., p. 41.

161   "as an autonomous lyrics throe": ibid., p. 44.

162   "solitary outriders": Werner, "Most Arrows," p. 16.

164   "Agoraphobia was her alibi": Werner, *Open Folios*, p. 27.

164   "Having abandoned the institution": Werner, "Most Arrows," p. 18.

164   "the spectacular commotion and turbulence": ibid., p. 1.

169   "is about not just whether there is a God": Faust, p. 208.

170   "infantry engagements, even as they grew": ibid., p. 41.

171   "it's not clear that God won": Hirschorn, Interview.

173   "the book is in a single word": James, p. 209.

173   "elaborately and massively dreary": ibid., p. 210.

173   *"He traveled"*: Flaubert, p. 455.

Eight: Nothing

175   "synesthesia of sight and sound": Bervin and Werner, p. 200.

176   "perhaps even pinned close": ibid., p. 200.

176   The first act of flight: ibid., p. 207.

176   "the isolate, piercing notes of a bird": ibid., p. 215.

176   "a whir of words": ibid., p. 200.

177   "We have to think of such fragments": Bervin and Werner, p. 8.

177   "When we say *small*, we often mean": ibid..

177   "These envelopes have been opened": ibid., p. 9.

177   "A message enclosed in an envelope": ibid., p. 212.

177   "Her own life was *reportless*": Werner, Interview.

178   "The envelope is the repository": Bervin and Werner, p. 213.

178   "The inaudible *whirring* of the envelopes": ibid., p. 213.

178   "My father first read": Werner, Interview.

182   "have dared to show us the ways": Bervin and Werner, p. 6.

182   "Viewing these 'envelopes' as visual objects": ibid., p. 7.

183   "regular irregularities": "Emily Dickinson's Visual Language," Farr, p. 250.

183   "an unrhymed shard of verse": ibid., p. 256.

183   "astonishing recklessness . . . by the snapping": Bervin and Werner, p. 205.

183   "promotes a curiously hypnotic effect": Werner, Interview.

183   "'Nothing' . . . was a totemic—and defiant–word": Bervin and Werner, p. 6.

184   "worked away from the audience": Howe, Interview.

184   "I was about nine": Thomas Gardner, p. 2.

185   "my father and I were undemonstrative shy": ibid., p. 140.

185   "I felt vividly how tiny and birdlike": ibid., p. 142.

185   "not only was he a lawyer": ibid., p. 144.

186   "I'm slightly agoraphobic": Howe, Interview.

186   "Noah Webster's pages bristle": Thomas Gardner, p. 157.

186   "Did she simply grab something at hand?" ibid., p. 159.

186   "Every mark on a page is acoustic": Howe, Interview.

186   "The sound of what you say sings": Thomas Gardner, p. 141.

187   "Emily Dickinson in sense had a happy life": Howe, Interview.

187   "with ink on her hands": Thomas Gardner, p. 147.

187   "They're erotic": Howe, Interview.

Nine: Cleopatra's Company

188   "daughters of Erin": Beecher and Stowe, p. 311.

188   "excessive exercise of the intellect": ibid., p. 258.

189   "It was at his dying bed": Stowe, *Annotated Uncle Tom's Cabin*, p. xxxv.

190   "Her writings flowed onto the paper": Wilson, *Patriotic Gore* p. 34.

190   "They come before us arguing and struggling": ibid., p. 6.

191   "Emily Dickinson was born to her talent": Emily Dickinson, *Poems of . . .* (1955), vol. 1, p. vii.

191   "like forty locked doors": Werner, *Open Folios*, p. 36.

191   "The primary project of the fascicles": Smith, *Rowing in Eden*, p. 92.

191   "The handwriting is fierce": ibid., p. 17.

191   "expectations created by typeface": ibid., p. 83.

192   "the trajectory of her desire": Werner, *Open Folios*, p. 4.

192   "If you follow the word": Howe, *The Birth-Mark*, p. 170.

192   "I think she may have chosen to enter": ibid.

193   "a dart that returns immediately": Bervin and Werner, p. 25.

193   "Freedom to roam poetically": Howe, *My Emily Dickinson*, p. 80.

193   "The poet is an intermediary hunting form": ibid., pp. 79–80.

193   "the aggression in God's yellow eye": ibid., p. 136.

193   "in holograph Dickinson's poems": Smith, *Rowing in Eden*, p. 80.

194   "into the blank and unfeeling": Vendler, 291.

194   "Writing traces the way": Werner, *Open Folios*, p. 22.

194   "Noticable change of appearance": Emily Dickinson, *Poems of . . .* (1955), vol. 1, pp. liv–lix

195   "word-paintings": Werner, *Open Folios*, p. 23.

195   "dangerous misssion": Shapiro, Letter.

195   "the spaces between the words": Shapiro, "Secrets of the Pen," p. 231.

196   "She was like a wounded animal": ibid.

196   "The cometary pace of her thought": Werner, *Open Folios*, p. 21.

197   *"Since Cleopatra died"*: Shakespeare, *Antony and Cleopatra*, act 4, scene 14.

198   "a dead spot: Benfey, Interview.

198   "and vanished into thin air": Benfey, *Summer of Hummingbirds*, p. 59.

198   "I remember her distinctly": Susan Dickinson.

199   "I knew she was taciturn": ibid.

199   *"Mrs. Harriet Beecher Stowe wrote"*: Smith, *Rowing in Eden*, p. 144.

201   "Why don't we talk": Benfey, Interview.

TEN: The Witch's Hour

203   "For motherhood . . . is the great mesh": Rich, p. 260.

203   "within the mothering role": ibid., p. 263.

204   "Talent hits a target": Andrew Solomon, p. 412.

204   "Every number has a kind of taste": Benfey, Interview.

204   "HAMLET: Do you see yonder": Shakespeare, *Hamlet*, act 3, scene 2.

204   "and for Dickinson": ": Benfey, Interview.

205   "the tiniest visual details": Sacks, pp. 195–197.

205   "absolute pitch": ibid., p. 199.

205   "Numbers for them are holy": ibid., p. 298.

205   "thought-scape": ibid., p. 211.

206   "There is no danger": Tanenhaus.

207   "Letters are scrawls, turnabouts": Howe, *The Birth-mark,* p. 141.

207   "Spaces between letters, dashes": ibid., p. 143.

208   "the brain begins by *disorganizing*": Andreasen, p. 78.

208   "associative links run wild": ibid.

209   "the cosmic microwave afterglow": Angier.

209   "If I ask, will there be a planet": ibid.

211   "It is the moral luck of making": Gopnik, "Van Gogh's Ear," p. 55.

Coda: Sam Carlo

216   "disappoinment in a much-too-loved woman friend": Emily
        Dickinson, *Bolts of Melody,* p. 4.

Selected Bibliography

Adams, Maureen. *Shaggy Muses: The Dogs Who Inspired Virginia Woolf, Emily Dickinson, Elizabeth Barrett Browning, Edith Wharton, and Emily Bronte*. New York: Ballantine, 2007.

Andreasen, Nancy. *The Creating Brain: The Neuroscience of Genius*. New York: Dana Press, 2005.

Angier, Natalie. "The Life of Pi, and Other Infinities." *New York Times*, January 1, 2013.

Ashton, Dore. *A Joseph Cornell Album*. Reprint. New York: Da Capo, 2002.

Barthes, Roland. *Writing Degree Zero*. Translated by Annette Lavers and Colin Smith. New York: Noonday, 1968.

Beecher, Catherine E., and Harriet Beecher Stowe. *The American Woman's Home*. New York: J. B. Ford, 1869.

Benfey, Christopher. Interview with the author, December 7, 2011.

———. *A Summer of Hummingbirds: Love, Art, and Scandal in the Intersecting Worlds of Emily Dickinson, Mark Twain, Harriet Beecher Stowe, & Martin Johnson Heade*. Reprint. New York: Penguin, 2009.

Bernhard, Mary Elizabeth Kromer. "Lost and Found: Emily Dickinson's Unknown Daguerreotypist." *The New England Quarterly*, 72, no. 4, (December 1999): pp. 594–601.

Bervin, Jen, and Marta Werner, eds. *The Gorgeous Nothings: Emily Dickinson's Envelope-Poems*. Limited Edition. New York: Granary Books, 2012; issued in a paperback edition, with a preface by Susan Howe, New York: New Directions, 2013.

Bianchi, Martha Dickinson. *Emily Dickinson Face to Face: Unpublished Letters with Notes and Reminiscences*. Boston: Houghton Mifflin, 1932.

———. *The Life and Letters of Emily Dickinson*. Boston: Houghton Mifflin, 1924.

Bingham, Millicent Todd. *Ancestors' Brocades: The Literary Debut of Emily Dickinson*. New York: Harper, 1945.

———. *Emily Dickinson: A Revelation*. New York: Harper, 1954.

———. *Emily Dickinson's Home: Letters of Edward Dickinson and His Family*. New York: Harper, 1955.

———, ed. "Prose Fragments of Emily Dickinson," *The New England Quarterly*, 28, no. 3 (September 1955): pp. 291–318.

Blackmur, R. P. "Emily Dickinson's Notation," *The Kenyon Review*, 18 (1956): pp. 224–37.

Bloom, Harold. *The Anxiety of Influence: A Theory of Poetry*. Reprint. New York: Oxford University Press, 1997.

———. *The Western Canon: The Books and School of the Ages*. Reprint. New York: Riverhead, 1995.

Browning, Elizabeth Barrett. *Aurora Leigh*. Reprint. New York: Oxford University Press, 1993.

Cody, John. *After Great Pain: The Inner Life of Emily Dickinson*. Cambridge: Harvard University Press, 1971.

Cornell, Joseph. *Joseph Cornell's Theater of the Mind: Selected Diaries, Letters, and Files*. Edited by Mary Ann Caws. London: Thames and Hudson, 1993.

———. Letter to Jay Leyda, June 19, 1953. Jay and Si-Lan Chen Leyda Papers and Photographs, Tamiment Library and Robert F. Wagner Labor Archives, Elmer Holmes Bobst Library, New York University.

Danly, Susan, ed. *Language as Object: Emily Dickinson and Contemporary Art*. Amherst: Mead Art Museum, Amherst College, 1997.

Dickinson, Edward, and Emily Norcross. *A Poet's Parents: The Courtship Letters of Emily Norcross and Edward Dickinson*. Edited by Vivian R. Pollak. Chapel Hill: University of North Carolina Press, 1988.

Dickinson, Emily. *Bolts of Melody: New Poems of Emily Dickinson*. Edited by Millicent Todd Bingham. New York: Harper, 1945.

———. *The Complete Poems of Emily Dickinson*. Edited by Thomas A. Johnson. Reprint. Boston: Back Bay, 1961.

————. *The Letters of Emily Dickinson.* Edited by Thomas A. Johnson. Cambridge: Harvard University Press, 1986.

————. *The Manuscript Books of Emily Dickinson.* 2 vols. Edited by R. W. Franklin. Cambridge: Harvard University Press, 1942.

————. *The Master Letters of Emily Dickinson.* Edited by R. W. Franklin. Amherst: University of Massachusetts Press, 1998.

————. *The Poems of Emily Dickinson.* 3 vols. Edited by Thomas H. Johnson. Cambridge: Harvard University Press, 1955.

————. *The Poems of Emily Dickinson,* Variorum Edition. 3 vols. Edited by R. W. Franklin. Cambridge: Harvard University Press, 1998.

————. *The Single Hound: Poems of a Lifetime.* Edited by Martha Dickinson Bianchi. Reprint. Gloucester, England: Dodo Press, 2008.

Dickinson, Susan. "Annals of the Evergreens." Dickinson Electronic Archives: www.emilydickinson.org/susan/tannals1.

Farr, Judith, ed. *Emily Dickinson: A Collection of Critical Essays.* Upper Saddle River, NJ: Prentice Hall, 1996.

Faust, Drew Gilpin. *This Republic of Suffering.* New York: Alfred A. Knopf, 2008.

Flaubert, Gustav. *A Sentimental Education.* translated by Douglas Parmée. Reprint. Oxford: Oxford University Press, 2008.

Gardner, Howard. *Creating Minds: An Anatomy of Creativity Seen Through the Lives of Freud, Einstein, Picasso, Stravinsky, Eliot, Graham, and Gandhi.* New York: Basic Books, 1993.

Gardner, Thomas, *A Door Ajar: Contemporary Writers and Emily Dickinson.* Oxford: Oxford University Presss, 2006.

Gilbert, Sandra M., and Susan Gubar. *The Madwoman in the Attic: The Woman Writer and the Nineteenth-Century Literary Imagination.* Reprint. New Haven: Yale University Press, 2000.

Gopnik, Adam. "Dog Story: How Did the Dog Become Our Master?" *The New Yorker,* August 8, 2011, pp. 46–53.

————. "Van Gogh's Ear: The Christmas Eve that Changed Modern Art." *The New Yorker,* January 4, 2010, pp. 48–55.

Gordon, Lyndall. *Lives Like Loaded Guns: Emily Dickinson and Her Family's Feuds.* New York: Viking, 2010.

Grabher, Gundrun, Roland Hagenbüchle, and Cristianne Miller, eds. *The Emily Dickinson Handbook*. Reprint. Amherst: University of Massachusetts Press, 2004.

Habegger, Alfred. *My Wars Are Laid Away in Books*. Reprint. New York: Modern Library, 2001.

Hart, Ellen Louise, and Martha Nell Smith, eds. *Open Me Carefully: Emily Dickinson's Intimate Letters to Susan Huntington Dickinson*. Ashfield, MA: Paris Press, 1998.

Higginson, Thomas Wentworth. *The Magnificent Activist*. Edited by Howard N. Meyer. New York: Da Capo, 2000.

———. "An Open Portfolio." *The Christian Union*, 42, (September 25, 1890): pp. 392–93.

Hirschhorn, Norbert. Interview with the author, September 28, 2011.

Hirschhorn, Norbert, and Polly Longsworth. " 'Medicine Posthumous': A New Look at Emily Dickinson's Medical Conditions." *The New England Quarterly*, 69, no. 2, (June 1996): pp. 299–316.

Howe, Susan. *The Birth-mark: Unsettling the Wilderness in American Literary History*. Middletown, CT: Wesleyan University Press, 1993.

———. Interview with the author, August 14, 2013.

———. *My Emily Dickinson*. Reprint. New York: New Directions, 2007.

James, Henry. *French Poets and Novelists*. London: Macmillan, 1904.

Kandel, Eric R.. *The Age of Insight: The Quest to Understand the Consciousness in Art, Mind, and Brain from Vienna 1900 to the Present*. New York: Random House, 2012.

Kent, Allegra. Interview with the author, December 4, 2012.

———. *Once a Dancer . . .* New York: St. Martin's Press, 1997.

Leyda, Jay. "Miss Emily's Maggie," in *New World Writing*. New York: New American Library, 1953, pp. 255–67.

———. *The Years and Hours of Emily Dickinson*. 2 vols. New Haven: Yale, 1960.

Longsworth, Polly. *Austin and Mabel: The Amherst Affair and Love Letters of Austin Dickinson and Mabel Loomis Todd*. Reprint. Amherst: University of Massachusetts Press, 1999.

———. Interview with the author, December 8, 2011.

———. "'Whose But Her Shy—Immortal Face': The Poet's Visage in the Popular Imagination," in Danly, pp. 35–41.

———. *The World of Emily Dickinson*. Reprint. New York: W. W. Norton, 1997.

Luce, William. *The Belle of Amherst: A Play Based on the Life of Emily Dickinson*. Boston: Houghton Mifflin, 1976.

McGann, Jerome. "Emily Dickinson's Visible Languages," in Farr, pp. 248–59.

McManus, Chris. *Right Hand, Left Hand: The Origins of Asymmetry in Brains, Bodies, Atoms, and Cultures*. Cambridge: Harvard University Press, 2002.

Mossberg, Barbara Antonina Clarke. *Emily Dickinson: When a Writer Is a Daughter*. Bloomington: Indiana University Press, 1982.

Murray, Aífe. *Maid as Muse: How Servants Changed Emily Dickinson's Life and Language*. Durham: University of New Hampshire Press, 2009.

Oates, Joyce Carol. *Wild Nights!* New York: HarperCollins, 2008.

Overbye, Dennis. "A Quantum of Solace." *New York Times*, July 2, 2013.

Paglia, Camile. *Sexual Personae: Art and Decadence from Nefertiti to Emily Dickinson*. New Haven: Yale University Press, 1990.

Patterson, Rebecca. *The Riddle of Emily Dickinson*. Boston: Houghton Mifflin, 1951.

Porter, David. "Assembling a Poet and Her Poems: Convergent Limit-Works of Joseph Cornell and Emily Dickinson," *Word & Image: A Journal of Verbal/Visual Enquiry*, 10, no. 3, (July-September 1994): pp 199–221.

Rich, Adrienne. *On Lies, Secrets, and Silence: Selected Prose*. Reprint. New York: W. W. Norton, 1995.

Sacks, Oliver. *The Man Who Mistook His Wife for a Hat and Other Clinical Tales*. Reprint. New York: Touchstone, 1998.

Sewall, Richard B. *Emily Dickinson: A Collection of Critical Essays*. Englewood Cliffs, NJ: Prentice Hall, 1963.

———. Letter to Jay Leyda, July 10, 1972. Jay and Si-Lan Chen Leyda Papers and Photographs, Tamiment Library and Robert F. Wagner Labor Archives. Elmer Holmes Bobst Library, New York University.

———. *The Life of Emily Dickinson.* Reprint. Cambridge: Harvard University Press, 1994.

Shapiro Susanne. Letter to the author's publicist, Lenore Riegel, April 4, 2012.

———. "Secrets of the Pen: Emily Dickinson's Handwriting." Emily Dickinson at Home: Proceedings of the Third International Conference of the Emily Dickinson Society, Mount Holyoke College, South Hadley, Massachusetts, August 12–15, 1999, pp. 235–38.

Simic, Charles. *Dime-Store Alchemy: The Art of Joseph Cornell.* Reprint. New York: New York Review Books, 2011.

Smith, Martha Nell. "Iconic Power and the New Daguerreotype of Emily Dickinson." Dickinson Electronic Archives: www.emilydickinson.org/node/20.

———. "A New Daguerreotype of Emily Dickinson?" *The Emily Dickinson International Society Bulletin*, 24, no. 2, (November/December 2012): pp. 4–5.

———. *Rowing in Eden: Rereading Emily Dickinson.* Austin: University of Texas Press, 1992.

Smith-Rosenberg, Carroll. "The Female World of Love and Ritual: Relations between Women in Nineteenth-Century America." *Signs*, 1, no. 1, (Autumn 1975): pp. 1–29.

Snively, Susan. Interview with the author, December 9, 2011.

———. "'Myself endued Balloon': Emily Dickinson and Balloons." [excerpted from a lecture delivered in Amherst in 2012].

Solomon, Andrew. *Far from The Tree: Parents, Children, and the Search for Identity.* New York: Scribner, 2012.

Solomon, Deborah. *Utopia Parkway: The Life and Work of Joseph Cornell.* Reprint. Boston: Museum of Fine Arts, 1997.

Sontag, Susan. "Alice in Bed: Scenes from a New Play." *The New Yorker*, May 31, 1993, pp. 142–49.

Starr, Sandra Leonard. *Joseph Cornell and the Ballet.* New York: Castelli, Feigen, Corcoran, 1983.

Stavans, Ilan. Interview with the author, December 7, 2011.

Stowe, Harriet Beecher. *The Annotated Uncle Tom's Cabin.* Edited by Henry Louis Gates, Jr. and Hollis Robbins. New York: W. W. Norton, 2007.

———. *Classics Illustrated Uncle Tom's Cabin.* Illustrated by Rolland H. Livingstone. New York: Gilberton Company, 1944.

Tannenhaus, Sam. "Write, Rewrite, Tweak: Updike at Work." *New York Times,* June 21, 2010.

Tate, Allen. *Collected Essays.* Denver: Allan Swallow, 1959.

Twain, Mark. *The Adventures of Huckleberry Finn.* Reprint. New York: New American Library, 1959.

Vendler, Helen. *Dickinson: Selected Poems and Commentaries.* Cambridge: Harvard University Press, 2010.

Waldman, Diane. *Joseph Cornell: Master of Dreams.* New York: Abrams, 2002.

Weber, Bruce. "Julie Harris, Celebrated Actress of Range and Intensity, Dies at 87." *New York Times,* August 24, 2013.

Werner, Marta. *Emily Dickinson's Open Folios: Scenes of Reading, Surfaces of Writing.* Ann Arbor: University of Michigan Press, 1995.

———. Interview with the author, June 30, 2013.

———. "Most Arrows." *Text* 10 (1997): pp. 41–72.

———. *Radical Scatters:Emily Dickinson's Late Fragments and Related Texts, 1870–1886.* University of Michigan, 1999–May 2007; University of Nebraska, Lincoln, June 2007–2010.

———. "'A Woe Of Ecstasy': On the Electronic Editing of Emily Dickinson's Late Fragments." *The Emily Dickinson Journal,* 16, no. 2, 2007, pp. 25–52.

White, Fred D. *Approaching Emily Dickinson: Critical Currents and Crosscurrents Since 1960.* Rochester, NY: Camden House, 2008.

Wilson, Edmund. *Patriotic Gore: Studies in the Literature of the American Civil War.* Reprint. New York: W. W. Norton, 1994.

———. *The Wound and the Bow.* New York: Oxford University Press, 1947.

Wineapple, Brenda. *White Heat: The Friendship of Emily Dickinson and Thomas Wentworth Higginson.* New York: Alfred A. Knopf, 2008.

Wolff, Cynthia Griffin. *Emily Dickinson.* Reprint. Reading, MA: Addison-Wesley, 1988.

Woolf, Virginia. *A Room of One's Own.* Reprint. Orlando, FL: Harvest, 1989.

Permissions

Index

BELLEVUE LITERARY PRESS is devoted to publishing literary fiction and nonfiction at the intersection of the arts and sciences because we believe that science and the humanities are natural companions for understanding the human experience. With each book we publish, our goal is to foster a rich, interdisciplinary dialogue that will forge new tools for thinking and engaging with the world.

To support our press and its mission, and for our full catalogue of published titles, please visit us at blpress.org.

BELLEVUE LITERARY PRESS
New York

EDITOR'S AFTERWORD

On June 21, 2001, the Shot at Dawn memorial was unveiled at the Memorial Arboretum in Staffordshire, England. It depicts a seventeen-year-old private who was condemned to death, without defence, in the summer of 1915. Behind the blindfolded figure stands a forest of 306 wooden stakes, each representing an executed Commonwealth soldier.

The death penalty for desertion and cowardice was abolished in 1930. In 1997 a review of the cases of the 306 Great War condemned men was begun. In 1998 it was suggested that the names of the executed soldiers might now be added to the country's war memorials. On Remembrance Day 2000, relatives and supporters of the executed soldiers joined the march and the two minutes' silence at the Cenotaph in Whitehall. However, the Secretary of State for Defence later stated that there would be no posthumous pardons for the men and boys who were shot at dawn.

Laurie R. King
Freedom, California

ABOUT THE AUTHOR

LAURIE R. KING is the *New York Times* best-selling author of nine Mary Russell mysteries, five contemporary novels featuring Kate Martinelli, and the acclaimed novels *A Darker Place, Folly, Keeping Watch,* and *Touchstone.* She is one of only two novelists to win the Best First Crime Novel awards on both sides of the Atlantic. She lives in northern California where she is at work on her Russell and Holmes mystery, *The Language of Bees.*

www.laurierking.com